Lecture Notes in Computer Science 13459

Wen Hua · Hua Wang · Lei Li (Eds.)

Databases Theory and Applications

33rd Australasian Database Conference, ADC 2022
Sydney, NSW, Australia, September 2–4, 2022
Proceedings

Editors
Wen Hua (iD)
The University of Queensland
Brisbane, QLD, Australia

Hua Wang (iD)
Victoria University
Footscray, VIC, Australia

Lei Li (iD)
The Hong Kong University of Science
and Technology (Guangzhou)
Guangzhou, Guangdong, China

ISSN 0302-9743   ISSN 1611-3349 (electronic)
Lecture Notes in Computer Science
ISBN 978-3-031-15511-6   ISBN 978-3-031-15512-3 (eBook)
https://doi.org/10.1007/978-3-031-15512-3

This Springer imprint is published by the registered company Springer Nature Switzerland AG
The registered company address is: Gewerbestrasse 11, 6330 Cham, Switzerland

Preface

It is our pleasure to present to you the proceedings of the 33rd Australasian Database Conference (ADC 2022), which took place in Sydney, Australia. ADC is an annual international forum for sharing the latest research advancements and novel applications of database systems, data-driven applications, and data analytics between researchers and practitioners from around the globe, particularly Australia and New Zealand. The mission of ADC is to share novel research solutions to problems of today's information society that fulfill the needs of heterogeneous applications and environments and to identify new issues and directions for future research and development work. ADC seeks papers from academia and industry presenting research on all practical and theoretical aspects of advanced database theory and applications, as well as case studies and implementation experiences. All topics related to databases are of interest and within the scope of the conference. ADC gives researchers and practitioners a unique opportunity to share their perspectives with others interested in the various aspects of database systems.

As in previous years, the ADC 2022 Program Committee accepted papers considered as being of ADC quality without setting any predefined quota. The conference received 36 submissions and accepted 9 full research papers, 8 short papers, and 2 invited papers. Each paper was peer reviewed in full by at least three independent reviewers, and in some cases four referees produced independent reviews. A conscious decision was made to select the papers for which all reviews were positive and favorable. The Program Committee that selected the papers consists of 37 members from around the globe, including Australia, China, New Zealand, and the UK, who were thorough and dedicated to the reviewing process.

We would like to thank all our colleagues who served on the Program Committee or acted as external reviewers. We would also like to thank all the authors who submitted their papers and the attendees. This conference is held for you, and we hope that with these proceedings, you can have an overview of this vibrant research community and its activities. We encourage you to make submissions to the next ADC conference and contribute to this community.

September 2022

Wen Hua
Hua Wang
Lei Li

General Chair's Welcome Message

On behalf of the organizers and Steering Committee for ADC 2022, I am honored to welcome you to the proceedings of the 33rd Australasian Database Conference (ADC 2022). In Australia and New Zealand, ADC is the premier conference on research and applications of database systems, data-driven applications, and data analytics. Over the past decade, ADC has been held in Dunedin (2021), Melbourne (2020), Sydney (2019), Gold Coast (2018), Brisbane (2017), Sydney (2016), Melbourne (2015), Brisbane (2014), Adelaide (2013), and Melbourne (2012). This year, the ADC conference was co-located with the 48th International Conference on Very Large Data Bases (VLDB 2022), with a joint PhD workshop co-organized in Sydney, Australia.

After careful consideration by the Program Committee, a total of 19 research papers were accepted for inclusion in the conference proceedings. We were very fortunate to have two keynote talks presented by world-leading researchers, Lei Chen from the Hong Kong University of Science and Technology and Divesh Srivastava from AT&T Labs – Research. In addition, we are grateful to Zhifeng Bao from the Royal Melbourne Institute of Technology, Lu Qin from the University of Technology Sydney, Jianxin Li from Deakin University, Renata Borovica-Gajic from the University of Melbourne, Jingwei Hou from the University of Queensland, and Alexander Zhou from the Hong Kong University of Science and Technology for their talks in the PhD school.

I wish to take this opportunity to thank all speakers, authors, and organizers. My special gratitude goes out to the Program Committee Co-chairs Wen Hua and Hua Wang for their dedication in ensuring a high-quality program, all members of the Program Committee for their commitment in providing high-quality reviews, Publication Chair Lei Li for his timely preparation of the conference proceedings, Web Chair Weitong Chen for his efforts in website maintenance, submission organization, and technical support, Publicity Co-chairs S. Venkatesan, Fan Zhang, and Rocky Chen for their efforts in disseminating our call for papers and attracting submissions in different regions, and Local Organization Co-chairs Dong Wen and Xin Cao for their efforts in covering every detail of the conference logistics. Without them, this year's ADC would not have been a success.

Sydney is a multi-cultural city and ADC 2022 was held on the main campus of the University of New South Wales, located on a 38-hectare site in the suburb of Kensington. We hope all contributors had a wonderful experience with the conference. We were pleased to welcome all participants of ADC 2022 to the conference, the campus, and the city.

Jeffrey Xu Yu

Organization

General Chair

Jeffrey Xu Yu · · · · · · · · · · · · · · · · · The Chinese University of Hong Kong, HKSAR

Program Committee Chairs

Wen Hua · · · · · · · · · · · · · · · · · The University of Queensland, Australia
Hua Wang · · · · · · · · · · · · · · · · · Victoria University, Australia

Publication Chair

Lei Li · · · · · · · · · · · · · · · · · The Hong Kong University of Science and
Technology (Guangzhou), China

Publicity Chairs

S. Venkatesan · · · · · · · · · · · · · · · · · Indian Institute of Information Technology,
Allahabad, India
Fan Zhang · · · · · · · · · · · · · · · · · Guangzhou University, China
Rocky Chen · · · · · · · · · · · · · · · · · The University of Queensland, Australia

Local Organization Chairs

Dong Wen · · · · · · · · · · · · · · · · · The University of New South Wales, Australia
Xin Cao · · · · · · · · · · · · · · · · · The University of New South Wales, Australia

Steering Committee

Rao Kotagiri · · · · · · · · · · · · · · · · · The University of Melbourne, Australia
Timos Sellis · · · · · · · · · · · · · · · · · RMIT University, Australia
Gill Dobbie · · · · · · · · · · · · · · · · · The University of Auckland, New Zealand
Alan Fekete · · · · · · · · · · · · · · · · · The University of Sydney, Australia
Xuemin Lin · · · · · · · · · · · · · · · · · University of New South Wales, Australia
Yanchun Zhang · · · · · · · · · · · · · · · · · Victoria University, Australia
Xiaofang Zhou · · · · · · · · · · · · · · · · · The University of Queensland, Australia

Program Committee

Tarique Anwar	University of York, UK
Jinli Cao	La Trobe University, Australia
Xin Cao	The University of New South Wales, Australia
Lijun Chang	The University of Sydney, Australia
Pingfu Chao	Soochow University, China
Muhammad Aamir Cheema	Monash University, Australia
Weitong Chen	The University of Queensland, Australia
Lu Chen	Swinburne University of Technology, Australia
Farhana Choudhury	The University of Melbourne, Australia
Junhao Gan	The University of Melbourne, Australia
Janusz Getta	University of Wollongong, Australia
Dan He	The University of Queensland, Australia
Rongyao Hu	Massey University, New Zealand
Wen Hua	The University of Queensland, Australia
Guangyan Huang	Deakin University, Australia
Md. Saiful Islam	Griffith University, Australia
Lei Li	The Hong Kong University of Science and Technology (Guangzhou), China
Wentao Li	University of Technology Sydney, Australia
Rong-Hua Li	Beijing Institute of Technology, China
Kewen Liao	Australian Catholic University, Australia
Sebastian Link	The University of Auckland, New Zealand
Guodong Long	University of Technology Sydney, Australia
Quoc Viet Hung Nguyen	Griffith University, Australia
Lu Qin	University of Technology Sydney, Australia
Jianfeng Qu	Soochow University, China
Afshin Rahimi	The University of Queensland, Australia
Yu Rong	Tencent AI Lab, China
Hua Wang	Victoria University, Australia
Junhu Wang	Griffith University, Australia
Weiqing Wang	Monash University, Australia
Miao Xu	The University of Queensland, Australia
Lina Yao	The University of New South Wales, Australia
Lin Yue	The University of Newcastle, Australia
Wenjie Zhang	The University of New South Wales, Australia
Ying Zhang	University of Technology Sydney, Australia
Wei Emma Zhang	The University of Adelaide, Australia
Rui Zhou	Swinburne University of Technology, Australia

Contents

Short Research Papers

Invited Papers

On International Chinese Education Index Ranking in a Global Perspective

Hui Chen[1]([⊠]) [iD], Zhengze Li[2], Yan Zhou[1], and Xiaoming Fu[2]([⊠]) [iD]

[1] Beijing Foreign Studies University, No. 2 Xisanhuan North Road, Haidian, Beijing 100089,
China
{chenhui,yanzhou}@bsfu.edu.cn
[2] University of Göttingen, Goldschmidtstr. 7, 37077 Göttingen, Germany
{zhengze.li,fu}@cs.uni-goettingen.de

Abstract. As one of the six official languages in the United Nations, Chinese language has received high attention. This paper studies a broad range of aspects related to international Chinese education (ICE) and develops an ICE index ranking system which assesses a set of indicators with their relevance to 33 aspects in 3 dimensions and 9 level-2 indicators that will help to understand the global situation of Chinese learning. The broader list of indicators (which we identified through a thorough review of the literature, taking account of data availability and representativeness) with various datasets is used to rank the global ICE index in over 150 countries. We conduct a comprehensive objective assessment of indicators rather than assigning weights to indicators based on experts' opinions. We find that the highest-ranked indicators across all 3 dimensions are mainly related to localization, followed by specialization, while collaboration plays the least but unneglectable role. The ranked and categorized indicators can be useful to understand the ICE development across the globe. The results show that different countries have widely varying patterns of ICE development with unique priorities for improvement. Through correlation study, we further find that countriess with **high FDI** from China generally score well on specialization and collaboration indicators. Countries with **more tourists** to China score usually higher, but the correlation is less significant. Our cross-country quantitative results can help policy makers to set improvement targets in specific countries and adopt new practices, while keeping track of the other aspects of ICE.

Keywords: International Chinese Education · Data analytics · Index ranking ·
Objective weight method · Correlation

1 Introduction

A number of languages have been increasingly studied as a second or foreign language in the world, including English, French, Spanish, Japanese, and Portuguese. The studies of teaching and learning such international languages have attracted more and more attention from governments, language policy makers, educators, researchers, and other

W. Hua et al. (Eds.): ADC 2022, LNCS 13459, pp. 3–20, 2022.
https://doi.org/10.1007/978-3-031-15512-3_1

stakeholders worldwide [1]. As one of the United Nation's six official languages, Chinese education is currently pursued in over 150 countries, of which 76 countries have incorporated Chinese into national education; over 200 million people learn Chinese as a foreign language, and over 4,000 colleges across the globe provide Chinese language courses in their curriculum [2]. However, there have been only limited studies on international Chinese education (ICE) on a global scale.

Researchers have studied ICE in 115 countries and selected regions, notably Thailand, the US, South Korea, Malaysia, Japan, Russia, the UK, Australia, France, and Germany, with a focus on microscopic issues such as Chinese language acquisition, teaching materials, teachers and pedagogy, as well as mesoscopic studies such as the development of Confucius Institutes and teaching resources [3]. However, few of these studies offer a global and macroscopic perspective on how different countries can be assessed with a set of common indicators.

In this paper, we collected extensive datasets of ICE in 153 countries to gain an understanding of the latest status of ICE learning around the world. To contribute to this ongoing examination and discussion, this paper presents our first step on an objective ICE index ranking method which is constructed using three categories of 33 indicators and explores a data-driven study on assessing the situations of ICE globally.

The development of an ICE index ranking method is important for the measurement and comparison, prediction, and reference for decision-making for ICE-related stakeholders. 1) By comparing and evaluating the level of Chinese education in each country, this index ranking system provides a useful tool for comparing and evaluating the level of ICE in a country. Cross-country assessment of the development level of ICE helps to estimate the overall ICE situation and relative position of a given country; 2) with a data-driven method for generalizing and measuring the level of ICE in a country in a global context based on the situation of *professional scale, domestic policy environment*, and *international cooperation and synergy* of ICE for the country, such an index can help effectively predict the development trend of ICE in the country; 3) a quantitative index framework provides an informative reference for national decision-making on ICE and potential improvements for countries to allocate relevant resources.

To allow a fair and objective assessment of items under study with multiple criteria (indicators), it is common to assign a weight to each indicator, deriving each indicator's score (index) with a weighted sum of its indicator values, and ranking them accordingly. Here, the ranking heavily depends on the weight, and a good ranking method shall be robust and stable, which means a ranked order shall not change if the weights are changed slightly [4]. We employ four objective weight methods independently to evaluate ICE index across countries. We show that the most important indicators for ICE are related to a country's local ICE development, with an overall contribution of 42% as the average of four weight methods. To mitigate the potential biases and instability in different weight methods, we further exploit the robust rank aggregation (RRA) method [5] which was originally proposed to address the robustness issue in gene ranking, to develop an integrated ranking for all individual objective weight methods.

We also perform correlation studies on the ICE index ranking results with a number of external factors, and find this ranking for over 150 countries is positively correlated to individual countries' foreign direct investment volume and international tourist numbers with China.

2 Related Work

2.1 Assessment of ICE

Gil [6] examined the current global standing of Chinese as a foreign language from two perspectives: the number of students learning Chinese and the number of universities and schools offering Chinese-related programs in the US, UK, New Zealand, Australia, South Korea, Thailand and Japan. Xiao [7] studies Chinese education in the United States by giving an overview of the National Security Language Initiative (NSLI) programs and Confucius Institute projects, the number of schools and organizations involved and the enrollments of students in these programs. Although quantitative analysis is used in these studies, the data displayed is far from exhaustive. In addition, they both focused on one specific country. Few researchers have focused on comparative analysis of the situation of Chinese teaching and learning as a second or foreign language across different countries on a global scale.

The notion of "index" which comprises a set of comprehensive indicators to compare the differences in the ICE development across countries in a horizontal manner can provide a basis for policy makers' decision making to promote the development of ICE and international exchange between countries. An "ICE Localization Development Index" [8] is constructed from 3 aspects: the integration of ICE into the national education system, the situation of Chinese language teachers and the situation of Chinese language teaching resources. Based on the assessment framework proposed in [5], which comprises 10 primary indicators and 52 secondary indicators, Wu [9] employs a hierarchical analysis method to develop an index system for assessing Confucius Institutes by analyzing the importance of each index. Wang and Han [4] present a "Global Confucius Institute Development Index" to characterize the overall development of Confucius Institutes. Wang and Chen [10] use a combination of quantitative and qualitative analysis to analyze the distribution of Confucius Institutes in countries along the "Belt and Road", based on the population, education and economy data to match the national conditions of the corresponding countries. These proposed index systems provide the basis for our work in this paper. Following the definition of the 3 primary indicators, this paper further refines them into 9 secondary indicators and 33 level-3 indicators, attempting to assess the current ICE situation in countries around the world from 3 dimensions: the level of specialization, the degree of localization and the degree of collaboration with China or Greater China.

2.2 Assessment Methods

A variety of assessment methods have been proposed to evaluating and comparing performance or development indicators (especially recent 2 decades on ranking universities), such as bi-clustering method [1], complex network analysis method [11], Linked

Open Data-based method [12], and gray relationship theory [13]. During the assessment, different assessment indicator weights may affect evaluation results. Therefore, to determine our assessment results exactly, indicator weights first need to be calculated.

The methods for determining the weight of assessment indicators can be broadly divided into subjective, objective and integrated weight methods. Subjective weight methods, such as Delphi method [14, 15], are mainly based on experts' subjective judgments instead of real data, which may lead to biases due to the subjective nature of different experts. Objective weight methods include principal components analysis (PCA) [16], CRITIC method [17], entropy weight method [18] and Coefficient of Variation (CV) method [19], which are mainly based on real data rather than expert judgments. The integrated weight method combines both types of methods into one, which not only reflects expert judgments but also real data. Since the subjective measures require a substantial coverage of expert opinions in each of the indicators, we adopt the following objective weight methods in this study. For all weight methods, the final step is to calculate a vector $W = \{w_1, w_2, \ldots w_m\}$ containing the weights w_j for index j. After calculating the rankings by each methods, we further aggregate them into an overall ranking.

Coefficient of Variation (CV). CV is a type of relative measure of dispersion, which quantifies the dispersion of data from the average or the mean value. It is defined as the ratio of the standard deviation to the mean, as a dimensionless quantity. When the original dataset has different units for different metrics, CV can be used to make a fair comparison among them. The details of CV method are as follows: first calculate the CV value of each index $CV_j = \frac{\sigma_i}{\mu_i}$, and then assigning the weight of each index according to the CV value:

$$w_j = \frac{CV_j}{\sum CV}.$$

Entropy Weight Method (EWM). EWM is a popular objective method to determine the weights of multiple assessment indicators [20]. Note the original data for each indicator needs to be first standardized using Min-Max normalization, which is achieved by

$$Y = \frac{x - \min(x)}{\max(x) - \min(x)}.$$

Then, EWM sets weights for each indicator by evaluating each indicator's importance; a larger entropy means the indicator is more important and the weight is higher. The entropy values of indicators are in inverse proportion to their entropy weight; if the data of one indicator vary substantially (i.e., that indicator can provide much useful information), its entropy would be low, and its entropy weight would be high.

Criteria Importance Through Intercriteria Correlation (CRITIC). The CRITIC method is another weight method [17]. It employs correlation analysis to calculate the contrasts between criteria, based on the standard deviation of normalized criterion values by columns and the correlation coefficients of all pairs of columns [21]. Like EWM, original data also needs to be standardized using Min-Max normalization, and then each column vector is recorded as y_i; the standard deviation of each column is recorded as σ_i; the linear correlation coefficient between vectors is calculated and recorded as r_{ij}, resulting in a symmetric matrix of size $m * m$. Then calculate a measure of the conflict created by criterion j with respect to the decision situation defined by the rest of criteria $\sum_{k=1}^{m}(1 - r_{jk})$, then determine the quantity of the information in relation to each criterion, namely $C_j = \sigma_i * \sum_{k=1}^{m}(1 - r_{jk})$. Then the final weight for indicator j can be calculated by normalizing these values to unity according to the following equation:

$$w_j = \frac{C_j}{\sum_{k=1}^{m} C_k}.$$

Principal Component Analysis (PCA). The PCA method is a technique which transforms a high-dimensional dataset into a low-dimensional one and removes redundant information [16]. It can identify the most important metrics for an index and derives the linear relationship between metrics by extracting the most relevant information in the dataset. PCA also requires Min-Max normalization of the data before use. The first five eigenvectors of the matrix $\{A_1, A_2, ..., A_5\}$ are calculated and the coefficients are weighted according to their variance contributions to obtain the weights C_j are calculated and the coefficients are weighted according to their variance contributions to obtain the weights:

$$w_j = \frac{C_j}{\sum_{k=1}^{m} C_k}.$$

Robust Rank Aggregation (RRA). The RRA method was initially developed to detect genes which are ranked consistently better than expected under null hypothesis of uncorrelated inputs and assign a significance score for each gene [22]. Using a probabilistic model, the algorithm parameters are made more robust to outliers, noise and errors. The significance scores further ensure only including the statistically relevant genes.

3 Dataset and Preprocessing

3.1 Data Sources and Choice of Indicators

Data Sources. The data sources for this paper mainly include:

Databases: "Chinese Language Globalization Database", BFSU Global Multilingual Textbook Resource Center Database, CNKI (https://www.cnki.net) and Duxiu Knowledge Base (https://www.duxiu.com).

Official Reports: International Chinese Language Teaching Resources Development Report, International Chinese Education Research Report, The Yearbook of Chinese Education in the World, Confucius Institute Annual Development Report, Index Global 2021; Language Education and Cooperation Annual Report (2017–2022); Statistical Yearbook of China's Culture and Tourism (2019), Statistical Bulletin of China's Outward Foreign Direct Investment (2019).

Relevant Non-governmental Organizations: Center for Language Education and Cooperation (http://www.chinese.cn/), China International Culture Association (http://en.chi naculture.org/cica/cn/), Chinese International Education Foundation (https://www.cief. org.cn), and The International Society for Chinese Language Teaching (http://www.shi han.org.cn).

Websites: Official websites of the ministries of education of various countries and provinces/states, Ministry of Foreign Affairs of the People's Republic of China (https:// www.fmprc.gov.cn), International Chinese Language Education Talents (http://zhaopin. jiaohanyu.com/company/c_show-id_2218.html), official websites of colleges and universities in various countries, authoritative higher education information websites such as UCAS.COM, and the official websites of relevant event organizers.

Others: Microsoft Bing, Google, Baidu search and web crawling, People's Daily Online (http://www.people.com.cn), Global Times (https://www.huanqiu.com), Xinhuanet (http://www.news.cn), Apple AppStore, GooglePlay and Huawei AppGallery.

The Choice of Indicators. The "International Chinese Education Development Index" proposed in this paper refers to the status or changes in the ICE development in countries around the world. Two general principles for the selection of indicators are as follows:

Combination of Comprehensiveness and Representativeness. For example, to measure the development level of ICE in a country, it is necessary to consider not only its independent development by its own strength, but also its development under the cooperation with the resources from China; both aspects indispensable when choosing indicators (i.e., ensuring the comprehensiveness). When measuring the development of Chinese resources in each country, the domestic textbooks and the student situation of Chinese majors in colleges and universities (which includes not only the number of universities offering Chinese majors, but also the proportion of these universities in all universities in the country) should be taken into consideration. To ensure this kind of comprehensiveness, both the number of students majoring in Chinese and the number of local learners in each country are chosen as indicators of the scale of learners. However, the latter includes the former. As the former data is not easy to find and the latter can be obtained through relevant databases, only the latter is selected. This is an example of representativeness.

Ensuring Data Coverage. Among the many optional indicators, those with high data coverage should be selected as much as possible. For example, Massive Open Online Courses (MOOCs) are important teaching resources, but only a few countries have produced local MOOCs for ICE. The data coverage is so low that the number of MOOCs is not considered as an indicator.

Based on the above principles and leveraging the previous index systems as well as relevant reports and papers (see Sect. 2.1 for details), we propose an International Chinese Education Index System, where candidate indicators are chosen based on their relevance to ICE and the availability of relevant data resources. As shown in Table 1, the index system comprises three dimensions (specialization, localization and collaboration) as the level-1 indicators. Each dimension contains three level-2 indicators, and each of which was then refined into a number of (currently 33) level-3 indicators. The selection of indicators includes both an overview of the current situation, such as the availability of ICE courses, and sustainable development, such as the number of scholarship/award-winning ICE teachers (who are sent to China for training), which indicates the growth potential of professional local teachers in the upcoming period. Thus, the proposed index system is expected to be able to systematically assess the current level, growth potential and international development of ICE from diverse perspectives.

Table 1. Hierarchical indicators and their meanings

Level-1 indicators	Level-2 indicators	Level-3 indicators (33)	CV weight	PCA weight	CRITIC weight	EWM weight
Specialization	The scale of specialized ICE education	No. of universities offering Chinese majors	2.68%	2.86%	2.46%	3.03%
		The percentage of universities offering Chinese majors	2.19%	2.70%	3.14%	2.67%
		Level of tertiary training (BA/MA/PhD)	1.62%	7.19%	2.42%	2.30%
		No. of ICE specialized organizations	2.84%	1.77%	2.55%	3.02%
	Teaching and research level	No. of academic publications	3.85%	2.16%	2.97%	4.08%
		No. of published academic papers	3.27%	2.10%	2.59%	3.46%
		No. of academic seminars	2.87%	1.39%	3.35%	3.28%
		No. of Chinese language and culture activities	5.88%	1.33%	2.96%	4.73%

(continued)

Table 1. (*continued*)

Level-1 indicators	Level-2 indicators	Level-3 indicators (33)	CV weight	PCA weight	CRITIC weight	EWM weight
	Resources development	No. of local ICE textbooks	3.65%	1.90%	2.85%	3.84%
		No. of ICE related publishing presses	3.21%	2.36%	2.54%	3.60%
		No. of ICE websites	5.68%	1.25%	3.02%	4.16%
		No. of ICE Apps	3.94%	1.17%	3.78%	4.02%
Localization	Policy environment/institutional assurance	Whether Chinese is included as part of education systems	1.13%	3.07%	3.35%	1.52%
		Which level of foreign language does ICE belong to	1.77%	2.56%	4.03%	2.45%
		Whether there is an official institutional setup and its guarantee system	1.33%	2.13%	4.32%	1.72%
	Education system	Whether Chinese as a foreign language is included in national syllabus	2.71%	1.90%	4.21%	3.50%
		Whether Chinese as a mother language is included in national syllabus	7.61%	1.75%	5.70%	7.17%

(*continued*)

Table 1. (*continued*)

Level-1 indicators	Level-2 indicators	Level-3 indicators (33)	CV weight	PCA weight	CRITIC weight	EWM weight
		Whether Chinese as a foreign language is included in national syllabus	7.14%	1.18%	5.04%	6.87%
		Whether Chinese as a mother language is included in regional syllabus	12.27%	1.14%	5.37%	8.95%
		Whether Chinese as a foreign language is included in global/regional syllabus	12.27%	1.03%	4.81%	8.95%
		Whether ICE is included in standard Chinese education in national education system	2.03%	0.79%	3.69%	2.96%
		Whether a formal assessment syllabus has been issued or Chinese language grade is included as part of the university selection criteria	2.92%	0.67%	3.62%	4.07%

(*continued*)

Table 1. (*continued*)

Level-1 indicators	Level-2 indicators	Level-3 indicators (33)	CV weight	PCA weight	CRITIC weight	EWM weight
	Scale of development	No. of ICE teachers	2.29%	3.42%	2.57%	2.87%
		No. of ICE learners	9.08%	5.72%	4.97%	6.76%
Collaboration	Official exchanges & collaborations in different levels	No. of official collaborative academic conferences	2.18%	0.42%	3.93%	2.89%
		No. of official cooperative education agreements	2.51%	0.27%	4.71%	3.34%
	Collaborations with professional organizations in China and/or Greater China	No. of collaborative academic conferences	2.99%	0.22%	3.79%	3.86%
		No. of board members of the International Society for Chinese Language Teaching	3.34%	0.18%	3.56%	4.09%
		No. of institutional members of the International Society for Chinese Language Teaching	3.04%	0.13%	4.80%	4.14%
	Collaboration with Chinese universities	No. of Confucius Institutes (2020)	2.65%	0.07%	3.56%	1.84%

(*continued*)

Table 1. (*continued*)

Level-1 indicators	Level-2 indicators	Level-3 indicators (33)	CV weight	PCA weight	CRITIC weight	EWM weight
		No. of learners enrolled in Confucius Institutes (2020)	3.49%	0.01%	3.57%	3.35%
		No. of ICE teachers sent to China for training (2018)	2.00%	0.02%	4.09%	2.20%
		No. of ICE teachers sent from China (2019)	3.26%	0.04%	4.20%	2.69%
Total	–	–	100%	100%	100%	100%

3.2 Data Preprocessing

We preprocessed all available data for all indicators for all countries in the following way: 1) filling in missing values with "0". 2) pre-processed the data according to the requirements of each of the four weighting methods, i.e. Min-Max normalization before CRITIC, PCA and EWM weighting to unify the order of magnitude of indexes, while keeping the original data for CV weighting computation.

4 Results

We calculate each indicator's weight using 4 methods, as shown in Table 1 (last 4 columns).

The weights of level-3 indicators are summed up to estimate the contribution of their corresponding level-1 indicators (as depicted in Table 1), as shown in Table 2. On average, the weights of localization/specialization/collaboration indicators are in a descending order.

Tables 1, 2 show localization indicators are of the highest importance in two weight methods (PCA and CRITIC) and of a slightly lower importance than specialization in two other methods (CV and EWM). Specialization indicators are of medium importance in all three algorithms, but specialization indicators are considered most important in the EWM algorithm, while collaboration indicators are given much lower weight. Overall, the three level indicators of localization, specialization and collaboration have a weighting of 42.38%, 36.67% and 20.94% respectively in the index calculation. For the ICE development, localization is the main goal, and specialization is a higher goal that can only be achieved after a certain degree of localization has been reached. From a practical

Table 2. The weights of the 33 level-3 indicators are cumulated to obtain the weights of the level-1 indicators of the different weighting methods

Level-1 indicators	CV	PCA	CRITIC	EWM	Average of four methods
Localization	41.67%	49.75%	39.03%	39.09%	**42.38%**
Specialization	41.68%	28.18%	34.65%	42.17%	**36.67%**
Collaboration	16.65%	22.07%	26.32%	18.74%	**20.94%**

point of view, the support of a language's home country has a huge impact on the spread of the language, especially in countries where there is a large shortage of local Chinese teachers and local teaching resources, and teachers and resources from China can play a significant role in supporting the development of local Chinese education. Collaborative support from the home country can be seen in the global spread of any language, such as the British Council of the U.K., the Alliance Française of France, the Goethe Institute of Germany, the Instituto Cervantes of Spain, and the Dante Institute of Italy.

Finally, the rankings using each method and the overall ranking after aggregation with the RRA method are calculated, and the results of the top 3 in different continents and top 20 overall rankings are shown in Tables 3, 4. The results of the three rankings, except for the PCA method, are identical in the top 10, with only minor differences in the lower ranked countries.

Table 3. ICE Top 3 countries from different continents (and their Global ICE Ranking)

	Africa	America	Asia	Europe	Oceania
Rank 1	Egypt (16)	U.S. (5)	South Korea (1)	U.K. (7)	Australia (6)
Rank 2	South Africa (21–50)	Canada (14)	Thailand (2)	France (11)	New Zealand (9)
Rank 3	Ghana (21–50)	Colombia (51–100)	Malaysia (3)	Russia (12)	Fiji (21–50)

Other countries are ranked in the form of following ranges: 21–50, 51–100, and 101+. The detailed list will be released publicly soon.

Noteworthy that most of high ranked countries are from Asia-Pacific/Pacific Rim region; their closer geographical distance to China is a possible reason. Since a closer geographical distance means higher interaction possibility such as trade and tourism, leading to a higher need of communication and language learning. Those topics will be further discussed in Sect. 5.

However the relationship between overall ranking and level-1 indicators remains unclear so far. To find the patterns between ICE level-1 indicators' ranking and overall ranking distribution varies across countries, radar charts are applied. As a commonly used tool to find the cluster, a radar chart consists of a sequence of equip-angular spokes, with each spoke representing one of the ranking of indicators in our case. The farther

Table 4. List of top 20 countries for ICE indicators based on the weights of 33 level-3 indicators, obtained by different weighting methods

Country	Continent	RRA	Rankings				
			CV	PCA	CRITIC	EWM	RRA
South Korea	Asia	1	1	1	1	1	1
Thailand	Asia	2	2	2	2	2	2
Malaysia	Asia	3	3	4	3	3	3
Japan	Asia	4	4	5	4	4	4
U.S.	America	5	5	3	5	5	5
Australia	Oceania	6	6	6	6	6	6
U.K.	Europe	7	7	7	7	7	7
Indonesia	Asia	8	8	10	8	8	8
New Zealand	Oceania	9	11	11	11	11	9
Philippines	Asia	10	10	12	10	10	10
France	Europe	11	9	13	9	9	11
Russia	Europe	12	13	14	14	12	12
Myanmar	Asia	13	12	15	15	13	13
Canada	America	14	15	9	13	14	14
Cambodia	Asia	15	14	16	16	16	15
Egypt	Africa	16	16	8	12	15	16
Spain	Europe	17	18	17	17	18	17
Germany	Europe	18	19	19	19	19	18
United Arab Emirates	Asia	19	17	20	18	17	19
Nepal	Asia	20	20	21	20	20	20

away the central point, the higher ranking. lines are drawn connecting the rankings for each indicator.

Four typical indicators' ranking distribution cases are shown in Fig. 1. Figure 1(a) represents the countries rankings are evenly distributed, for example Spain (ranking of specialization/ localization/ collaboration/ overall is **14/16/20/17**, same format below), thus the lines make up equilateral triangles. Some exemplar countries whose specialization ranking is relatively low such as New Zealand (**31**/12/8/9) could be found in Fig. 1(b). Since localization takes the largest percentage of overall ranking, the difference between its ranking and overall ranking is relatively small as shown on Fig. 1(c); Egypt (22/**34**/4/16) is an example of this. Figure 1(d) shows several countries' relatively low collaboration ranking drags down their overall ranking, where Vietnam (7/22/**114**/29) is a representative example.

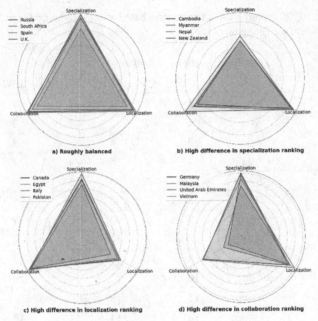

Fig. 1. Radar charts of selected countries

5   Impact of the Number of Tourists and Foreign Direct Investments on ICE Ranking

According to Sapir [23], there is something behind the language and language cannot exist without culture. Language international education is determined by the *political status of its home country, economic and trade relations, cultural interactions,* and *educational exchanges* [3]. The relationship between language international education and the above four factors has been well studied, but there have been few data-driven studies on the relationship between ICE and economic and trade relations. [10] is among the few studies which examines the relationship between the distribution of Confucius Institutes and the scale of Chinese exports along the Belt and Road. To explore the correlation between ICE and Sino-foreign economic and trade relations, we propose to analyze both foreign direct investments and tourism. Top 10 ranked lists of our collection of outbound tourists to China and inward FDI from China (2019) are given in Table 5 and Table 6, respectively.

We calculate the Spearman correlation coefficient and test the RRA aggregated ICE ranking with the number of tourists, and the FDI in 2019, and the results are shown in Table 7. The results show that the index ranking of international Chinese education is significantly and positively correlated with the number of tourist arrivals and the amount of FDI from China, i.e., the higher the number of outbound tourists to China in a country, the higher the level of Chinese education development and vice versa; the higher inward FDI from China, the higher the level of ICE and vice versa. Foreign language learning and economic and trade development have a relationship of mutual achievement. The direct experience of outbound tourism promotes their learning of the country's language, and the improvement of their language skills motivates them to achieve outbound tourism. Helping other countries in the world that want to attract FDI (e.g., from China) can strengthen the level of development of foreign language education in their country (e.g., Chinese) and create a language-friendly investment environment; while investment in the local area directly contributes to related employment and foreign language demand, and therefore can promote the spread of the language of the investing country locally. Therefore, strengthening foreign language learning is a mutually beneficial option for both sides and is important for economic and trade development. This is in line with the findings of another article [10] - which found that for each additional Confucius Institute established by China in a region along the Belt and Road, China's exports to the region increased by US$20,000.

Table 5. Top-10 countries with outbound tourists to China (Source: Statistical Yearbook of China's Culture and Tourism 2019)

Rank	Country	Outbound tourists to China (million)
1	Myanmar	1242.18
2	Vietnam	794.87
3	South Korea	434.66
4	Russia	272.26
5	Japan	267.63
6	U.S.	240.67
7	Mongolia	186.23
8	Malaysia	138.35
9	Philippines	117.77
10	Singapore	100.85

Table 6. Top-10 countries with inward foreign direct investment from China (Source: Statistical Bulletin of China's Outward Foreign Direct Investment)

Rank	Country	Inward FDIs from China (USD million)
1	Cayman Islands	276,145.06
2	British Virgin Islands	141,878.84
3	United States	77,797.50
4	Singapore	52,636.56
5	Australia	38,068.38
6	Netherlands	23,854.82
7	U.K.	17,143.90
8	Indonesia	15,132.55
9	Germany	14,233.99
10	Canada	14,091.47

Table 7. Correlation result between tourism/FDI and RRA rank (***: p < 0.001)

	The number of outbound tourists to China (million)	Share of outbound tourists to China (%)	China's outward FDI Stock in 2019 (USD million)
RRA rank reverse	0.63***	0.63***	0.53***

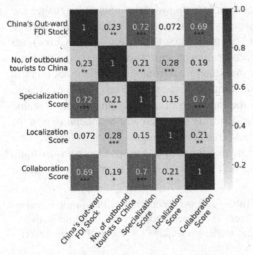

Fig. 2. Correlation between level-1 ICE indicators and external factors

A correlation matrix for the level-1 ICE indicators and tourists/FDI amounts in Pearson correlation coefficient is given in Fig. 2. It shows China's outward FDI stock has highly significant positive correlations with the specialization score (0.72, p < 0.001) and the collaboration score (0.69, p < 0.001). Similarly, the number of outbound tourists to China has low but extreme significant positive correlation with the localization score (0.28, p < 0.001) and specialization (0.21, p < 0.01), and low positive correlation with the collaboration score (0.19, p < 0.05) in some extent. Interestingly there is highly significant correlation between specialization and collaboration, while there is no significant linear correlation between specialization score and localization.

6   Conclusions and Further Discussions

This paper proposes four objective-based comprehensive rankings and introduces the RRA method to multiple ranking methods to ensure the reliability of the rankings and apply them to ICE indicator rankings. We further analyze the impact contribution values of each factor. Our findings show that the U.S., Thailand, and Australia rank in the top three in ICE indicators, followed by the U.K., Egypt, and South Korea, and Canada, Russia, Italy, and New Zealand are also in the top ten rankings. The most important indicators for ICE in a country are related to the country's domestic ICE development, with an overall contribution of 42%.

We further find through Spearman correlation analysis that the level of international Chinese education development is significantly and positively correlated with its tourist population entering China and the amount of Chinese outward investment.

Given that Hong Kong, Macau and Taiwan invest much less in ICE than mainland China, even most of the data we collected focuses on the situation related to mainland China, it should also reflect the overall development and promotion of ICE in the whole Greater China region.

Future work includes correlation analysis with data on countries' GDP, residents' income, import/export volume with China/Greater China and media attention on ICE topics and experimenting with other weight methods and ranking methods.

Acknowledgement. This research is funded by the Fundamental Research Funds for the Central Universities (Grant No. 2020JJ014), 2021 International Chinese Education Research Project "Big Data Analysis of International Chinese Education Network Video Resources" (Grant No. 21YH13C). The data in this article comes from the BFSU "International Chinese Education Index Report" database, which was completed by more than 100 faculty members and graduate students. Their contributions and efforts are highly appreciated.

References

1. Macaro, E., Woore, R. (eds.): Debates in Second Language Education. Routledge, New York (2022)
2. Yin, D.: How to improve the quality of international Chinese language education products. People's Daily (Overseas Edition) (2021). http://paper.people.com.cn/rmrbhwb/html/2021-03/26/content_2040175.htm
3. Li, B.: Study on the International Chinese Language Spread Based on Bibliometrics, Liaoning Normal University Press, Shanghai (2022)
4. Wang, H., Han, J.: The construction of the development index for confucius institutes worldwide. J. Yunnan Normal Univ. (Teach. Learn. Chin. Foreign Lang. Ed.) Editorial **2** (2021)
5. Wu, Y.: On the index system of confucius institute assessment. Educ. Res. **32**(8), 30–34, 92 (2011)
6. Gil, J.: A comparison of the global status of English and Chinese: towards a new global language?: Will Chinese really replace English as the world's lingua franca? English Today **27**(1), 52–59 (2011)
7. Xiao, Y.: Chinese education in the United States: players and challenges. Global Chin. **2**(1), 23–50 (2016)
8. Guo, J.: Research on localization development index construction of international Chinese education. J. Res. Educ. Ethnic Minorities **3** (2021)
9. Wu, C.: Research on the evaluation index system of Confucius Institute based on hierarchical analysis. Asia-Pac. Educ. **36**, 265–267 (2016)
10. Wang, H., Chen, Y.: A study of the distribution of the Confucius Institutes in the Belt-and-Road countries based on big data. J. Yunnan Normal Univ. (Teach. Learn. Chin Foreign Lang. Ed.) **1** (2019)
11. Bellantuono, L., Monaco, A., Amoroso, N., et al.: Territorial bias in university rankings: a complex network approach. Sci. Rep. **12**, 4995 (2022). https://doi.org/10.1038/s41598-022-08859-w
12. Meymandpour, R., Davis, J.G.: Ranking universities using linked open data. In: Proceedings of WWW 2013 Workshop on Linked Data on the Web (LDOW 2013), Rio de Janeiro, Brazil (2013)
13. Ertuğrul, I., Öztaş, T., Özçil, A., Öztas, G.Z.: Grey relational analysis approach in academic performance comparison of university a case study of Turkish universities. Eur. Sci. J. **12**(10), 128–139 (2016)
14. Dachyar, M., Dewi, F.: Improving university ranking to achieve university competitiveness by management information system. IOP Conf. Seri.: Mater. Sci. Eng. **83**, 012023 (2015)

15. Gordon, T.J.: The Delphi method in futures research methodology. AC/UNC Millennium Proj. **2**(3), 1–30 (1994)
16. Pearson, K.F.R.S:. On lines and planes of closest fit to systems of points in space. London Edinb. Dublin Philos. Mag. J. Sci. **2**(11), 559–572 (1901). https://doi.org/10.1080/147864 40109462720
17. Diakoulaki, D., Mavrotas, G., Papayannakis, L.: Determining objective weights in multiple criteria problems: the CRITIC method. Comput. Oper. Res. **22**(7), 763–770 (1995)
18. Zhu, Y., Tian, D., Yan, F.: Effectiveness of entropy weight method in decision-making. Math. Probl. Eng. **2020**, 3564835 (2020)
19. Tzeng, G.-H., Teng, M.-H., Chen, J.-J., Opricovic, S.: Multicriteria selection for a restaurant location in Taipei. Int. J. Hosp. Manag. **21**(2), 171–187 (2002)
20. Li, L.-H., Mo, R.: Production task queue optimization based on multi-attribute evaluation for complex product assembly workshop. PLoS ONE **10**, e0134343 (2015)
21. Madic, M., Radovanović, M.: Ranking of some most commonly used nontraditional machining processes using ROV and CRITIC methods. UPB Sci. Bull. Ser. D **77**(2), 193–204 (2015)
22. Kolde, R., Laur, S., Adler, P., Vilo, J.: Robust rank aggregation for gene list integration and meta-analysis. Bioinformatics **28**(4), 573–580 (2012). https://doi.org/10.1093/bioinform atics/btr709
23. Sapir, E.: Language: An Introduction to the Study of Speech. The Commercial Press (1985)
24. Asudeh, A., Jagadish, H.V., Miklau, G., Stoyanovich, J.: On obtaining stable rankings. Proc. VLDB **12**, 237–250 (2018)
25. Kosztyán, Z.T., Banász, Z., Csányi, V.V., Telcs, A.: Rankings or leagues or rankings on leagues? - Ranking in fair reference groups. Tert. Educ. Manag. **25**(4), 289–310 (2019). https://doi.org/10.1007/s11233-019-09028-x
26. Kanoksilapatham, B.: National survey of teaching Chinese as a foreign language in Thailand. Southeast Asian Ministers of Education Organization (2011)
27. Osborne, C., Zhang, Q., Xia, Y.: The past and present of Chinese language teaching in Ireland. Chin. Lang. Teach. Methodol. Technol. **2**(1), 32 (2019)

Multi-objective Social Network Detection - A Graph Database Supported NSGA-II Based Approach

Josh Trueman[1], Hui Ma[1(✉)], Aaron Chen[1], and Sven Hartmann[2]

[1] Victoria University of Wellington, Wellington, New Zealand
{hui.ma,aaron.chen}@ecs.vuw.ac.nz
[2] Clausthal University of Technology, Clausthal-Zellerfeld, Germany
sven.hartmann@tu-clausthal.de

Abstract. Community detection in social networks is an emerging concept in the realm of artificial intelligence. It helps organizations to offer targeted services based on community predispositions. Social networks require effective community detection methods to detect clusters of users with dense inner community connections and sparse external connections. Numerous approaches have been taken in accomplishing this challenge. However many existing algorithms suffer from scalability issues when the network contains extensive and highly connected data. Furthermore, the definition of a community encourages a multi-objective approach in which both the external and internal connections of communities must be considered. In this paper, we propose a multi-objective approach that uses Non-dominated Sorting Genetic Algorithm (NSGA-II) supported by a graph database to overcome the inherent scalability problems. This graph database-supported, non-dominated sorting genetic algorithm (GD-NSGA-II) has been developed and shown to be effective in consistently finding high-quality community structures in social networks.

1 Introduction

Social networking has attracted billions of users. A social network consists of a set of objects connected by a set of interconnections. These objects can be users, groups and pages while the interconnections are the social relations between them such as common interests, friend status or page visits.

Information regarding the community structures of social networks can be used by many organizations to target their services to suitable users or customers. Community detection aims to identify such community structures within a social network. Specifically, *Community detection* partitions networked data (nodes) into clusters based on intrinsic similarities [1]. This is especially important in social network analysis as it allows for marketing to be targeted to selected groups based on user relations and interests.

Numerous approaches to community detection in complex networks have been reported recently [2,3]. However the effectiveness of many existing

© The Author(s), under exclusive license to Springer Nature Switzerland AG 2022
W. Hua et al. (Eds.): ADC 2022, LNCS 13459, pp. 21–33, 2022.
https://doi.org/10.1007/978-3-031-15512-3_2

approaches are only evaluated on small networks with no underlying ground truth and no clear-cut community definition. In this paper, the community defined in [4] is utilized to systematize the community detection process. Previous research focused mainly on the modularity metric to evaluate the quality of community structures. However, recent studies reveal that using modularity as the only objective often leads to limited resolution and imbalance inconveniences [5].

Different from previous works, we believe the community detection problem can be naturally defined as a multi-objective optimization problem. Therefore in this paper we study the community detection problem as a multi-objective problem in which conflicting objectives are optimized to produce a set of *Pareto optimal solutions*. The proposed approach is supported by a graph database to allow for the use of large datasets such as the "ego-Facebook" dataset and expedite query processing compared to conventional database structures. Additionally, the proposed approach utilizes the seeding technique to promote the generation of strong individuals in the initial genetic population.

In this paper, we aim to propose a graph database supported approach for community detection by using a modified Fast and Elitist Non-Dominated Sorting Algorithm (NSGA-II) algorithm [6] that can effectively handle multiple conflicting objectives during the optimization process. Driven by this goal, we are targeted to achieve the following four objectives:

1. Design a graph database model to facilitate the construction and analysis of social networks such that relevant node and connection information can be stored and queried efficiently.
2. Develop a seeding technique that uses the Label Propagation Algorithm to identify high-quality community structures to be embedded into the initial genetic population for the purpose of improving the algorithm performance.
3. Design and implement the GD-NSGA-II algorithm to detect community structures in social networks queried from the graph database.
4. Evaluate the performance and scalability of the implemented algorithm and compare its effectiveness against several existing multi-objective algorithms.

Organization. This paper is structured as follows. Section 2 reviews related work in community detection. Section 3 defines the problem of multi-objective social network detection. Section 4 presents our new graph database-supported NSGA-II-based approach, named GD-NSGA-II, including the data model used for storing social network data in a graph database and the NSGA-II-based algorithm seeded with the output of the graph database. Section 5 presents the results of the experimental evaluation of our proposed approach. Section 6 concludes the paper and discusses future work.

2   Related Work

Various clustering algorithms have been proposed to solve the community detection problem through partitioning nodes into a predefined number of non-overlapping clusters. In [7], the popular K-means clustering algorithm has been utilized for this purpose. While this clustering algorithm has proven to be efficient at clustering large datasets [8], it poses major problems when clustering social network data. Specifically, it is difficult to determine the suitable value of k in advance before clustering any social networks. Additionally, the definition of "means" limits the application domain to numerical variables. While this would work with data such as edge weighting, social network data includes relationships such as "friends with" or "follows" which is difficult to determine an appropriate numerical value to.

Propagation clustering algorithms such as the Label Propagation Algorithm (LPA) [9] utilize the concept of "message passing" between nodes in a graph to identify community structures. Nodes are assigned identical labels based on the labels of the majority of its neighbors as a means of inferring their belongings to any communities [10,11]. Propagation algorithms are extremely fast and require minimal knowledge of the network topology. However, they often fail to identify near-optimal communities in practice [10].

Evolutionary Computation (EC) algorithms have been utilized to detect communities in social networks [12–14]. These approaches can be categorized into single-objective and multi-objective approaches. Single-objective EC algorithms have the goal to identify desirable community structures that optimize a single objective [15,16]. Meanwhile, multi-objective EC algorithms have been applied to optimize multiple objectives with promising results. In both [13,14], multi-objective EC algorithms outperformed many single-objective EC and non-EC community detection algorithms. The most popularly used multi-objective algorithm in literature is the Fast and Elitist Non-Dominated Sorting Algorithm (NSGA-II).

Graph databases use graph structures to store entities and relationships between entities and have been used to tackle community detection problems [17]. As shown in [18], Neo4j [19], the most popular graph database used worldwide [20], performs significantly better than its competitors OrientDB [21], Titan [22] and DEX (now Sparksee) [23], in terms of both loading datasets and traversal of the graph network. Additionally, Neo4j offers community detection methods, e.g., Label Propagation algorithm [9].

To the best of our knowledge, existing community detection approaches are not efficient as they compute connection data frequently during the search process. This issue is addressed in this paper by using a graph database that can be queried efficiently for node and relationship information. Existing methods from graph databases are greedy methods and may stuck at local optima. We further evolve the initial solutions from a graph database with NSGA-II, which is effective in evolving high quality global optimal solutions for multi-objective optimization problems.

3 Preliminaries

In this section, we introduce the terminology and notations used in this paper. Then we give a formal definition of the multi-objective social network community detection problem that considers both internal and external connections.

A social network can be modeled as a graph $G = (V, E)$ with a set V of nodes and a set E of edges. The nodes represent entities, while the edges represent relationships between entities. In this paper, the focus is on finite, undirected and unweighted graphs. Various scoring functions have been proposed for community detection. According to [24], they fall into four categories: a) *Scoring based on internal connectivity*, b) *Scoring based on external connectivity*, c) *Scoring based on both internal and external connectivity*, and d) *Scoring based on a network model*. In research and practice, modularity is one of the most popular scoring functions that takes both internal and external connections into account.

Let $\mathcal{M}$ be a partition of graph G, i.e., a collection $M_1, \ldots, M_k$ of non-empty subsets of node set V so that each node of G belongs to exactly one subset in $\mathcal{M}$. The subsets in $\mathcal{M}$ are often called modules or clusters or communities, and $\mathcal{M}$ is also called a *clustering*. Let G_M denote the subgraph of G induced by node set M, i.e., two nodes form an edge in G_M just when they form an edge in G. Let L_M denote the number of edges of G_M. Let $K_M = \sum_{v \in M} deg_v$ denote the total degree of M in G where deg_v is just total degree of node v, i.e., the number of edges G that v belongs to. The *modularity* $Q(\mathcal{M})$ of $\mathcal{M}$ is defined in Eq. (1c).

$$Q^{intra}(\mathcal{M}) = \sum_{M \in \mathcal{M}} \frac{L_M}{L_V} \tag{1a}$$

$$Q^{inter}(\mathcal{M}) = \sum_{M \in \mathcal{M}} \left(\frac{K_M}{2L_V}\right)^2 \tag{1b}$$

$$Q(\mathcal{M}) = Q^{intra}(\mathcal{M}) - Q^{inter}(\mathcal{M}) = \sum_{M \in \mathcal{M}} \left[\frac{L_M}{L_V} - \left(\frac{K_M}{2L_V}\right)^2\right] \tag{1c}$$

For more detailed formal definitions we refer to [25]. When analyzing the community structure of a graph, one is interested in a clustering with maximum modularity. Modularity values are in the range between −1 and 1 where a value close to 1 indicates strong community structure [24].

The maximum modularity problem for graphs was proven to be NP-hard in [25]. Modularity in Eq. (1c) can be easily split two naturally conflicting objectives $Q^{intra}(\mathcal{M})$ and $Q^{inter}(\mathcal{M})$ which will be maximized and minimized, respectively. The first objective in Eq. (1a) aims to find a clustering with the maximum fraction of edges within the communities, while the second objective in Eq. (1b) aims to divide the graph into many communities with small total degree.

4   Graph Database-Supported NSGA-II Approach

This section develops a new algorithm GD-NSGA-II for multi-objective community detection. We start with an algorithm overview, followed by a detailed description of each algorithmic component.

Algorithm Overview. The design of GD-NSGA-II combines concepts of NSGA-II and Neo4j, allowing social networks to be stored in a graph database and queried using Neo4j's Cypher query language. Figure 1 depicts a high level algorithm overview.

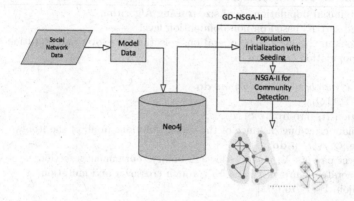

Fig. 1. Overall framework of our GD-NSGA-II approach

According to Fig. 1, data is pre-processed to fit the data requirements of Neo4j. The network model stores the properties of nodes and relationships between nodes. The individuals in the social network are modeled as nodes, and the relationships between individuals as edges. After appropriate pre-processing, a social network is stored in a Neo4j database. We then use Neo4j's built-in LPA algorithm to seed the initial genetic population and set the maximum number of communities.

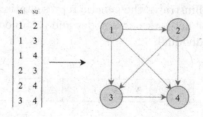

Fig. 2. An illustration of a social network imported into Neo4j

Figure 2 shows a sample of a social network. On the left is the edge list of the graph that was provided. The columns represent the nodes connected by a relationship and the rows represent an instance of a relationship. On the right, the Neo4j representation of this sample is illustrated by which nodes are connected based on the edge list on the left. Although the Neo4j representation is illustrated by a directed relationship, this is disregarded at run-time and any connection between two nodes is considered to be unweighted and undirectional. More details about GD-NSGA-II are described below.

Algorithm 1. GD-NSGA-II for Community Detection

Generate initial population P_0 of size n using Algorithm 2
Rank and sort P_0 based on non-domination level
Apply domain-specific genetic operations selection, crossover and mutation to create a child population Q_0 of size n
$i \leftarrow 0$
while $i < numberOfGenerations$ **do**
    $R_i \leftarrow P_i \cup Q_i$
    Partition R_i into fronts $F_1, F_2, \ldots$
    Calculate crowding distance of the sorted solutions in all of the fronts
    while $|Q_{i+1}| \leq n$ **do**
        Select parents X_1 and X_2 through binary tournament selection
        Generate offsprings Y_1 and Y_2 through crossover and mutation
        Adjoin Y_1, Y_2 to Q_{i+1}
    end while
    Evaluate all solutions in Q_{i+1} using the objective functions in Eq. (1a) and (1b)
    $i \leftarrow i + 1$
end while

Genetic Representation. For GD-NSGA-II, we develop a suitable representations of any community detection solution as a chromosome. This is an important design decision in genetic algorithms as it has direct impact of the effectiveness and efficiency of the algorithm. We decide that an individual is composed of n directly encoded genes where n is just the number of nodes of the graph. Consequently, each gene is assigned an integer value corresponding to the community it belongs to. Figure 3 illustrates the genetic representation of a sample individual. In this example the network has 8 nodes and each node is differentiated by its placement in the individual.

Fig. 3. The genetic representation of individuals

Seeding Method of Population Initialization. For GD-NSGA-II, we adopt a novel method that uses both randomly generated solutions as well as solutions obtained from the baseline algorithm to create the initial genetic population, in order to balance the quality and diversity of the initial population. Particularly, we propose to use the LPA algorithm supported by Neo4j [9] to seed 5% of the initial population.

Fitness Functions. For GD-NSGA-II, we choose the objective functions defined in Eq. (1a) and (1b) to evaluate the fitness of evolved solutions in any of the populations. It is crucial for the performance of the algorithm that this can be done very efficient utilizing the underlying Neo4j database.

Algorithm 2. Population Initialization with Seeding

$i \leftarrow 0$
$popSize \leftarrow 40$
$population \leftarrow []$
while $i < popSize$ **do**
  if i mod $popSize/(popSize * 0.05) = 0$ **then**
    $individual \leftarrow generateLPAIndividual()$
  else
    $noOfCommunites \leftarrow random(1, noOfNodes)$
    $individual \leftarrow generateIndividual(noOfCommunities)$
    Adjoin $inidividual$ to $population$
  end if
end while

Genetic Operators. Next, we develop suitable domain-specific methods for effectively and efficiently performing the genetic operators crossover, mutation, and selection on the genetic populations throughout our approach. For GD-NSGA-II, we use a *uniform crossover operation* to generate new offspring from candidate parents, as illustrated in Fig. 4a. Due to uniform crossover, for each gene of a parent chromosome, there is a 50% chance that the gene is inherited by the offspring. Otherwise the gene is inherited from the second parent.

For GD-NSGA-II, we utilize *mutation* as an adequate means of maintaining genetic diversity in a genetic population. We achieve this by randomly changing the community to which a node is assigned, based on the given mutation rate, as illustrated in Fig. 4b.

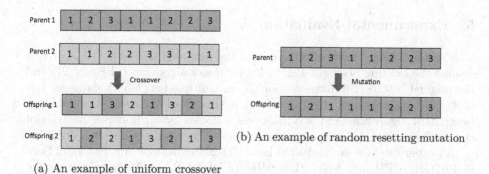

(a) An example of uniform crossover

(b) An example of random resetting mutation

Fig. 4. An illustration of crossover and mutation in GD-NSGA-II

For GD-NSGA-II, we use *binary tournament selection* to select parents. The process first selects two random parents from the population. This is followed by applying a chain comparator composed of a dominance comparator and a crowded distance comparator. The first compares the two candidates by Pareto dominance. A solution x^1 is said to dominate another solution x^2 if both the following conditions are true: The solution x^1 is no worse than x^2 in all objectives and The solution x^1 is strictly better than x^2 in at least one objective [26]. If no dominant solution can be found from the two candidate parents, the latter is used to compare the crowding distance of the two solutions. The crowding distance measures the distance between a solution and its two neighboring solutions. The solution with the larger crowding distance will be selected as the tournament winner. The binary tournament selection process is illustrated in Fig. 5.

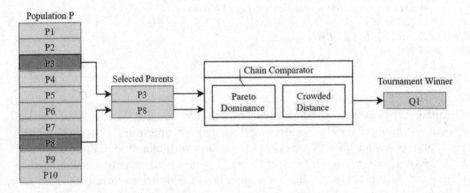

Fig. 5. An illustration of binary tournament selection in GD-NSGA-II

In summary, GD-NSGA-II uses a graph database to store social networks and generate some initial solutions. NSGA-II are further exploited to evolve Pareto optimal solutions.

5   Experimental Evaluation

This section evaluates the effectiveness of the proposed GD-NSGA-II approach against the existing Strength Pareto Evolutionary algorithm (SPEA2) [27] and the original NSGA-II implementation [6] on multiple benchmark datasets. Initially, the evaluation configuration will be discussed including the datasets, benchmark algorithms and specifications, followed by an in-depth analysis of the results produced through hyper volume and inverted generational distance.

All experiments were conducted on a Mid-2018 Macbook Air with Intel Core i5 1.6 GHz CPU and 8 GB 2133 MHz LPDDR3 RAM. Prior to testing the algorithms performance, a reference set is generated from an aggregation of 30 seeds of each algorithm in which the hypervolume and IGD are calculated using.

Datasets. The data component of the artifacts architecture refers to the collection of datasets used in this project. The datasets included are the ego-Facebook social circles database provided by Stanford's large network dataset collection, the Zachary Karate club dataset used in part to establish the Girvan-Newman algorithm [28] and the Dolphin Social network dataset [29]. All three datasets are undirected and unweighted. The Zachary Karate Club dataset describes a social network with 34 members and 78 connections between them. Additionally, there exists two key nodes in which the remaining nodes hinge on. The Dolphin Social Network dataset [29] describes a social network of frequent associations between 62 bottlenose dolphins in a community living off Doubtful Sound, New Zealand. The nodes of the network represent the dolphins while the edges represent the relationship between two dolphins. The 'ego-Facebook' data [24] contains a total of 4,039 nodes and 88,234 edges by combining 10 smaller ego-networks. The data was collected from survey participants and has been made anonymous by concealing feature values.

Table 1. Datasets used for evaluation with relevant network information

DataSet	No. of nodes	No. of edges
Zachary Karate Club	34	78
Dolphins Social Network	62	159
ego-Facebook	4039	88234

The table above illustrates the size and density of connection across all of the datasets used in this project.

Baseline Algorithms. We use two multi-objective algorithms, i.e., SPEA2 and NSGA-II, as the baseline algorithms to determine the efficiency and effectiveness of GD-NSGA-II. Additionally, the parameter settings defined in the next section will also be applied to both baselines.

All competing algorithms are evaluated on 3 different datasets of varying node and edge density (see Table 1). It is expected that the performance of the algorithms will change based on the size of the dataset, therefore both the mean and standard deviation of the evaluation metrics hypervolume and inverted generational distance (IGD) are calculated to provide a fair comparison. Additionally, the algorithms were run for 30 times to accommodate the calculation of these metrics. Results that are significant are marked in bold.

Experimental Parameters. The parameter values for GD-NSGA-II were analytically chosen through both preliminary research and experimental analysis. The population size was set as 50 to ensure a strong mating pool can be maintained without slowing the algorithms performance significantly. The number of generations was established as 100 given the search space for detecting community structures is significant, thus the time taken to convergence will be longer.

Crossover and mutation rates were set as 1 and 0.5 respectively to maintain genetic diversity from one generation to the next.

Results and Analysis. We use the metrics *hypervolume* and *Inverted generational distance* (IGD) to analyze the effectiveness of our proposed approach in comparison to the baseline methods. *IGD* and *hypervolume* are commonly used performance evaluation metrics for multi-objective optimization [30]. IGD measures the distance from the nearest point of the non-dominated population generated from the proposed approach to the reference set which has been obtained by aggregating all of the approaches. Hypervolume measures the dominated volume covered by a reference point and the front evolved by each algorithm. In Table 2, the top performing IGD and Hypervolume values are marked in bold.

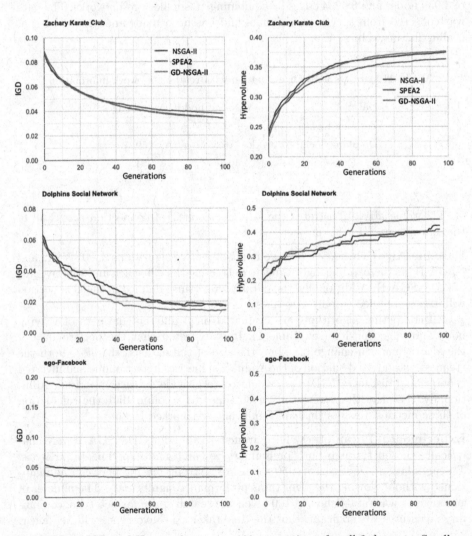

Fig. 6. Mean IGD and Hypervolume over 100 generations, for all 3 datasets. Smaller IGD values indicate better quality. Larger Hypervolume values indicate better quality.

Table 2. Mean IGD and hypervolume over 30 runs of each approach on the three datasets

Dataset	Inverted generational distance			Hypervolume		
	NSGA-II	SPEA2	GD-NSGA-II	NSGA-II	SPEA2	GD-NSGA-II
Zachary	**0.05 ± 0.01**	**0.05 ± 0.01**	**0.05 ± 0.01**	**0.35 ± 0.03**	0.34 ± 0.03	**0.35 ± 0.03**
Dolphins	0.03 ± 0.01	0.03 ± 0.01	**0.02 ± 0.01**	0.35 ± 0.06	0.35 ± 0.05	**0.39 ± 0.06**
Facebook	0.05 ± 1e–3	0.18 ± 2e–3	**0.03 ± 1e–3**	0.35 ± 7e–3	0.2 ± 5e–3	**0.4 ± 8e–3**

Comparison of IGD and Hypervolume. Figure 6 illustrates the mean IGD and hypervolume for each generation across 30 runs of each approach on each data set. The experimental results show that GD-NSGA-II outperforms the standard NSGA-II and SPEA2 in terms of the hypervolume and IGD the generated Pareto-optimal solutions. We note that as size of the data set increases, the difference in both IGD and hypervolume between GD-NSGA-II, NSGA-II and SPEA2 also increases. This highlights the effectiveness of both the seeding based initialization and the maximum community limit to reduce the search space of detecting community structures in the network, which means our proposed approach scales significantly better than both the NSGA-II and SPEA2 algorithms on large datasets.

6   Conclusions

This paper presented a new GD-NSGA-II algorithm for multi-objective community detection on large social networks. To achieve high scalability and performance, we further adopted the Neo4j graph database to expedite the query and processing of network information stored in the database. Using the built-in LPA algorithm of Neo4j, a new seeding approach was also developed in this paper to boost the search for Pareto optimal community structures in our algorithm. Extensive experiments have been performed in this paper. Our experiments clear showed that GD-NSGA-II is more effective than several existing methods in generating a set of Pareto optima solutions for users to choose according to their preferences. Future work can explore different objective functions.

References

1. Nettleton, D.F.: Data mining of social networks represented as graphs. Computer Science Review **7**, 1–34 (2013)
2. Zhang, Y., et al.: Community detection in networks with node features. Electr. J. Stat. **10**, 3153–3178 (2016)
3. van Gennip, Y., et al.: Community detection using spectral clustering on sparse geosocial data. SIAM J. Appl. Math. **73**, 67–83 (2013)
4. Radicchi, F., et al.: Defining and identifying communities in networks. Proc. NAS **101**, 2658–2663 (2004)

5. Guerrero, M., et al.: Multi-objective evolutionary algorithms to find community structures in large networks. Mathematics **8**, 2048 (2020)

6. Deb, K., et al.: A fast and elitist multiobjective genetic algorithm: NSGA-II. IEEE Trans. Evol. Comput. **6**, 182–197 (2002)

7. Xu, R., Wunsch, D.: Survey of clustering algorithms. IEEE Trans. Neural Netw. **16**, 645–678 (2005)

8. Sreedhar, C., et al.: Clustering large datasets using k-means modified inter and intra clustering (KM-I2C) in hadoop. J. Big Data **4** (2017)

9. Raghavan, U.N., et al.: Near linear time algorithm to detect community structures in large-scale networks. Phys. Rev. E **76**(3) (2007)

10. Poaka, V., Hartmann, S., Ma, H., Steinmetz, D.: A link-density-based algorithm for finding communities in social networks. In: Link, S., Trujillo, J.C. (eds.) ER 2016. LNCS, vol. 9975, pp. 76–85. Springer, Cham (2016). https://doi.org/10.1007/978-3-319-47717-6_7

11. Shi, X., et al.: An overlapping community discovery algorithm based on label propagation. In: CISCE. IEEE, pp. 395–398 (2019)

12. Wen, X., et al.: A maximal clique based multiobjective evolutionary algorithm for overlapping community detection. IEEE Trans. Evol. Comput. **21**, 363–377 (2017)

13. Pizzuti, C.: A multiobjective genetic algorithm to find communities in complex networks. IEEE Trans. Evol. Comput. **16**, 418–430 (2012)

14. Gong, M., et al.: Complex network clustering by multiobjective discrete particle swarm optimization based on decomposition. IEEE Trans. Evol. Comput. **18**, 82–97 (2014)

15. Yun, L., et al.: A genetic algorithm for community detection in complex networks. J. Central South Univ. **20**, 1269–1276 (2013)

16. Bucur, D., Iacca, G.: Influence maximization in social networks with genetic algorithms. In: Squillero, G., Burelli, P. (eds.) EvoApplications 2016. LNCS, vol. 9597, pp. 379–392. Springer, Cham (2016). https://doi.org/10.1007/978-3-319-31204-0_25

17. Ariadi, A., et al.: A graph database supported GA-based approach to social network analysis. In: IEEE SSCI, pp. 01–08 (2020)

18. Jouili, S., Vansteenberghe, V.: An empirical comparison of graph databases. In: International Conference on Social Computing, pp. 708–715. IEEE (2013)

19. Neo4j: Neo4j - the world's leading graph database. [Online]. https://neo4j.com/

20. DB-Engines: Historical trend of graph DBMS popularity [Online]. https://db-engines.com/en/ranking_trend/graph+dbms

21. OrientDB: Orientdb community [Online]. https://orientdb.org/

22. Titan: Titan: distributed graph database [Online]. https://titan.thinkaurelius.com/

23. Sparsity-Technologies: Out-of-core graph database for edge computing. [Online]. https://www.sparsity-technologies.com/

24. Yang, J., Leskovec, J.: Defining and evaluating network communities based on ground-truth. Knowl. Inf. Syst. **42**, 181–213 (2015)

25. Brandes, U., et al.: On modularity clustering. IEEE Trans. Knowl. Data Eng. **20**, 172–188 (2007)

26. Ghosh, A., Das, M.K.: Non-dominated rank based sorting genetic algorithms. Fundamenta Informaticae **83**, 231–252 (2008)

27. Zitzler, E., et al.: SPEA2: Improving the strength pareto evolutionary algorithm. TIK-report, vol. 103 (2001)

28. Girvan, M., Newman, M.E.: Community structure in social and biological networks. Proc. NAS **99**, 7821–7826 (2002)
29. Lusseau, D.: The emergent properties of a dolphin social network. Proc. R. Soc. Lond. B Biol. Sci. **270**, S186–S188 (2003)
30. Jiang, S., et al.: Consistencies and contradictions of performance metrics in multi-objective optimization. IEEE Trans. Cybernetics **44**, 2391–2404 (2014)

Full Research Papers

A Top-Down Scheme for Coverage Centrality Queries on Road Networks

Yehong Xu[1]([✉]) [ID], Mengxuan Zhang[2] [ID], Ruizhong Wu[3], and Lei Li[1,4] [ID]

[1] The Hong Kong University of Science and Technology, Hong Kong, Hong Kong
yxudi@connect.ust.hk, thorli@ust.hk
[2] Iowa State University, Ames, USA
mxzhang@iastate.edu
[3] Guangzhou University, Guangzhou, China
wrz@e.gzhu.edu.cn
[4] The Hong Kong University of Science and Technology (Guangzhou),
Guangzhou, China

Abstract. Coverage Centrality is an important metric to evaluate the node importance in road networks. However, the current solutions have to compute the coverage centrality of all the nodes together, which is resource-wasting especially when only some nodes' centrality is required. In addition, they have poor adaption to the dynamic scenario because of the computation inefficiency. In this paper, we focus on the coverage centrality query problem and propose an efficient algorithm to compute the centrality of a single node efficiently in both static and dynamic scenarios, with the help of the intra-region pruning, inter-region pruning, and top-down search. Experiments validate the efficiency and effectiveness of our algorithm compared with the state-of-the-art method.

Keywords: Coverage Centrality · Road network · Shortest path

1 Introduction

Coverage Centrality (CC) is a centrality metric that evaluates the importance of a node in terms of its contribution to the shortest paths of the underlying network. Knowing the *CC* value of a node (essentially intersections) over a road network is important, as it indicates the extra travel cost might be incurred due to an intersection's blocking [9,23]. Obviously, this knowledge is quite helpful in traffic management and control. However, *CC* is time-consuming to compute and inefficient to maintain. Therefore, in this paper, we study the problem of efficient *CC* computation for a single vertex.

CC is formally defined as followed. Given an undirected weighted road network $G(V, E, W)$ composed of the vertex set V, the edge set $E \subseteq V \times V$, and the weights $W \to \mathbf{R}^+$ associating each edge $e(u, v) \in E$ with a non-negative value $w(u, v)$. Denote by n, m the # vertices and edges, i.e. $n = |V|$ and $m = |E|$. A path $p = \langle v_1, ..., v_k \rangle$ is a sequence of vertices where $(v_i, v_{i+1}) \in E$ for all

© The Author(s), under exclusive license to Springer Nature Switzerland AG 2022
W. Hua et al. (Eds.): ADC 2022, LNCS 13459, pp. 37–49, 2022.
https://doi.org/10.1007/978-3-031-15512-3_3

$i \in [1, k - 1]$ $(k > 1)$. The length of a path $l(p)$ is defined as the sum of edge weights, i.e. $l(p) = \sum_{i=1}^{k-1} w(v_i, v_{i+1})$. Let $p_{s,t}$ denote any path between a vertex pair (s, t). The shortest path $\hat{p}_{s,t}$ is a path among all $p_{s,t}$ with the minimum length. The *Coverage Centrality* of one vertex v is defined as the sum number of vertex pairs that have at least one shortest path passes through v:

$$CC(v) = \sum_{s,t \in V, s \neq t \neq v} \delta_{s,t}(v) \tag{1}$$

where $\delta_{s,t}(v)$ equals to 1 if there exists a shortest path between s and t that passes through v; otherwise 0.

CC values can be obtained/estimated using two branches of methods. The first branch orders only CC ranks but does not calculate the centrality directly [27], so it is out of our consideration. The second branch is based on *Betweenness Centrality (BC)*, whose definition is quite similar to CC with $\delta_{s,t}(v)$ defined as $\delta_{s,t}(v) = \frac{|\hat{p}_{s,t}(v)|}{|\hat{p}_{s,t}|}$ where $\hat{p}_{s,t}$ and $\hat{p}_{s,t}(v)$ denote the shortest path between s, t and the shortest path between s, t passing v, respectively. The fundamental BC algorithm is *Brandes* [3] whose time complexity is $O(m + n^2 log n)$ where n and m are the number of vertices and edges. Clearly, *Brandes* is prohibitive for large graphs. Although there come other strategies improving its scalability [4,5,10, 19,20,25], these strategies could hardly apply to road networks, as analyzed in Sect. 2.2. Therefore, only *Brandes* could be extended to estimate CC [18].

Motivation. *Brandes*-based CC either obtains the centrality of all vertices or none of them, resulting in heavy computation. However, in many cases, we are only interested in the centrality of certain vertices. Besides, the network is dynamic with traffic conditions keep changing [28,29,31], understanding the evolution of vertices' CC values is quite useful. In most real cases, we only need to monitor the evolution of certain interested vertices, while current centrality maintenance algorithms [12,14,15] which are all based on *Brandes* have to pay high costs to keep track of all vertices. Then a question comes naturally: why not focusing on developing a CC calculation algorithm for *single* vertices that can be easily adapted to *dynamic* graphs as it provides a chance to relieve the computation compared to *Brandes*-based methods?

Challenges. Here, we introduce the CC query: given a vertex v, the CC query $q(v)$ asks the CC value of v. According to Formula 1, to answer a CC query, $O(n^2)$ pairs of vertices need to be checked to see whether they pass through v. Then it takes $O(n^2 \times \tau)$ time in total, where τ is the time of checking whether one vertex pair (a, b) passes through v. We call it as the *dependency check* for (a, b). This naive calculation is obviously time-consuming. Therefore, our first challenge is to reduce the # dependency checks. Our second challenge is how to design the algorithm to make it be scalable to dynamic graphs.

Our Ideas. As for the first challenge, given a CC query $q(v)$, we observe that the shortest paths of such vertex pairs (a, b) cannot pass v if $\hat{p}_{v,a}$ and $\hat{p}_{v,b}$ share any common vertex other than v (i.e. overlap). Thus, we do not need check (a, b)

for v. To detect such vertex pairs, the shortest paths from v to all other vertices are required. We find that the *Shortest Path Tree (SPT)* rooted at v (denoted as T_v, Fig. 1) is a perfect structure to organize all these paths, which is formally defined below.

Definition 1 *(Shortest Path Tree (SPT))*. *A shortest path tree rooted at $v \in V$, denoted as T_v is a spanning tree of G such that any simple path from v to another vertex u in T_v corresponds to one of the shortest paths $\hat{p}_{v,u}$ in G.*

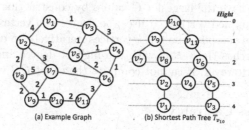

(a) Example Graph   (b) Shortest Path Tree $T_{v_{10}}$

Fig. 1. Example graph and its shortest path tree $T_{v_{10}}$

The vertices that are descendants of the same tree node define a region [24]. As shortest paths to v from vertices in the same region overlap, vertex pairs (a, b) formed by endpoints in the same region can be pruned. We call it *Intra-Region Pruning*. Nevertheless, there remain vertex pairs to check with two endpoints in different regions. According to the *Subpath Property*, those vertex pairs whose shortest path passes through v tend to be closer to the tree root rather than leaves, so we propose the *Top-Down Search* mechanism to check vertex pairs. We further incorporate *Inter-Region Pruning* during the traversal. As for the second challenge, we propose to avoid constructing any index over the given graph such that the algorithm is naturally dynamic.

Contributions. To the best of our knowledge, we are the first to study the efficient CC computation from the aspect of vertex pairs pruning and the first to compute the accurate CC of a single vertex. Specifically, we utilize SPT as the carrier of CC calculation and propose *intra-region pruning* and *inter-region pruning* to prune those vertex pairs with endpoints in two different regions. Finally, we conduct extensive experiments in real-life road networks and the experimental results demonstrate the superiority of our approaches.

2   Related Work

The definition of *Coverage Centrality* was first proposed in [11]. However, the authors did not provide a concrete algorithm to compute it. As proved in [7], CC is equivalent to *Betweenness Centrality (BC)* for a vertex s if every pair of vertex has exactly one shortest path. In this section, we briefly summarize the existing works about CC and BC, along with algorithms for shortest distance queries which is a fundamental operation in our algorithm.

2.1 Coverage Centrality

The only existing method that computes CC is proposed in [1], where CC values are used to derive a vertex order to build a smaller hub-labeling index. The authors assume that every shortest path is unique such that BC and CC are equal. Given a road network G, they first compute SPT T_s for all $s \in V(G)$, which costs $O(nm + n^2 logn)$ time. CC of a vertex v is the sum of # descendants of v in all T_s, which can be obtained by running the depth-first-search algorithm from s over every T_s. This step further costs $O(n^2 + mn)$ time. [27] finds the top-k vertices that have the largest CC values by constructing a hypergraph H which consists of sampled vertices. It uses the degree of a vertex in H to approximate CC value and compute the top-k vertices iteratively. In each iteration, the algorithm first searches the vertex with the highest degree and removes it and its edges from H. However, it cannot compute the exact CC value.

2.2 Betweenness Centrality

The fastest exact BC algorithm is *Brandes* [3]. It runs the *Dijkstra's* algorithm from each vertex v and constructs the corresponding directed acyclic graph (DAG), which encodes all the shortest paths starting from v. The BC value of one vertex is obtained by accumulating the paths' contributions to it through the backward propagation in each DAG. Its time complexity is $O(nm + n^2 logn)$. Partitioning the graph into multiple components could improve the scalability of *Brandes*, and the BC value is obtained by summing up its local BC values within each components [4,25,26]. However, these algorithms fail to improve the time complexity of *Brandes*. Besides, their decomposition methods are not suitable for road networks. Another line of research scales up BC computation through approximation. It derives a subgraph G' from G by various sampling methods [21,22]. BC values are computed by running (modified) *Brandes* over G'. The algorithms focus on finding an error-bounded sampling method such that BC values can be accurately approximated based on a small sample graph G'. Nevertheless, the existing solutions have not fully achieved this goal.

2.3 Shortest Path Algorithms

The shortest distance computation is the building block of our CC computation. Given a CC query $q(v)$, it facilitates us to perform the dependency check for the given vertex pair (a, b) to see if there is any $\hat{p}_{a,b}$ passing through v. The fundamental shortest distance algorithm is *Dijkstra's* [6,17], which finds the shortest path in a *breadth-first search* manner with time complexity $O(m + nlogn)$. Nevertheless, it is not efficient enough, especially for large graphs. Then auxiliary information is stored to accelerate the computation including shortcuts in *Contraction Hierarchy (CH)* [8] and distance labels in *Hub Labeling (HL)* [2,16]. Since the latter approach is generally more efficient even in dynamic graphs [28–30], we use *HL* as our shortest distance index.

3   Algorithm

In this section, we introduce how to calculate the CC of a vertex s using T_s. We first demonstrate the computation framework, then we present our algorithm that traverses and prunes the vertex pairs in T_s.

3.1   Framework

Given a road network G and $q(s)$, our framework employs an SPT rooted at s (T_s) and a *HL*-based shortest distance index $\mathcal{L}$ of G. Every vertex pair (u, v) in the T_s needs either to be checked if it depends on s by the shortest distance algorithm *SPA* based on $\mathcal{L}$, or be pruned based on the structural characteristics of T_s introduced in the following sections. The complexity of building T_s is $O(m + n \log n)$ with *Dijkstra*'s, and # dependency check is $O(n^2)$. Such that the time complexity of our algorithm is $O(n^2 \tau)$, where $O(\tau)$ is the time complexity of *SPA*. Therefore, the total complexity is $O(m + n \log n + n^2 \tau)$, which is normally smaller than *Brandes*'s $O(mn + n^2 \log n)$. The following paragraphs introduce our methods to prune vertex pairs which address our first challenge. Besides, our framework do not construct any index, therefor it can be applied to dynamic graphs simply by adapting a dynamic *SPA* and $\mathcal{L}$ [28,29]. Thereby, our second challenge is also addressed.

3.2   Intra-region Pruning

Definition 2 (Region). *In a tree T_s rooted at s, a region is the set of vertices from subtree $T_s(v)$, $v \in cld(s)$.*

where $T_s(v)$ denotes the subtree rooted at v and $cld(v)$ denotes the children of v. Let M_v be the number of v' children, i.e. $M_v = |cld(v)|$.

   Then V is partitioned into regions $T_s^1, \ldots, T_s^{M_s}$. Particularly, we call a vertex pair (u, w) *intra-region* vertex pair if u and w are located in a same region or otherwise *inter-region* pair. All intra-region vertex pairs can be safely pruned from dependency checking as they definitely do not depend on s according to the following lemma.

Lemma 1. *For any vertex pair in the same region of T_s, i.e. $u, w \in T_s(v)$ ($v \in cld(s)$), then $s \notin \hat{p}_{u,w}$.*

Proof. We can prove it by contradiction. Assume that there exist a shortest path p_1 between u, w in G that contains s. Then the length of p_1 must equal $l(\hat{p_{u,s}}) + l(\hat{p_{s,w}})$. Meanwhile, since u and w are in the same subtree $T_s(v)$, there must exist a path p_2 between u, w that is the concatenation of $\hat{p}_{u,v}, \hat{p}_{v,w}$. Given that $l(\hat{u, v}) < l(\hat{u, s})$ and $l(v, \hat{w} < v, \hat{s})$, we have $l(p_2) < l(p_1)$. Thus, p_1 cannot be a shortest path between u, w, this contradicts to our assumption. We thereby proved that $s \notin \hat{p}_{u,w}$.   ∎

   Suppose the # vertices in each region of T_s is $n_1, \ldots, n_{M_s}$, then there are $\sum_{1 \leq i \leq M_s} n_i^2$ vertex pairs being pruned from the dependency checking.

3.3 Inter-region Pruning

Following the *intra-region pruning*, there left only the *inter-region* vertex pair for dependency checks. That is, we only need to check the vertex pair (u, v) with $u \in T_s^i, v \in T_s^j$ $(1 \leq i < j \leq M_s)$. How could we check those $\sum_{1 \leq i < j \leq M_s} n_i \times n_j$ vertex pairs efficiently? The naive solution is to check them one by one, however, some vertex pairs could avoid being checked if their *parent vertex pairs* (defined as follows) do not have a shortest path passing s, as illustrated in Lemma 2.

Definition 3 (Parent Vertex Pair). *Given a vertex $v \in V$, we use $v.p$ to denote the parent of v in T_s. For a vertex pair(u, v), its right parent vertex pair is $(u, v.p)$ and its left parent vertex pair is $(u.p, v)$.*

Lemma 2. *A vertex pair (u, v) does not have any shortest path passing s if neither parent vertex pairs of (u, v) does.*

Proof. Suppose the right parent vertex pair $(u, v.p)$ does not depend on s. We denote $p_{u,v.p}$ as a path concatenated by $\hat{p}_{u,s}, \hat{p}_{s,v.p}$, and $p_{u,v}$ is concatenated by $\hat{p}_{u,s}, \hat{p}_{s,v.p}$ and the edge $(v.p, v)$. Clearly, $p_{u,v.p}$ is a subpath of $p_{u,v}$. Since $p_{u,v.p}$ is not the shortest path, $p_{u,v}$ cannot be either, and shortest paths between (u, v) do not pass s. This reason also applies to the left parent vertex pair. ∎

Top-Down Traversal. To avoid unnecessary vertex pair checking, for a vertex pair, we could check its parent vertex pairs first and then decide whether to check it based on its parent vertex pairs' results. In other words, we can check the *inter-region* vertex pair by traversing the *SPT* in a top-down manner, and we call this way of vertex pair checking as *top-down traversal*. And we use *transmission route* to embody the traversal and define it as follows.

Definition 4 (Transmission Route). *A transmission route Tra is to encode the sequence of movements to get from an inter-region vertex pair (u, v) $(u \in T_s^i, v \in T_s^j$ and $i < j)$ to its descendant vertex pairs, where each movement is a downward hop in T_s^i or T_s^j via an edge in T_s. Without loss of generality, we use 0 (resp. 1) to denote the downward hop in T_s^i (resp. T_s^j).*

For example, $(v_9, v_{11}) \xrightarrow{Tra} (v_7, v_{11}), (v_8, v_{11})$ with $Tra = \{0\}$ and $(v_9, v_{11}) \xrightarrow{Tra} (v_7, v_6), (v_8, v_6)$ with $Tra = \{10, 01\}$.

For the inter-region vertex pairs across two regions T_s^i, T_s^j $(i \neq j)$, we initialize the traversal by first checking the vertex pair (v_i, v_j) where v_i (resp. v_j) is the root of T_s^i (resp. T_s^j), then push down the traversal by checking its child vertex pairs $\{(v_i', v_j)|\forall v_i' \in cld(v_i)\}$ and $\{(v_i, v_j')|\forall v_j' \in cld(v_j)\}$. It can be easily seen that every vertex pair between the two regions have the chance to be checked. Nevertheless, some vertex pairs could be checked more than once according to the following Lemma 3, which results in a significant amount of redundant computation.

Lemma 3. *Suppose that the dependency check on the vertex pair (u, v) $(u \in T_s^i, v \in T_s^j$ and $i \neq j)$ propagates to vertex pair (u', v') with $h_s(u') - h_s(u) = a, h_s(v') - h_s(v) = b$, then (u', v') could be repeatedly checked for C_{a+b}^a times.*

where $h_s(v)$ denotes the height of v in T_s $(h_s(s) = 0)$.

Proof. To traverse (u', v') downwards from (u, v), the movements in transmission route $(u, v) \xrightarrow{Tra} (u', v')$ contains a 0s and b 1s. Whereas, the order of movements in T_s^i or T_s^j does not make any difference. Therefore, there are C_{a+b}^a different transmission routes such that (u', v') would be repeatedly checked for C_{a+b}^a times. ∎

The question then becomes how to skillfully avoid redundant dependency checks without the need to label if a vertex pair has been checked already.

Theorem 1. *For $(u, v) \xrightarrow{Tra} (u', v')$ with $h_s(u') - h_s(u) = a, h_s(v') - h_s(v) = b, a + b > 1$, if we exclude all Tras that contain the subsequence "10", then there left only one Tra.*

Proof. We only need to prove that there exists only one Tra that does not contain any subsequence "10". This is intuitively right because Tra can only be in the format $Tra = \{0\}^i \{1\}^j$ where $i, j \geq 0, i + j = a + b$. ∎

For example (Fig. 1), in $(v_9, v_{11}) \xrightarrow{Tra} (v_2, v_6)$, $Tra = \{100, 010, 001\}$. And $Tra = \{001\}$ after the "10" restriction.

Algorithm 1: Top-down traversal

Input: $T_s, C_s \leftarrow \infty$
Result: $CC(s)$
1 $CC(s) = 0; H \leftarrow \{(u, v, 0) | u, v \in cld(s), u \neq v\}$
2 **while** H *is not empty* **do**
3     $u, v, ant \leftarrow H.pop()$
4     $dc \leftarrow DC(u, v, s)$ //dependency check
5   **if** dc **then**
6        $CC(s) \leftarrow CC(s) + 1$
7   **if** $C(s) \geq C_s$ **then**
8   Break
9   **foreach** $w \in cld(v)$ **do**
10           $H.insert((u, w, 1))$
11   **if** $ant = 0$ **then**
12   **foreach** $w \in cld(u)$ **do**
13              $H.insert((w, v, 0))$

14 **return** $CC(s)$

We could avoid the repetitive dependency checks by complying with Theorem 1, which indicates that we will not check the left child vertex pair of the right child vertex pair. Along with Lemma 2, we could prune the unnecessary vertex pairs and terminate the traversal as soon as possible. With all these theoretical directions, we illustrate our *top-down traversal* in Algorithm 1. Specifically, we first construct a shortest path tree T_s and initialize a heap H by pushing into a triple $(u, v, 0)$ with $u, v \in cld(s)$ (line 1). $DC(u, v, s)$ is the dependency check function and we use dc to denote the dependency check result. dc is true if s depends on (u, v), otherwise false. If s depends on (u, v), we insert its child vertex pair into H according to Theorem 1 (line 5–13). We further adopt a stop condition (line 7–8) where the threshold C_s can be set to an extremely large value (e.g. $\geq 10^8$). This design is based on the fact that accurate CC calculation is no longer needed when the value is certainly up to some level.

4   Experiments

4.1   Experiment Setting

Datasets. We test on four real-world road networks [13] as shown in Table 1.

Table 1. Real-world road networks

Name	Region	# Vertices n	# Edges m
DG	Dongguan	8,315	11,128
WH	Wuhan	21,560	30,008
SZ	Suzhou	46,094	62,190
SH	Shanghai	78,560	106,728

Queries. We randomly sampled 1,000 vertices from all vertices in each road network. To inspect the CC distribution of the randomly selected vertices, we group these vertices by CC values and summarize the proportion of them in each group. Specifically, we divide the selected vertices into 10 groups Q_1 to Q_{10} where Q_1 constitutes of those whose CC values are ≤ 1 and Q_i ($2 \leq i \leq 10$) constitutes of those whose CC values are in the range of $[10^{i-1}, 10^i)$. Figure 2 shows the cumulative distribution of randomly selected vertices over these groups. Clearly that in all road networks, most vertices fall into query groups from Q_1 to Q_8. Besides, we recorded the CC values C_{10} that ranked at the top $10th$ percentile in each road network.

Algorithms. Our top-down algorithm adopts PLL [2] to facilitate dependency checks (Algorithm 1 line 4). Besides, the termination threshold C_s is set to C_{10} of corresponding road networks. As for the baseline, since there is no algorithm that computes exact CC nor an algorithm for CC or BC query processing, we could only compare the efficiency of our algorithm with states-of-art algorithms that collectively compute BC values for all vertices in the given graph. Here, we choose *Brandes* [3] as our baseline. All algorithms are implemented in C++ and compiled with GNU GCC 9.2.0 with full optimization and conducted on a machine with an Intel Xeon CPU with 2.20 GHz and 1 TB main memory running Linux.

Metrics. To evaluate the efficiency of our algorithm, we recorded the # dependency checks done by our algorithm when processing each CC query. This is because dependency checks dominate the efficiency of our algorithm. We also recorded the running time of processing each CC query. As for the *Brandes* algorithm, we record its running time for processing each road network.

4.2   Experimental Results

The experimental results when grouping the randomly selected query vertices by their CC values (as described in Sect. 4.1) are shown in Fig. 3 and Fig. 4.

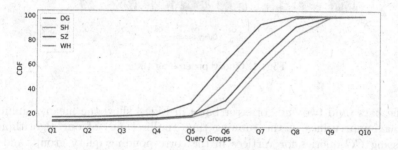

Fig. 2. CC cumulative distribution of 1,000 randomly selected vertices on all road networks.

Specifically, Fig. 3 shows the mean, minimum, and maximum values of # dependency checks executed by our algorithm for processing the CC queries for vertices in the corresponding query group. Observing Fig. 3 we find that when the CC value increases, the # dependency checks tend to increase in all road networks. This is because our algorithm only prunes those vertex pairs whose left (or right) parent vertex pair in the T_s does not depend on the query vertex s (Lemma 2). While s with a large CC value must have a relatively small number of vertex pairs not depending on it. Such that the top-down traversal over T_s can only prune a small number of vertex pairs. Hence, # dependency checks are large. We also find that vertices that have similar CC values tend to have similar # dependency checks even though they are in road networks with varying sizes, which reflects that the graph size does not dominate the efficiency of our algorithm. However, this does not mean that they are not correlated. Indeed, a vertex in a larger graph is more likely to have a big CC value (Fig. 2), thus more likely to require abundant dependency checks.

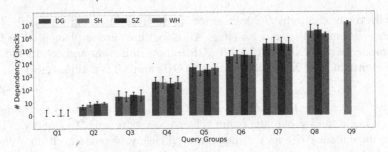

Fig. 3. # of dependency check

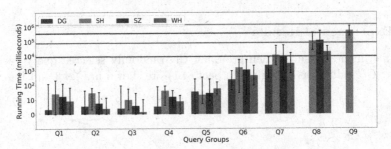

Fig. 4. Query processing time

The bars (and two ends of error bars) in Fig. 4 show the mean, minimum, and maximum values of the running time (millisecond) of our algorithm for processing CC queries for vertices in the corresponding query group, and the horizontal lines denote the running time of the *Brandes* algorithm for processing the road networks. We have the following observations. First, in Q_1 the minimum running time in all road networks is nearly 0. Note that processing a CC query by our algorithm must involve an SPT construction while may not incur any dependency check. This means that the minimum running time of our algorithm is the time cost for the SPT construction. Since it could be nearly 0, the overhead of the SPT construction in our algorithm can be ignored. Second, when CC values increase, the running time in all road networks also tends to increase. This is because # dependency checks of our algorithm increases as the CC value of a vertex increases. Thereby, a longer time is needed. Third, for vertices in the same query group, it generally takes a longer time for our algorithm to process those from a large road network. Fourth, our algorithm is faster than *Brandes* in orders of magnitude for processing most (at least 90%) of the vertices, especially for those with low CC values (Q_1 to Q_4). Therefore, we can derive that our algorithm is feasible for processing most CC queries.

5   Conclusion

In this paper, we study the problem of efficient computation of the CC value of individual vertices in the road network. We propose pruning strategies that significantly shrink the search space for CC computation. We also propose a novel CC computation algorithm adapting these strategies. The experimental results demonstrate that our approach achieves a speedup of orders of magnitude for most query vertices compared to the baseline.

References

1. Abraham, I., Delling, D., Goldberg, A.V., Werneck, R.F.: A Hub-based labeling algorithm for shortest paths in road networks. In: Pardalos, P.M., Rebennack, S. (eds.) SEA 2011. LNCS, vol. 6630, pp. 230–241. Springer, Heidelberg (2011). https://doi.org/10.1007/978-3-642-20662-7_20
2. Akiba, T., Iwata, Y., Yoshida, Y.: Fast exact shortest-path distance queries on large networks by pruned landmark labeling. In: Proceedings of the 2013 ACM SIGMOD International Conference on Management of Data, pp. 349–360 (2013)
3. Brandes, U.: A faster algorithm for betweenness centrality. J. Math. Sociol. 25(2), 163–177 (2001)
4. Daniel, C., Furno, A., Goglia, L., Zimeo, E.: Fast cluster-based computation of exact betweenness centrality in large graphs. J. Big Data 8 (2021)
5. De Meo, P., Ferrara, E., Fiumara, G., Provetti, A.: Generalized Louvain method for community detection in large networks. In: 2011 11th International Conference on Intelligent Systems Design and applications, pp. 88–93. IEEE (2011)
6. Dijkstra, E.W., et al.: A note on two problems in connexion with graphs. Num. Math. 1(1), 269–271 (1959)
7. Freeman, L.C.: A set of measures of centrality based on betweenness. Sociometry 40, 35–41 (1977)
8. Geisberger, R., Sanders, P., Schultes, D., Delling, D.: Contraction hierarchies: faster and simpler hierarchical routing in road networks. In: McGeoch, C.C. (ed.) WEA 2008. LNCS, vol. 5038, pp. 319–333. Springer, Heidelberg (2008). https://doi.org/10.1007/978-3-540-68552-4_24
9. Henry, E., Bonnetain, L., Furno, A., El Faouzi, N.E., Zimeo, E.: Spatio-temporal correlations of betweenness centrality and traffic metrics. In: 2019 6th International Conference on Models and Technologies for Intelligent Transportation Systems (MT-ITS), pp. 1–10. IEEE (2019)
10. Hoang, L., Pontecorvi, M., Dathathri, R., Gill, G., You, B., Pingali, K., Ramachandran, V.: A round-efficient distributed betweenness centrality algorithm. In: Proceedings of the 24th Symposium on Principles and Practice of Parallel Programming, pp. 272–286 (2019)
11. Ishakian, V., Erdös, D., Terzi, E., Bestavros, A.: A framework for the evaluation and management of network centrality. In: Proceedings of the 2012 SIAM International Conference on Data Mining, pp. 427–438. SIAM (2012)
12. Jamour, F., Skiadopoulos, S., Kalnis, P.: Parallel algorithm for incremental betweenness centrality on large graphs. IEEE Trans. Parall. Distrib. Syst. 29(3), 659–672 (2017)

13. Karduni, A., Kermanshah, A., Derrible, S.: A protocol to convert spatial polyline data to network formats and applications to world urban road networks. Sci. Data **3**(1), 1–7 (2016)
14. Kourtellis, N., Morales, G.D.F., Bonchi, F.: Scalable online betweenness centrality in evolving graphs. IEEE Trans. Knowl. Data Eng. **27**(9), 2494–2506 (2015)
15. Lee, M.J., Lee, J., Park, J.Y., Choi, R.H., Chung, C.W.: QUBE: a quick algorithm for updating betweenness centrality. In: Proceedings of the 21st International Conference on World Wide Web, pp. 351–360 (2012)
16. Li, L., Wang, S., Zhou, X.: Time-dependent hop labeling on road network. In: 2019 IEEE 35th International Conference on Data Engineering (ICDE), pp. 902–913. IEEE (2019)
17. Li, L., Zhang, M., Hua, W., Zhou, X.: Fast query decomposition for batch shortest path processing in road networks. In: ICDE, pp. 1189–1200. IEEE (2020)
18. Li, Y., U, L.H., Yiu, M.L., Kou, N.M.: An experimental study on hub labeling based shortest path algorithms. Proc. VLDB Endow. **11**(4), 445–457 (2017)
19. Madduri, K., Ediger, D., Jiang, K., Bader, D.A., Chavarria-Miranda, D.: A faster parallel algorithm and efficient multithreaded implementations for evaluating betweenness centrality on massive datasets. In: 2009 IEEE International Symposium on Parallel & Distributed Processing. pp. 1–8. IEEE (2009)
20. Puzis, R., Zilberman, P., Elovici, Y., Dolev, S., Brandes, U.: Heuristics for speeding up betweenness centrality computation. In: 2012 International Conference on Privacy, Security, Risk and Trust and 2012 International Confernece on Social Computing, pp. 302–311. IEEE (2012)
21. Riondato, M., Kornaropoulos, E.M.: Fast approximation of betweenness centrality through sampling. Data Mining Knowl. Discov. **30**(2), 438–475 (2015). https://doi.org/10.1007/s10618-015-0423-0
22. Riondato, M., Upfal, E.: ABRA: approximating betweenness centrality in static and dynamic graphs with Rademacher averages. ACM Trans. Knowl. Discov. Data **12**(5), 1–38 (2018)
23. Rupi, F., Bernardi, S., Rossi, G., Danesi, A.: The evaluation of road network vulnerability in mountainous areas: a case study. Netw. Spat. Econ. **15**(2), 397–411 (2015)
24. Samet, H., Sankaranarayanan, J., Alborzi, H.: Scalable network distance browsing in spatial databases. In: Proceedings of the 2008 ACM SIGMOD International Conference on Management of Data, pp. 43–54 (2008)
25. Sariyüce, A.E., Saule, E., Kaya, K., Çatalyürek, Ü.V.: Shattering and compressing networks for betweenness centrality. In: Proceedings of the 2013 SIAM International Conference on Data Mining, pp. 686–694. SIAM (2013)
26. Suppa, P., Zimeo, E.: A clustered approach for fast computation of betweenness centrality in social networks. In: 2015 IEEE International Congress on Big Data, pp. 47–54. IEEE (2015)
27. Yoshida, Y.: Almost linear-time algorithms for adaptive betweenness centrality using hypergraph sketches. In: Proceedings of the 20th ACM SIGKDD International Conference on Knowledge Discovery and Data Mining, pp. 1416–1425 (2014)
28. Zhang, M., Li, L., Hua, W., Mao, R., Chao, P., Zhou, X.: Dynamic hub labeling for road networks. In: 2021 IEEE 37th International Conference on Data Engineering (ICDE), pp. 336–347. IEEE (2021)
29. Zhang, M., Li, L., Hua, W., Zhou, X.: Efficient 2-hop labeling maintenance in dynamic small-world networks. In: 2021 IEEE 37th International Conference on Data Engineering (ICDE), pp. 133–144. IEEE (2021)

30. Zhang, M., Li, L., Zhou, X.: An experimental evaluation and guideline for path finding in weighted dynamic network. Proc. VLDB Endow. **14**(11), 2127–2140 (2021)
31. Zhou, A., Wang, Y., Chen, L.: Butterfly counting on uncertain bipartite graphs. Proc. VLDB Endow. **15**(2), 211–223 (2021)

Personalized Arrhythmia Detection Based on Lightweight Autoencoder and Variational Autoencoder

Zhaoyi Zhong[1,2], Le Sun[1,2(✉)], and Sudha Subramani[3]

[1] Engineering Research Center of Digital Forensics, Ministry of Education, Nanjing University of Information Science and Technology, Nanjing, China
{20201221065,LeSun1}@nuist.edu.cn
[2] Department of Jiangsu Collaborative Innovation Center of Atmospheric Environment and Equipment Technology (CICAEET), Nanjing University of Information Science and Technology, Nanjing 210044, China
[3] Victoria University, Footscray, Australia
Sudha.Subramani@vu.edu.au

Abstract. Arrhythmia has become one of the important causes of human death. The research on arrhythmia detection has great medical value. In reality, patients' arrhythmia heartbeat is much less than the normal heartbeat. Supervised classifiers often have the problem of imbalanced training data. Therefore, we propose an unsupervised personalized arrhythmia detection system, called PerAD. PerAD trains a lightweight autoencoder ShaAE for each user for arrhythmia detection. ShaAE only needs to use the user's personal normal data for training. The encoder and decoder of ShaAE are composed of a lightweight network ShaRNN. ShaRNN is a two-layer RNN structure that can process data in parallel. Thus, ShaAE is easy to deploy to edge wearable devices. We also design a fast-inference variational autoencoder to generate normal simulation samples to assist in training ShaAE. We test ShaAE on MIT-BIH Arrhythmia Database. ShaAE without using simulation data to assist training can achieve 96.86% accuracy. ShaAE using simulation samples to assist training can achieve accuracy of 97.11% and has 6.19% higher performance than state-of-the-art for f1 score.

Keywords: Deep learning · Arrhythmia detection · Unsupervised learning · Lightweight autoencoder · Variational autoencoder

1 Introduction

The rapid development of the Internet of things has provided a lot of data for smart medicine [13]. Researchers began to use various machine learning or deep

This work is partially supported by the National Natural Science Foundation of China (Grants No. 61702274), PAPD and the Major Key Project of PCL (Grant No. PCL2022A03, PCL2021A02, PCL2021A09).

learning methods based on big data to help diagnose various diseases [10, 20, 26, 31, 32, 34]. Arrhythmia is a common cardiovascular disease. Arrhythmia causes millions of deaths every year [19]. In the past, arrhythmia detection requires professional instruments to collect ECG signals, and professional doctors to make judgments according to the collected ECG signals. This not only aggravates the burden of doctors, but also fails to diagnose whether the patient has arrhythmia in time.

Recently, the research on arrhythmia detection based on machine learning and deep learning has received great attention. Many scholars have used machine learning methods to detect arrhythmia. For example, Salam [30] and Chen [8] used support vector machine (SVM) to classify normal heartbeats and arrhythmia heartbeats. The method of arrhythmia detection based on machine learning has high requirements for training data. In reality, the arrhythmia heartbeat of patients is generally far less than the normal heartbeat. So the training data often have the class imbalance problem [17]. Methods based on deep learning are often keen to train a large comprehensive deep classification model for arrhythmia detection. Rajpurkar [28] and Acharya [1] proposed a deep neural network with 34 and 11 revolution layers to classify heartbeat respectively. Yao [39] proposed a convolution neural network based on attention mechanism for 12 lead ECG signal arrhythmia detection. The methods mentioned above used a large amount of data to train a large comprehensive model to detect arrhythmia for all users. And the cost of training a large comprehensive model is very high. And these methods still have the class imbalance problem during the training phase.

In order to avoid the class imbalance problem, some methods choose to use unsupervised model to detect arrhythmia. The unsupervised model only needs to be trained with normal heartbeat data. Autoencoder (AE) is a classical unsupervised model. AE has been widely used in time series data analysis. For example, Yin et al. [40] build an autoencoder based on convolution neural network to detect anomalies in the time series data of the Internet of things. Xu et al. [38] used variational autoencoder (VAE) to detect anomaly in KPIs data flow of web application of Internet company. Some scholars have applied AE to arrhythmia detection. For example, Keiichi et al. [25] used the denoising autoencoder as a feature extractor to detect arrhythmia based on the extracted features. Thill et al. [35] designed an autoencoder based on temporal convolution network (TCN) for arrhythmia detection. Hou et al. [15] designed an autoencoder based on long short-term memory network (LSTM) to detect arrhythmia. Generic antigenic neural networks (GANs) is also a unsupervised model. Zhou et al. [41] uses GANs to detect arrhythmia. Both GANs and VAE belong to the generation model. However, the training of GANs is more unstable and the training time is longer. VAE with simple structure can train faster.

In order to solve the above problems, this paper proposes an unsupervised personalized arrhythmia detection system, called PerAD. The core of PerAD includes a lightweight autoencoder ShaAE and a fast-inference variational autoencoder. PerAD provides each user with a ShaAE for arrhythmia detection. The fast-inference variational autoencoder (VAE) is used to generate normal simulation data to assist in training ShaAE. PerAD has good performance on MIT-BIH arrhythmia database. And PerAD can be easily deployed on personal edge devices. The main contributions of this paper are as follows:

* We propose a lightweight autoencoder ShaAE for arrhythmia detection. ShaAE is built by a lightweight structure based on RNN. ShaAE can process data in parallel and can be easily deployed to edge wearable devices.
* We propose an unsupervised personalized arrhythmia detection system, called PerAD. PerAD provides each user with a separate ShaAE for arrhythmia detection. There will be no problem of unbalanced data during the training phase. And the overall system is more flexible.
* We use a fast influence VAE to assist in training ShaAE. This VAE has little inference time. And the performance of ShaAE with training assisted by simulation samples is greatly improved.

The rest of this paper is organized as follows: Sect. 2 summarizes the related work of arrhythmia detection and anomaly detection. Section 3 introduces our proposed system PerAD. Section 4 introduces the experiments and analyzes the performance of PerAD; and Sect. 5 summarizes the paper.

2   Relate Work

2.1   Arrhythmia Detection

Machine learning and deep learning methods are widely used in arrhythmia detection. Recurrent neural network (RNN) is good at extracting the contextual features of time series data. Long short-term memory network (LSTM) and gate recurrent unit (GRU) are two common RNNs. Chauhan et al. [5] used LSTM to classify different categories of arrhythmias. Pandey et al. [27] used convolutional autoencoder to extract ECG features. Then, the bidirectional long short-term memory network (BiLSTM) was used to detect arrhythmias. The author also compared many models commonly used in time series data classification with the model they proposed. Xu et al. [37] used 1D convolution and GRU to build a system for arrhythmia classification. This system is used to classify five different arrhythmias. And the system can process variable length ECG data.

2.2   Anomaly Detection

Many machine learning and deep learning methods have been frequently used in anomaly detection. For example, one-class SVM [11] is a common tool for anomaly detection. One-class SVM uses only positive samples (normal data) to train the model. One-class SVM maps data to feature space and uses hyperplane to distinguish normal data from abnormal data. Some deep one-class networks are also trained to learn the boundary between normal data and abnormal data [4,29]. Autoencoder (AE) [3] is a powerful tool in the field of anomaly detection. It belongs to unsupervised neural network. AE uses only normal data to train according to the reconstruction error. When abnormal data is input during the test phase, the reconstruction error will be large. Therefore, the reconstruction error value can be used as an index to distinguish whether the input data is abnormal data. Recently, AE is also widely used in anomaly detection problems such as medical time series and images [7,12]. Variational autoencoder (VAE) [18] is a special autoencoder. The decoder of VAE can generate simulation data similar to the training data. Therefore, it is also a generation model.

3 Our Proposed Methodology

3.1 Problem Definition

Table 1. Meaning of the main notations

Notation	Meaning
$X = \{X_1, X_2 \ldots X_n\}$, $\{X\}_{normal}$ and $\{X\}_{abnormal}$	$X = \{X_1, X_2 \ldots X_n\}$ is an ECG record containing n heartbeats. X is divided into two sets $\{X\}_{normal}$ and $\{X\}_{abnormal}$. $\{X\}_{normal}$ contains only the heartbeat without arrhythmia. $\{X\}_{abnormal}$ contains only the heartbeat with arrhythmia
$\{X\}_{source}$, $\{X\}_{simulation}$, $\{X\}_{train}$ and $\{X\}_{test}$	$\{X\}_{source}$ is the collection of ECG records of the user after preprocessing. $\{X\}_{simulation}$ is the simulation data set generated using VAE. $\{X\}_{train}$ is the training set of ShaAE. $\{X\}_{source}$ and $\{X\}_{simulation}$ are merged into $\{X\}_{train}$. $\{X\}_{test}$ is the test set of ShaAE
$x = [x_1, \ldots x_T]$, $z = [z_1, \ldots z_P]$ and $\hat{x} = [\hat{x}_1, \ldots \hat{x}_T]$	x is a heartbeat vector containing a total of T data points. z is the encoding result of x. z contains a total of P data points. $\hat{x}$ is the reconstruction result of x. In this paper, the input data, coding results and reconstruction results of all autoencoders are represented by x, z and $\hat{x}$
$f(\bullet)$, $f_{encoder}(\bullet)$ and $f_{decoder}(\bullet)$	$f(\bullet)$ is a standard autoencoder. $f_{encoder}(\bullet)$ is the encoder of $f(\bullet)$. $f_{decoder}(\bullet)$ is the decoder of $f(\bullet)$
$F(\bullet)$, $F_{encoder}(\bullet)$ and $F_{decoder}(\bullet)$	$F(\bullet)$ is a ShaRNN based AutoEncoder (ShaAE). $F_{encoder}(\bullet)$ is the encoder of $F(\bullet)$. $F_{decoder}(\bullet)$ is the decoder of $F(\bullet)$
$G(\bullet)$, $G_{encoder}(\bullet)$ and $G_{decoder}(\bullet)$	$G(\bullet)$ is a fast-inference VAE. $G_{encoder}(\bullet)$ is the encoder of $G(\bullet)$, $G_{encoder}(\bullet)$ is the decoder of $G(\bullet)$

Table 1 shows the main notations used in this paper. We regard arrhythmia detection as anomaly detection. Heartbeat with arrhythmia is classified as abnormal heartbeat. Heartbeat without arrhythmia is classified as normal heartbeat. Given a single lead ECG record containing n heartbeats, $X = \{X_1, X_2 \ldots X_n\}$, we divide x into two sets, namely $\{X\}_{normal}$ and $\{X\}_{abnormal}$. The heartbeat in $\{X\}_{normal}$ is a normal heartbeat, and the heartbeat in $\{X\}_{abnormal}$ is an abnormal heartbeat with arrhythmia.

3.2   Encoder and Decoder

Autoencoder is a common tool in the field of anomaly detection. A standard autoencoder $f(\bullet)$ usually consists of encoder $f_{encoder}(\bullet)$ and decoder $f_{decoder}(\bullet)$. Encoder is often used to compress the dimensions of input data to obtain the coding result. The encoding result can also represent the meaningful features extracted by the encoder from the input data. The decoder reconstructs the encoding result to obtain the reconstruction result. We define the data input to the autoencoder as $x = [x_1, \ldots x_T]$. Input x into encoder $f_{encoder}(\bullet)$ to get encoding result $z = [z_1, \ldots z_P]$. Usually $P \ll T$. Input z into decoder $f_{decoder}(\bullet)$ to get reconstruction result $\hat{x} = [\hat{x}_1, \ldots \hat{x}_T]$. This process can be represented by Eq. 1

$$
\begin{aligned}
z &= f_{encoder}(x), x \in R^T, z \in R^P \\
\hat{x} &= f_{decoder}(z), \hat{x} \in R^T
\end{aligned}
\tag{1}
$$

Usually, the reconstruction error $Loss_{recon}$ of autoencoder needs to be calculated in training and testing phase. we use the l_2-norm based mean square error (MSE) to calculate $Loss_{recon}$, see Eq. 2

$$
MSE(x, \hat{x}) = \|x - \hat{x}\|_2^2.
\tag{2}
$$

The autoencoder uses only normal data for training. Therefore, it will only learn the patterns of normal data. In the testing phase, abnormal data input into the trained autoencoder will obtain larger reconstruction loss than normal data. Therefore, we can use a threshold to distinguish between normal and abnormal data.

3.3   PerAD

We express the training set and test set as $\{X\}_{train}$ and $\{X\}_{test}$ respectively. $\{X\}_{train}$ only contains the normal heartbeats of the user. Our aim is to use $\{X\}_{train}$ to train a lightweight autoencoder $F(\bullet)$ for personalized arrhythmia detection. Given an arrhythmia threshold AT, $F(\bullet)$ can divide any ECG record x provided by a user into $\{X\}_{normal}$ and $\{X\}_{abnormal}$.

We propose a system for personalized arrhythmia detection called PerAD. Figure 1 shows the overall framework of PerAD. In the training phase, firstly, the user's normal ECG record is divided into multiple heartbeats in preprocessing to form a set $\{X\}_{source}$. Then a fast-inference variational autoencoder (VAE) $G(\bullet)$ is trained to generate normal simulation samples to form a set $\{X\}_{simulation}$. Finally $\{X\}_{source}$ and $\{X\}_{simulation}$ are combined into a training set $\{X\}_{train}$ to train a lightweight autoencoder $F(\bullet)$ for the user. In the testing phase, the trained $F(\bullet)$ will calculate the reconstruction loss $Loss_{recon}$ of the user's test set $\{X\}_{test}$. If $Loss_{recon} > AT$, $F(\bullet)$ will classify the heartbeat as abnormal heartbeat. If $Loss_{recon} \leq AT$, $F(\bullet)$ will classify the heartbeat as normal heartbeat.

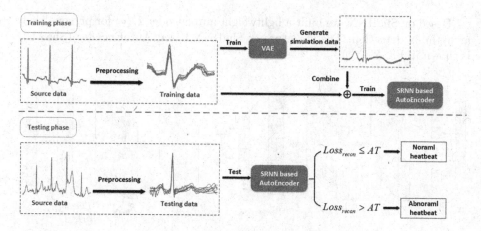

Fig. 1. Overall framework of PerAD.

Preprocessing. Different ECG records may have the problems of inconsistent sampling rate and having noise. Therefore, we first resample the continuous ECG record 360 Hz [33]. Then, the ECG record will be denoised by wavelet denoising [21]. In order to segment the continuous ECG signal into multiple heartbeats, we use the R peak detection algorithm [22] to locate the R peak of each heartbeat. Finally, by intercepting 99 and 200 data points before and after the R peak, we divide the continuous ECG signal into a set composed of multiple heartbeats.

ShaRNN Based AutoEncoder. Recurrent neural network (RNN) is good at extracting contextual features of sequential data. RNN has been widely used in time series prediction and classification. Although RNN has a good performance in time series processing, it requires a large training and inference cost. Therefore, this paper introduces a lightweight RNN structure, ShaRNN [9], which processes the input data in parallel and can significantly reduce the inference cost. Specifically, ShaRNN is mainly composed of two-layer structure. Given an input sequence data $x = [x_1, x_2 \ldots x_T]$, the first layer structure $L^{(1)}$ of ShaRNN divides x into independent data blocks first. Note that the set composed of all data blocks is $B = [B_1, \ldots, B_{T/k}]$, where B_i is each data block and k is the size of each data block. After that, all data blocks will be input into the same standard RNN cell $(R^{(1)})$ to get the output $v^{(1)} = [v_1^{(1)}, \ldots, v_{T/k}^{(1)}]$, see Eq. 3.

$$v_i^{(1)} = R^{(1)}(B_i), i \in [T/k]. \tag{3}$$

The second layer structure $L^{(2)}$ of ShaRNN includes a standard RNN cell $(R^{(2)})$ and a full connection layer (*linear*). Input $v^{(1)}$ into $R^{(2)}$ to get $v^{(2)}$, see Eq. 4.

$$v_{T/k}^{(2)} = R^{(2)}\left(\left[v_1^{(1)}, \ldots, v_{T/k}^{(1)}\right]\right). \tag{4}$$

The final output result of *linear* is $y = linear(v^{(2)})$.

Based on ShaRNN, we built a lightweight autoencoder $F\left(\bullet\right)$ for personalized arrhythmia detection. The structure of ShaRNN based AutoEncoder (ShaAE) is shown in Fig. 2.

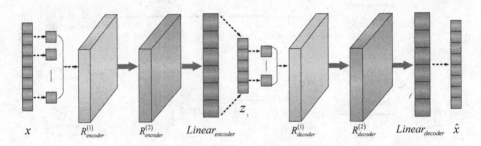

Fig. 2. Structure of ShaAE.

As shown in Fig. 2, both encoder $F_{encoder}$ and decoder $F_{decoder}$ are composed of a two-layer structure of ShaRNN. On the whole, $F\left(\bullet\right)$ has a symmetrical structure. In our model, the shape of the input data x satisfies the form of $[batchsize, length]$, where $batchsize$ is the number of heartbeats contained in a batch in the training or testing phase, and $length$ is the length of heartbeats. In this paper, $length = 300$. In order to enable the encoder $F_{encoder}$ and decoder $F_{decoder}$ to encode and reconstruct the input data, we adjust the hidden state dimension of RNN cell and the dimension of $linear$ layer in $F_{encoder}$ and $F_{decoder}$. Specifically, $F_{encoder}$ and $F_{decoder}$ include six main structures: $R_{encoder}^{(1)}$, $R_{encoder}^{(2)}$, $R_{decoder}^{(1)}$, $R_{decoder}^{(2)}$, $Linear_{encoder}$ and $Linear_{decoder}$ (see Fig. 2). We set the hidden state dimension of $R_{encoder}^{(1)}$, $R_{encoder}^{(2)}$, $R_{decoder}^{(1)}$ and $R_{decoder}^{(2)}$ to 200. We set the output dimension of $Linear_{encoder}$ and $Linear_{decoder}$ to 100 and 300 respectively. Therefore, the encoder $F_{encoder}$ encodes input data $x = [batchsize, 300]$ and outputs the encoding result $z = [batchsize, 100]$. The decoder decodes z and outputs the reconstruction result $\hat{x} = [batchsize, 300]$. The loss function of ShaAE is reconstruction loss, see Eq. 5:

$$Loss_{recon} = \frac{1}{batchsize * length} \sum_{i}^{batchsize} \sum_{j}^{length} \left(x_{ij} - \hat{x}_{ij}\right)^2. \qquad (5)$$

4   Experiment and Discussion

4.1   Experimental Environment and Dataset

Our experiment is run on a computer with an Intel(R)Core (TM) i9-9900 CPU and a GPU of 8.0 GB memory (RTX 2080).

We test the performance of our proposed system on the MIT-BIH Arrhythmia Database (MIT-BIH) [23]. MIT-BIH is a database of arrhythmia provided by

Massachusetts Institute of Technology. MIT-BIH contains 48 ECG dual channel records from 47 subjects. We only use the data of the first channel for each record. Because some records contain too few normal heartbeats or abnormal heartbeats (less than 100), we only use part of records in the experiment. We divide each record into training set, test set and validation set according to the ratio of 4:1:1. In the test set and validation set, the number of normal heartbeat and abnormal heartbeat is the same.

We used five evaluation indicators to measure the performance of our proposed PerAD. The five evaluation indicators are accuracy (ACC), f1 score (F1), recall (REC), precision (PRE) and area under curve (AUC). AUC is an indicator specially used to measure the performance of binary classification model. AUC is the area under ROC curve. The vertical axis of ROC curve is true positive rate (TPR) and the horizontal axis is false positive rate (FPR).

4.2 Experiment 1: Test the Influence of the Number of Simulation Data on Training ShaAE

We compare the performance of ShaAE trained with different number of samples generated by VAE. We first show the implicit space transformation of VAE. Figure 3 shows the implicit variables of a heartbeat encoded on our trained VAE.

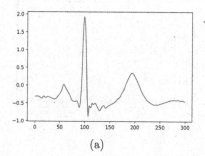 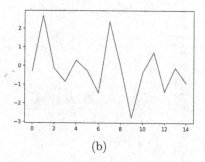

(a)   (b)

Fig. 3. An example of (a) a heartbeat and (b) its corresponding implicit variable.

Before the trained ShaAE classifies the test data, it is necessary to determine a threshold AT. We select the threshold that can maximize $(TPR - FPR)$ on the validation set as AT. Figure 4 shows the results.

We can find that the more the number of simulation samples generated by VAE is used, the better the performance of ShaAE. When the number of simulation samples reaches 500, the accuracy of ShaAE is greatly improved, reaching 97.11%, and then stabilized. In order to balance accuracy and efficiency, we choose ShaAE using 500 simulation samples to assist training as an example to compare with other methods in Experiment Sect. 4.3. Figure 5 shows an example of reconstruction errors on ShaAE trained without using simulation samples and ShaAE using 500 simulation samples to assist training for a set of normal and

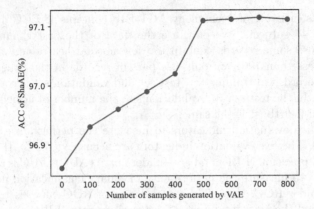

Fig. 4. Average ACC of ShaAE trained by different number of samples generated by VAE.

abnormal samples, respectively. We can find that ShaAE using 500 simulation samples to assist training can more effectively distinguish abnormal points from normal points.

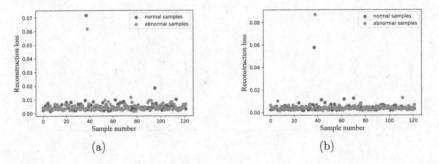

Fig. 5. An example of reconstruction errors on (a) ShaAE trained without using simulation samples and (b) ShaAE using 500 simulation samples to assist training.

4.3   Experiment 2: Evaluate PerAD with Other Methods

We compared the performance of our proposed system with other methods on MIT-BIH. The ShaAE line is the performance of ShaAE trained without using simulation samples to assist training. The ShaAE+VAE line is the performance of ShaAE using 500 simulation samples to assist training. The comparison results of the experiment are shown in Table 2.

Table 2. Performance comparison between ShaAE and State-of-the-Art methods based on MIT-BIH

Work	Model size	ACC (%)	F1 (%)	REC (%)	PRE (%)	AUC (%)
ShaAE	Lightweight personalized	96.86	97.98	96.90	99.13	98.92
ShaAE+VAE	Lightweight personalized	97.11	98.14	97.15	99.21	99.00
BeatGAN [41]	Large comprehensive	–	–	–	–	94.75
Chen et al. [6]	Large comprehensive	98.92	–	–	–	–
Homaeinezhad et al. [14]	Large comprehensive	98.20	–	–	–	–
Javadi et al. [16]	Large comprehensive	96.02	–	–	–	–
Nagarajan et al. [24]	Lightweight	91.70	91.95	95.67	94.97	–
Rahhal et al. [2]	Large comprehensive	98.00	–	–	–	–
Kiranyaz et al. [36]	Large comprehensive	98.90	–	–	–	–

We can find that ShaAE trained without the simulation samples generated by VAE can reach a relatively good level: the ACC is higher than 96%. The ACC of ShaAE using 500 simulation samples to assist training can reach 97.11%. The F1 of our method is 6.19% higher than the baseline. More importantly, our proposed method provides each user with a separate lightweight personalized autoencoder for arrhythmia detection. Such a strategy has more practical application value. For example, our model can be easily deployed on wearable edge devices and can be easily modified.

5 Conclusion

This paper proposes a system for personalized arrhythmia detection, called PerAD, which provides a lightweight autoencoder ShaAE for each user for arrhythmia detection. PerAD also trained a fast-inference variational autoencoder to assist in training ShaAE. PerAD only needs to use the user's normal heartbeat for train networks, which is a great advantage in the context of the difficulty of collecting a large amount of arrhythmia data. High flexibility is also a highlight of PerAD. Unlike most methods based on deep learning, PerAD does not train a large comprehensive deep neural network to provide arrhythmia detection services for any user, but provides each user with a separate lightweight model for arrhythmia detection. Therefore, it is very convenient to adjust the model according to the specific needs of a user. In addition, ShaAE for arrhythmia detection is a lightweight autoencoder. Therefore, PerAD is very suitable to be deployed to edge devices and has great practical application value. The experiment demonstrate that the accuracy of PerAD on MIT-BIH arrhythmia database can reach more than 97.11%.

References

1. Acharya, R.U., Fujita, H., Oh, L.S., Hagiwara, Y., Tan, J.H., Adam, M.: Application of deep convolutional neural network for automated detection of myocardial infarction using ECG signals. Inf. Sci. **415**, 190–198 (2017)

2. Al Rahhal, M.M., Bazi, Y., AlHichri, H., Alajlan, N., Melgani, F., Yager, R.R.: Deep learning approach for active classification of electrocardiogram signals. Inf. Sci. **345**, 340–354 (2016)
3. Borghesi, A., Bartolini, A., Lombardi, M., Milano, M., Benini, L.: Anomaly detection using autoencoders in high performance computing systems. In: Proceedings of the AAAI Conference on Artificial Intelligence, vol. 33, pp. 9428–9433 (2019)
4. Chalapathy, R., Menon, K.A., Chawla, S.: Anomaly detection using one-class neural networks. arXiv: Learning (2018)
5. Chauhan, S., Vig, L.: Anomaly detection in ECG time signals via deep long short-term memory networks. In: Proceedings of the 2015 IEEE International Conference on Data Science and Advanced Analytics (IEEE DSAA 2015), pp. 834–840 (2015)
6. Chen, X., et al.: Atrial fibrillation detection based on multi-feature extraction and convolutional neural network for processing ECG signals. Comput. Methods Programs Biomed. **202**, 106009 (2021)
7. Chen, Y., Zhang, H., Wang, Y., Yang, Y., Zhou, X., Wu, M.J.Q.: MAMA Net: multi-scale attention memory autoencoder network for anomaly detection. IEEE Trans. Med. Imaging **40**, 1032–1041 (2021)
8. Chen, Z., et al.: An energy-efficient ECG processor with weak-strong hybrid classifier for arrhythmia detection. IEEE Trans. Circuits Syst. II Express Briefs **65**, 948–952 (2017)
9. Dennis, K.D., et al.: Shallow RNNs: a method for accurate time-series classification on tiny devices. In: Advances in Neural Information Processing Systems (NIPS 2019), vol. 32 (2019)
10. Du, J., Michalska, S., Subramani, S., Wang, H., Zhang, Y.: Neural attention with character embeddings for hay fever detection from twitter. Health Inf. Sci. Syst. **7**, 1–7 (2019)
11. Fujiwara, Y., Kanai, S., Arai, J., Ida, Y., Ueda, N.: Efficient data point pruning for one-class SVM. In: Proceedings of the AAAI Conference on Artificial Intelligence, vol. 33, pp. 3590–3597 (2019)
12. Gong, D., et al.: Memorizing normality to detect anomaly: Memory-augmented deep autoencoder for unsupervised anomaly detection. In: 2019 IEEE/CVF International Conference On Computer Vision (ICCV 2019), pp. 1705–1714 (2019)
13. He, J., Rong, J., Sun, L., Wang, H., Zhang, Y., Ma, J.: A framework for cardiac arrhythmia detection from IoT-based ECGs. World Wide Web **23**, 2835–2850 (2020)
14. Homaeinezhad, R.M., Atyabi, A.S., Tavakkoli, E., Toosi, N.H., Ghaffari, A., Ebrahimpour, R.: ECG arrhythmia recognition via a neuro-SVM-KNN hybrid classifier with virtual QRS image-based geometrical features. Expert Syst. Appl. **39**, 2047–2058 (2012)
15. Hou, B., Yang, J., Wang, P., Yan, R.: LSTM-based auto-encoder model for ECG arrhythmias classification. IEEE Trans. Instrum. Meas. **69**(4), 1232–1240 (2019)
16. Javadi, M., Arani, S.A.A.A., Sajedin, A., Ebrahimpour, R.: Classification of ECG arrhythmia by a modular neural network based on mixture of experts and negatively correlated learning. Biomed. Signal Process. Control **8**(3), 289–296 (2013)
17. Jiang, H., Zhou, R., Zhang, L., Wang, H., Zhang, Y.: Sentence level topic models for associated topics extraction. World Wide Web **22**, 2545–2560 (2019)
18. Kingma, P.D., Welling, M.: Auto-encoding variational Bayes. CoRR (2013)
19. Kiranyaz, S., Ince, T., Gabbouj, M.: Personalized monitoring and advance warning system for cardiac arrhythmias. Sci. Rep. **7**, 1–8 (2017)

20. Lee, J., Park, J.S., Wang, K.N., Feng, B., Tennant, M., Kruger, E.: The use of telehealth during the coronavirus (COVID-19) pandemic in oral and maxillofacial surgery - a qualitative analysis. EAI Endorsed Trans. Scalable Inf. Syst. (2021)
21. Madan, P., Singh, V., Singh, D.P., Diwakar, M., Kishor, A.: Denoising of ECG signals using weighted stationary wavelet total variation. Biomed. Signal Process. Control **73**, 103478 (2022)
22. Merah, M., Abdelmalik, A.T., Larbi, H.B.: R-peaks detection based on stationary wavelet transform. Comput. Methods Programs Biomed. **121**, 149–160 (2015)
23. Moody, G.B., Mark, R.G.: The impact of the MIT-BIH arrhythmia database. IEEE Eng. Med. Biol. Mag. **20**(3), 45–50 (2001)
24. Nagarajan, V., Vijayaraghavan, V., et al.: End-to-end optimized arrhythmia detection pipeline using machine learning for ultra-edge devices. arXiv preprint arXiv:2111.11789 (2021)
25. Ochiai, K., Takahashi, S., Fukazawa, Y.: Arrhythmia detection from 2-lead ECG using convolutional denoising autoencoders. In: Proceedings of the KDD, pp. 1–7 (2018)
26. Pandey, D., Wang, H., Yin, X., Wang, K., Zhang, Y., Shen, J.: Automatic breast lesion segmentation in phase preserved DCE-MRIs. Health Inf. Sci. Syst. **10**, 1–19 (2022)
27. Pandey, K.S., Janghel, R.R.: Automated detection of arrhythmia from electrocardiogram signal based on new convolutional encoded features with bidirectional long short-term memory network classifier. Phys. Eng. Sci. Med. **44**, 173–182 (2021). https://doi.org/10.1007/s13246-020-00965-1
28. Rajpurkar, P., Hannun, Y.A., Haghpanahi, M., Bourn, C., Ng, Y.A.: Cardiologist-level arrhythmia detection with convolutional neural networks. arXiv: Computer Vision and Pattern Recognition (2017)
29. Ruff, L., et al.: Deep one-class classification. In: ICML, pp. 4390–4399 (2018)
30. Salam, A.K., Srilakshmi, G.: An algorithm for ECG analysis of arrhythmia detection. In: 2015 IEEE International Conference on Electrical, Computer and Communication Technologies (2015)
31. Sarki, K.R., Ahmed, K., Wang, H., Zhang, Y.: Convolutional neural network for multi-class classification of diabetic eye disease. EAI Endorsed Trans. Scalable Inf. Syst. (2019)
32. Sarki, R., Ahmed, K., Wang, H., Zhang, Y.: Automated detection of mild and multi-class diabetic eye diseases using deep learning. Health Inf. Sci. Syst. **8**(1), 1–9 (2020). https://doi.org/10.1007/s13755-020-00125-5
33. Sun, L., Zhong, Z., Qu, Z., Xiong, N.: PerAE: an effective personalized autoencoder for ECG-based biometric in augmented reality system. IEEE J. Biomed. Health Inform. **26**, 2435–2446 (2022)
34. Supriya, S., Siuly, S., Wang, H., Zhang, Y.: Automated epilepsy detection techniques from electroencephalogram signals: a review study. Health Inf. Sci. Syst. **8**(1), 1–15 (2020). https://doi.org/10.1007/s13755-020-00129-1
35. Thill, M., Konen, W., Wang, H., Bäck, T.: Temporal convolutional autoencoder for unsupervised anomaly detection in time series. Appl. Soft Comput. **112**, 107751 (2021)
36. Vatti, R.A., Vinoth, K., Sneha, Y.: Edge intelligence for predicting and detecting cardiac pathologies by analyzing stress and anxiety. J. Crit. Rev. **7**(18), 2816–2822 (2020)
37. Xu, G., Xing, G., Jiang, J., Jiang, J., Ke, Y.: Arrhythmia detection using gated recurrent unit network with ECG signals. J. Med. Imaging Health Inform. **10**, 750–757 (2020)

38. Xu, H., et al.: Unsupervised anomaly detection via variational auto-encoder for seasonal KPIs in web applications. In: Proceedings of the 2018 World Wide Web Conference, pp. 187–196 (2018)
39. Yao, Q., Wang, R., Fan, X., Liu, J., Li, Y.: Multi-class arrhythmia detection from 12-lead varied-length ECG using attention-based time-incremental convolutional neural network. Inf. Fusion **53**, 174–182 (2020)
40. Yin, C., Zhang, S., Wang, J., Xiong, N.N.: Anomaly detection based on convolutional recurrent autoencoder for IoT time series. IEEE Trans. Syst. Man Cybern. Syst. **52**(1), 112–122 (2020)
41. Zhou, B., Liu, S., Hooi, B., Cheng, X., Ye, J.: BeatGAN: anomalous rhythm detection using adversarially generated time series. In: IJCAI, pp. 4433–4439 (2019)

Efficient kNN Join over Dynamic High-Dimensional Data

Nimish Ukey, Zhengyi Yang$^{(\boxtimes)}$, Guangjian Zhang, Boge Liu, Binghao Li, and Wenjie Zhang

The University of New South Wales, Sydney, NSW 2052, Australia
{n.ukey,zhengyi.yang,guangjian.zhang,boge.liu,binghao.li,
wenjie.zhang}@unsw.edu.au

Abstract. Given a user dataset U and an object dataset I in high-dimensional space, a kNN join query retrieves each object in dataset U its k nearest neighbors from the dataset I. kNN join is a fundamental and essential operation in applications from many domains such as databases, computer vision, multi-media, machine learning, recommendation systems, and many more. The datasets in real world often update dynamically on insertion or deletion of objects. However, existing algorithms of dynamic kNN join lack support for deletion and batch update, which are important in real-life applications. In this paper, we propose a new method of kNN join over dynamic high-dimensional data. Specifically, our method features lazy updates, batch operations, and optimised deletions. Experiments on real-world datasets show that our method outperforms the existing algorithms of naive RkNN join and HDR Tree by up to 5 and 4 times, respectively.

Keywords: kNN join · Dynamic data · High-dimensional data

1 Introduction

The k-Nearest Neighbor (kNN) join problem is fundamental in many data analytic and data mining applications, such as classification, clustering, outlier detection, similarity search, etc. Specifically, given a query dataset U and an object dataset I in high-dimensional space, a kNN join query retrieves each object in dataset U its k nearest neighbors from I. For example, social applications (e.g., Youtube, Netflix, Twitter, Instagram, etc.) uses kNN join to provide recommendation to users based on their interest, by representing users and contents as feature vectors in a high-dimensional space. Similarly, e-commerce recommendation systems use kNN join to suggest products for consumers to increase the chance of buying them. In many applications of kNN join nowadays, including the scenarios mentioned above, data is generated in a very high velocity. As reported by Twitter, about $350,000$ tweets are sent per minute in 2020. To fully make use of newly generated data to provide a fresh and timely recommendation, there emerges the demand of efficient kNN join on highly dynamic data.

W. Hua et al. (Eds.): ADC 2022, LNCS 13459, pp. 63–75, 2022.
https://doi.org/10.1007/978-3-031-15512-3_5

Motivations. If we look at the existing works, most existing kNN join approaches [3,14,16] work on static data. To handle dynamic data, such approaches recompute kNN join from scratch upon every update (i.e., insertion) of the object dataset, which resulting in a very high time cost and latency. Cui Yu et al. [17] come up with the high-dimensional kNN Join+ algorithm for dynamically updating the new data points to allow incremental updates on kNN join results. Being a disk-based approach, however, it was unable to meet the real-time requirements. Further work by Yang, C., et al. [15] proposes the index structure of HDR Tree (High-dimensional R-tree) on dynamic kNN join. It identifies data nodes whose kNN are affected by the inserted data and updates only the affected data points to avoid redundant computation. In addition, HDR Tree performs dimensionality reduction through Principal Component Analysis (PCA) and clustering to further prune candidates.

We found two major drawbacks of existing solutions for kNN join over dynamic high-dimensional data as presented in the following.

1. *Lack of Support for Deletions.* While the two fundamental update operations are insertion and deletion, all existing algorithms work only on insertions. For each deletion of object data, they need to recompute the kNN for all query points as in static solutions, which results in a high time-complicity and inefficiency.
2. *Lack of Support for Batch Updates.* Existing algorithms updates the results of kNN join for each insertion of the new data. However, none of them supports batch updates. With the rapid growth of high-velocity streaming data, such design significantly limits the performance of dynamic kNN join on large datasets. In many real-world applications, it is common to batch multiple updates into a single group to improve the throughput.

Our Solution and Contributions. To address the two problems of existing algorithms as mentioned above, we present a new algorithm for kNN join over dynamic high-dimensional data in this paper. Our method supports efficient deletions and batch updates. It computes kNN join in main memory and adopts the HDR Tree in [15] to reduce in-memory search cost. Additional optimisations are proposed in this paper to improve the efficiency of our method. Specifically, our contributions in this paper are summarised as follows:

1. *Lazy Updates.* We design a lazy update mechanism. It identifies the users whose kNN should be updated on insertions and deletions and mark them as "dirty" node in the HDR Tree. The actual computation of updating is delayed until the kNN values of affected users are needed.
2. *Batch Operations.* Given a batch of updates (i.e., insertions and deletions), we propose to not update the results immediately for each of the new items. Instead, we identify all user affected by the batch of updates before updating them to avoid redundant computation.
3. *Optimised Deletions.* Item deletions in kNN join is costly. When an item is deleted, we need to search all affected users and update their kNN list. In our

approach, we propose to maintain a reversed kNN table for all items to speed up the process of searching for affected users.

4. *Extensive Experiments.* We perform an extensive experimental analysis of real-time kNN join using real-world high-dimensional datasets. To summary, our method outperforms the naive RkNN join and HDR Tree by up to 5 and 4 times, respectively.

Paper Organization. The remainder of the paper is organized as follows. In Sect. 2, we define the problem and discuss preliminaries. Section 3 reviews the related work. We dedicate Sect. 4 for a brief summarization of the HDR Tree. In Sect. 5 and Sect. 6, we describe our lazy updates and batch updates techniques. In Sect. 7, we introduce deletion optimization. Experimental analysis is presented in Sect. 8, followed by a conclusion in Sect. 9.

2   Background

2.1   Problem Definition

This section provides the definitions for kNN join and the Reverse kNN join operations. We refer to U and I as the *User* and *Item* sets for a kNN join operations throughout this paper. A summary of frequently used symbols is given in Table 1. We focus on the problem of continuously processing a kNN join while handling a *sliding window* of items. For each user in $U = \{u_1, u_2, \ldots, u_n\}$ we search for the k nearest neighbor items in the item set $I = \{i_1, i_2, i_3, \ldots, i_k\}$ in d-dimensional. We formally define kNN join in Definition 1.

Definition 1 (kNN Join). *In the d-dimensional space, given query point set $U = \{u_1, u_2, \ldots, u_n\}$ as user point set and object point set $I = \{i_1, i_2, i_3, \ldots, i_m\}$ as items point set, the kNN join is the process of finding the kNN item points for the set of user points in d-dimensional space. That is, $U_{kNN}I = \{kNN(u_i)| u_i \in U \wedge kNN(u_i) \subset I\}$.*

For any update operation in dynamic data, it is necessary to search for the affected users [15]. This refers to a *reverse kNN (RkNN) join* as defined below.

Definition 2 (Reverse kNN Join). *Given user point set $U = \{u_1, u_2, \ldots, u_n\}$ and item point $I = \{i_1, i_2, \ldots, i_m\}$, the Reverse kNN join is the process of finding all the points from U which contains item i_j as their kNN in d-dimensional space. That is, $U_{RkNN}I = \{RkNN(i)|i \in I \wedge RkNN(i) \subset U\{\forall u \in RkNN(i) : u \in U \wedge i \in kNN(u)\}\}$*

We use RkNN [5] to check for the set of users affected by an item's insertion/deletion operation and update the kNN result accordingly.

Problem Definition. Given a user dataset U and an item dataset I, our goal is to dynamically output the kNN join results of U in I upon every update of I (i.e., insertions and deletions).

Table 1. Summary of Symbol and Definitions

Symbols	Definitions
U, I	User set and Item set
u, i	User and Item
W	Sliding window
k	Number of nearest neighbors
d, r	Dimensionality of original and reduced dataset
R, Rp	KNN and RkNN set
f	Fanout
l	Level of tree
L	Height of tree
C_i	The ith Cluster
$dist$	Distance
$dist_{pca}$	Distance after PCA transformation
$dknn$	Distance to the kth nearest neighbor
$maxdknn$	Maximum distance between dknn
X, V, T	Matrix
n, m, N, M	The size of a set

2.2 Dynamic kNN Join

We denote kNN join over dynamic data as *Dynamic kNN (DkNN) Join*. In DkNN join, a recommendation list R is maintained for every user u_i, containing its k nearest neighbors. We also used the sliding window to monitor the item stream and only the items within the sliding window are recommended. Every time an item is updated, the sliding window must be updated as well. According to the pruning strategy, any newly inserted item will affect the set of users if and only if the newly added item falls within the $dknn$ range of the user.

If any existing item is removed or expired, then we have to check for the set of affected users. Accordingly, we update the recommendation list of those affected users. Similarly, when any new item is inserted into the sliding window, then it looks for the affected user and updates its recommendation list. It must be updated dynamically in a real-time system.

Lemma 1. *The user is affected by the newly inserted item i' or the expired item i_1 if and only if it falls within the user's dknn radius range.*

3 Related Work

The dimensionality reduction is the transformation of the high dimensional to low dimensional dataset while keeping some useful properties of the original dataset. It helps to improve the performance of the kNN for the higher dimensional dataset. Various approaches have been proposed to deal with the issue of the curse of dimensionality like Pyramid Technique [2], iDistance [11], Δ-tree [8],

VA-File [13], iMinMax [12], LSH [9], LSHI [10], etc. It usually helps to improve the performance of the kNN for higher dimensional dataset.

In the literature, many studies have been carried out on index structures that can handle kNN join. Böhm et al. [3] present a kNN join problem, which finds the kNN for a set of queries in a single run operation. The work on kNN join techniques like MuX(Multi-page Indexing) [3], Gorder(G-ordering kNN) [14], and iJoin [16] involves the nested loop searching strategy for high dimensional datasets. Böhm and Krebs proposed a novel approach for computing the kNN join using MuX, a special index structure for similarity joins. MuX and iJoin utilize an index nested loop join technique whereas Gorder is a block nested loop join approach. However, they performed the operation on a static dataset, so when updating it they have to perform the kNN computation on all the users, which is a very costly process.

Processing a kNN join queries on high-dimensional data, Yu, C. et al. introduced the kNN Join+ technique [17]. Four different types of data structures were used in this study: the RkNN join table, kNN join table, iDistance [11], and Sphere tree. The Sphere tree is modeled upon the concept of the M-Tree [7]. It's structured similarly to an R-tree, but rather than rectangles, it deals with spheres. The iDistance indexing is used to find the kNN for newly inserted point p while on the other hand sphere tree is used to look for RkNN i.e. points having p as their kNN. The iDistance approach used the Pyramid Technique [2] to convert a high-dimensional space into a one-dimensional value. In this work, they develop a shared query optimisation strategy in order to improve performance but being a disk-based approach it was difficult to meet the real-time requirements. Yang, C. et al. [15] provide two different data structures in continuous kNN join, namely exact (HDR-tree) and approximate (HDR*-tree) solutions. HDR Tree utilizes the PCA [4] and clustering approach for dimensionality reduction. On the other hand, HDR*-Tree employs the Random Projection [1] method. It uses a random matrix to translate the data from d to r dimensions. The experimental result shows that HDR* Tree is faster than HDR Tree but with lesser accuracy. In this paper, we only focus on exact kNN queries.

4   HDR Tree

To handle dynamic kNN join in high-dimensional data, we adopt the HDR Tree [15] as the index structure in our method. HDR Tree performs dimensionality reduction via Principal Component Analysis and clustering. In this section, we briefly introduce HDR Tree.

4.1   Principal Component Analysis

PCA approach is basically used to reduce the cost of computation in the tree structure. Considering the dataset $X_{N.d}$, where N denotes the number of rows and d as the dimensionality of the dataset. To transform the dataset from d dimension to r dimension we have to follow a certain process. The value of r is

$0 < r < d$. While processing the dimensionality reduction the direction having the highest variance is considered as the first principal component and followed by the second component in descending order. The 1st dimension of the tree structure consists of the values with high variance.

1. The covariance matrix of the input dataset(X) is first calculated.
2. Using the covariance matrix, eigenvalues and their associated eigenvectors are computed as follows.

$$COV = \frac{\sum_{i=1}^{n} (X_i - \bar{x})(Y_i - \bar{y})}{n - 1}$$

3. Sort the eigenvalue and associated eigenvectors in descending order.
4. The transformed matrix (T) will be used to transform the newly inserted point to the required dimension.

This different dimensionality approach provides us the better pruning power which helps us to reduce the computation overhead.

4.2   Structure of Tree

A demonstration of the HDR Tree is given in Fig. 1. With the help of eigenvalues, we use different dimensionality at each level. The high-dimensional dataset was partitioned into clusters using the K-Means clustering method. Other clustering approaches can also be utilized. The root level (i.e. level 1) set with d_1 dimensionality, and based on the fanout value f we cluster the root node (i.e. $C_1, C_2, ...C_f$). In the next level (i.e. level 2) the dimensionality d_2 is set. Every cluster from the root node is sub-clustered. In our case, cluster $C1$ is sub-divided into the $C_{11}, C_{12}, ...C_{1f}$. The dimensionality increases at every level. The leaf node will be with its complete dimensionality d_l in level l.

In Fig. 1 the internal nodes and the root node have the same structure which is represented by a tuple $(C, maxdknn, l, num, r, ptr)$. Where C is the center of sub-cluster, $maxdknn$ is the maximum distance between the users and its kNN, l is the level of node, num is considered as the number of users, r is the radius of sub-cluster and ptr is the pointer to the next node.

4.3   Construction

To construct the HDR Tree, the estimated height of the three is calculated using $L = [log_f N]$. The fixed fanout size is used but the threshold value θ is adjusted in such a way that the height of the tree should not exceed the L too much. For each level, the dimensionality is calculated and stored for further process. Initially, the cluster with d_1 dimensionality is created along with the $maxdknn$ value. The $maxdknn$ of the cluster can be termed as the maximum distance between the users in the clusters and their k-th nearest neighbor items. While constructing a tree, it checks for the number of users within a cluster. If it is less than a θ then it creates the Leaf Node (LN) else it creates the Non-Leaf Node (NLN) using the new incremental dimensionality approach.

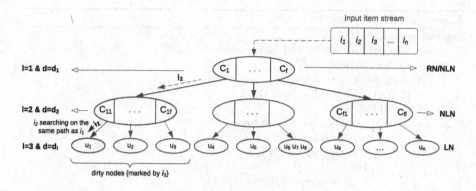

Fig. 1. Example of lazy updates on HDR-tree

4.4   Search

The search algorithm looks for the affected users in a leaf node. It directly computes the distance between user and item in LN. Contrary, non-leaf nodes check for the pruning condition and if it satisfies then only it continues the search process. It checks if the distance between the transformed item and cluster is greater than the *maxdknn* value (i.e. $dist_{pca}(i, C_j) \geq maxdknn$), then we prune that cluster as users within the cluster will not be affected by the item i's update operation. Thus, its child nodes need not be visited further.

5   Lazy Updates

For every new item, we identify the users whose kNN should be updated. However, we do not update the HDR Tree immediately. Instead, we mark the nodes along the search tree as "dirty", meaning that the radius information on these nodes is not tight. We only update them when another new item accesses the same search path.

Example 1. If $I = \{i_1, i_2, ..., i_n\}$ is set of new items and $U = \{u_1, u_2, .., u_m\}$ is a user set. So, we will consider the users affected by update operations i_1, i_2, and i_3 are: $i_1 = \{u_1, u_2, u_3\}, i_2 = \{u_1, u_5, u_9, u_{16}\}, i_3 = \{u_3, u_7, u_{19}\}$. For newly inserted item i_1, we search for the users which are affected by the update operation {i.e. u_1, u_2, u_3}. We mark all the newly affected user nodes as dirty nodes. During the next insertion of an item i_2, it will check for the other affected users. In this case item i_2 it affecting the u_1, u_5, u_9, and u_{16}. As we can see that it is searching on the same path because it also consists of the u_1. Hence, as it is trying to access the same path we will update it. Basically, we are updating the node if and only if there is a necessity to do so.

As mentioned in Algorithm 1, lines 1–4 check for the affected users within the leaf node. Line 5–10 examines the status of the node i.e. whether it was

---

Algorithm 1. LazySearch

Ensure: node $node$, item i
Require: affected user set R_p and Lazy nodes
1: **if** $node$ is a LN **then**
2:     **for** each users u_j in LN **do**
3:         **if** $dist(i, u_j) \leq u_j \rightarrow dknn$ **then**
4:             add u_j in R_p;
5:             **if** $u_j \rightarrow dirty == true$ **then**
6:                 **if** $u_j \rightarrow R.size() < k$ **then**
7:                     $computekNN(W)$;
8:                 **else**
9:                     $u_j \rightarrow computeDirtykNN(I)$;
10:                    $u_j \rightarrow dirty = false$;
11: **else**
12:     $C_p = NLN \rightarrow clusters$;
13:     **for** each clusters $C_j : C_p$ **do**
14:         **if** $dist_{node.dimension}(i, Cj) < Cj \rightarrow maxdknn$ **then**
15:             LazySearch $(NLN \rightarrow children[j], i, m)$;

---

previously marked as dirty? If the node was marked as dirty then we update the node and also need to update the HDR Tree. On the other hand, lines 12–15 deal with the non-leaf node. Basically, it works on the pruning approach of the HDR Tree. The cluster is pruned if the distance is less than the $maxdknn$ value which helps to improve the efficiency of an algorithm.

6 Batch Updates

The HDR Tree Search algorithm returns the set of affected users set R_p. The recommendation list of those affected users is updated. It is observed that the sequential update method is a bit costly. Therefore, we come up with the batch approach to save the computation cost.

When there is a batch of new items, we identify the affected users but do not update the search path immediately for each of the new items. We process all updates at the node left before updating the parameters on the internal level to help save the cost.

Example 2. For instance, $\{i_1, i_2, ...i_n\}$ are the stream of new items. If an item i_1 is affecting the user u_1, u_8, u_{11} and the next item from input stream i_2 is affecting the $u_8, u_{11}, u_{18}, u_{25}$ then updating the search path immediately after every new item will be computationally expensive. If we process it in batch then it helps us to save the cost as it can be seen in the above example that i_1 and i_2 are affecting some same users u_8, u_{11}. So, rather than processing the separate updates, we go with the batch updates.

Algorithm 2 is used to perform the batch update operation on all the affected nodes. The R_{p-ins} is a set of all affected nodes. For every node amongst all the affected nodes, it calculated the kNN to update the recommendation list, the *dknn* value of the cluster, and to further update the *maxdknn* value. The AdjustMaxDkNN method is used to update the HDR Tree structure.

Algorithm 2. Batch Update for Insertion Operation

Require: Affected user set R_{p-ins}
Ensure: Updated $R, DkNN$ and $maxDkNN$
1: **for** each u_j in R_{p-ins} **do**
2:     **for** each i in $u_j \to R$ **do**
3:         $D \leftarrow dist(i, u_j)$;
4:         $V \leftarrow tuple(D, i)$
5:     $computekNN(V)$;
6:     $u_j \to dknn = V[k]$;
7:     **while** $u_j \to R.size() > k$ **do**
8:         pop u_j from R;
9: $AdjustMaxDkNN()$;

In the Batch Update Deletion Algorithm, the R_{p-del} is a set of affected nodes by deletion operation. In Algorithm 3, lines 1–3, check for the affected node and perform an update operation by computing its kNN and then finally adjust the *maxdknn* value of HDR Tree. The computekNN method is used to calculate the k nearest neighbor user vector with the help of sliding window items streams. Initially, it calculates the distance between user and item vector and based on the distance finds the k nearest neighbors for the desired user and also set the *dknn* value of the user. The deletion operation is very costly as compared to insertion and hence optimization is necessary to improve the performance. For the same reason, we come up with the Lazy Updates and Batch Optimization for both insertion and Deletion operations.

Algorithm 3. Batch Update for Deletion Operation

Require: Affected user set R_{p-del}
Ensure: Updated $R, dknn$ and $maxdknn$
1: **for** each u_j in R_{p-del} **do**
2:     **if** $uj \to R.size() < k$ **then**
3:         $computekNN(V)$;
4: $AdjustMaxDkNN()$;

---

7   Deletion Optimization

Without the assistance of other data structures, we need to re-compute the RkNN join of an item by the HDR tree when that item is being deleted. The re-computation of RkNN join based on the HDR tree when the deletion is time costly. As a result, we apply a structure called an RkNN table [17] which continuously maps the items in the sliding window to their RkNN lists to reduce time cost. With the assistance of an RkNN table, we can directly gain the RkNN list of a deleted item without repeating the RkNN join process on the HDR tree.

An RkNN table contains rows of data, where the number of rows is equal to the size of the sliding window. To map every item to its RkNN list, each row in an RkNN table contains the index of an item and the RkNN list of that item. A RkNN list of an item means a list that contains the indexes of all the users that have that item in their kNN lists. The algorithm is given in Algorithm 4.

Algorithm 4. Update RkNN table

Require: The updating of an item i
Ensure: The updated $RkNN$ table
1: **if** updating=$Deletion$ **then**
2:      **for** each user u_j in $RkNN(i)$ **do**
3:          Update $kNN(u_j)$
4:          Add u_j to $RkNN$(the k-th nearest neighbor of u_j)
5:      Cancel $RkNN(i)$ from the $RkNN$ table
6: **else**
7:      Gain $RkNN(i)$ by the HDR Tree
8:      Add $RkNN(i)$ to the $RkNN$ table
9:      **for** each user u_j in $RkNN(i)$ **do**
10:          Cancel u_j from $RkNN$(the k-th nearest neighbor of u_j)
11:          Update $kNN(u_j)$

---

8   Performance Evaluation

In this section, we present our experimental results. All experiments are conducted on a computer with an Intel Core i5-4210U 2.4 GHz processor, 12 GB RAM, running Windows 10 OS. All methods are implemented in C++. We compare our work with the two baseline algorithms:

1. *NaiveRkNN*: The naive approach of searching affected users without index. It calculates the distance between the item and all the users within U and decides whether to update the recommendation list of users or not.
2. *HDR Tree*: The HDR Tree [15] method that searches for the affected users caused by any update operation as discussed in Sect. 4.

We performed most of the experiments on the 128 Dimensional NUS-WIDE Image DataSet [6] which consist of 269,648 records from the Flickr dataset. A 128-dimensional dataset is used by default. We build the sliding window which acts as an item stream. The default sliding window W size is kept at 200000 and 50000 random users are selected. We set the default value of k to 10 and the fanout f to 5.

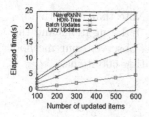

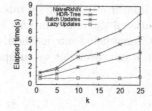

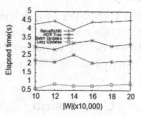

Fig. 2. Vary number of updated items

Fig. 3. Vary the number of k

Fig. 4. Vary the number of W

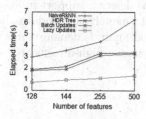

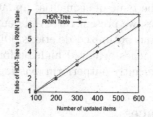

Fig. 5. Vary the number of features

Fig. 6. HDR tree vs RkNN table in deletion

Exp-1: Varying the Number of Updated Items. We compare the effect of updated items by varying it from 1 to 600. Figure 2 shows that the cost for searching the affected items is linearly increasing for all the approaches, but the batch update and lazy update outperform the baseline approaches. The batch update and lazy update are about 1.5 and 3 times faster than the HDR Tree.

Exp-2: Varying $|W|$ and k. In Fig. 3 it can be seen that when increasing the k size, the elapsed time increases in all the approaches. But lazy update and batch update gives better results than baseline approaches. If we increase the k size the $maxdknn$ also increases which results in more affected users. As shown in the Fig. 4, with an increase in the sliding window size W the time cost increases for all the approaches as the computation cost increases.

Exp-3: Varying the Number of Features. We conduct experiments on other datasets in the NUS-WIDE Image DataSet collection with different dimensions. The dimension varies from 128 to 500. Figure 5 illustrates that with the increase of dimensionality, the execution time increases because the time required for distance computation increases. As shown in the figure, our approaches outperform existing ones.

Exp-4: The Effect of Deletion Optimisation. We compare the effectiveness of our deletion optimisation with the naive HDR Tree in this experiment. For the HDR Tree method, we use the HDR Tree to find the RkNN list of a being deleted item. In our method (denoted as the RkNN Table in Fig. 6), we directly extract the RkNN list of a deleted item from the RkNN table. Note that we normalize the time cost as the ratio between the real-time cost for updating items and the time cost for updating 100 items using our method. As observed, our method achieves about 15% percent of improvement when updating 600 items.

9   Conclusion

In this paper, we study kNN join over dynamic high-dimensional data. We are using the main-memory indexing HDR Tree structure to search a chunk of affected users for every update operation and update the kNN result. To address the issue of sequential updates and lack of deletion support in existing approaches, we present three different optimisations, namely lazy updates, batch updates and optimized deletions. Our experimental analysis demonstrates that our approaches achieved high performance for dynamic high-dimensional data and significantly outperform existing approaches.

References

1. Achlioptas, D.: Database-friendly random projections. In: Proceedings of the twentieth ACM SIGMOD-SIGACT-SIGART Symposium on Principles of Database Systems, pp. 274–281 (2001)
2. Berchtold, S., Böhm, C., Kriegal, H.P.: The pyramid-technique: towards breaking the curse of dimensionality. In: Proceedings of the 1998 ACM SIGMOD International Conference on Management of Data, pp. 142–153 (1998)
3. Böhm, C., Krebs, F.: The k-nearest neighbour join: Turbo charging the KDD process. Knowl. Inf. Syst. 6(6), 728–749 (2004)
4. Chakrabarti, K., Mehrotra, S.: Local dimensionality reduction: a new approach to indexing high dimensional spaces. In: VLDB Conference (2000)
5. Cheema, M.A., Zhang, W., Lin, X., Zhang, Y.: Efficiently processing snapshot and continuous reverse k nearest neighbors queries. VLDB J. 21(5), 703–728 (2012)
6. Chua, T.S., Tang, J., Hong, R., Li, H., Luo, Z., Zheng, Y.: Nus-wide: a real-world web image database from national university of Singapore. In: Proceedings of the ACM International Conference on Image and Video Retrieval, pp. 1–9 (2009)
7. Ciaccia, P., Patella, M., Zezula, P.: M-tree: an efficient access method for similarity search in metric spaces. In: VLDB, vol. 97, pp. 426–435 (1997)
8. Cui, B., Ooi, B.C., Su, J., Tan, K.L.: Contorting high dimensional data for efficient main memory KNN processing. In: Proceedings of the 2003 ACM SIGMOD International Conference on Management Of Data, pp. 479–490 (2003)
9. Gionis, A., et al.: Similarity search in high dimensions via hashing. In: VLDB, vol. 99, pp. 518–529 (1999)
10. Hu, Y., Yang, C., Zhan, P., Zhao, J., Li, Y., Li, X.: Efficient continuous KNN join processing for real-time recommendation. Personal Ubiquit. Comput. 25(6), 1001–1011 (2021)
11. Jagadish, H.V., Ooi, B.C., Tan, K.L., Yu, C., Zhang, R.: iDistance: an adaptive B+-tree based indexing method for nearest neighbor search. ACM Trans. Database Syst. (TODS) 30(2), 364–397 (2005)

12. Ooi, B.C., Tan, K.L., Yu, C., Bressan, S.: Indexing the edges-a simple and yet efficient approach to high-dimensional indexing. In: Proceedings of the Nineteenth ACM SIGMOD-SIGACT-SIGART Symposium on Principles of Database Systems, pp. 166–174 (2000)
13. Weber, R., Schek, H.J., Blott, S.: A quantitative analysis and performance study for similarity-search methods in high-dimensional spaces. In: VLDB, vol. 98, pp. 194–205 (1998)
14. Xia, C., Lu, H., Ooi, B.C., Hu, J.: GORDER: an efficient method for KNN join processing. In: Proceedings of the Thirtieth International Conference on Very Large Data Bases, vol. 30, pp. 756–767 (2004)
15. Yang, C., Yu, X., Liu, Y.: Continuous KNN join processing for real-time recommendation. In: 2014 IEEE International Conference on Data Mining, pp. 640–649. IEEE (2014)
16. Yu, C., Cui, B., Wang, S., Su, J.: Efficient index-based KNN join processing for high-dimensional data. Inf. Softw. Technol. **49**(4), 332–344 (2007)
17. Yu, C., Zhang, R., Huang, Y., Xiong, H.: High-dimensional KNN joins with incremental updates. Geoinformatica **14**(1), 55–82 (2010)

Diverse Shortest Paths in Game Maps: A Comparative User Study and Experiments

Lingxiao Li[1]([✉]), Muhammad Aamir Cheema[1], Mohammed Eunus Ali[2],
Hua Lu[3], and Huan Li[4]

[1] Faculty of Information Technology, Monash University, Melbourne, Australia
{lingxiao.li,aamir.cheema}@monash.edu
[2] Bangladesh University of Engineering and Technology, Dhaka, Bangladesh
eunus@cse.buet.ac.bd
[3] Department of People and Technology, Roskilde University, Roskilde, Denmark
luhua@ruc.dk
[4] Department of Computer Science, Aalborg University, Aalborg, Denmark
lihuan@cs.aau.dk

Abstract. Computing diverse shortest paths requires finding a set of k alternative paths (including the shortest path) between a given source s and a target t. Intuitively, these paths should be significantly different from each other and meaningful/natural (e.g., must not contain loops or unnecessary detours). While finding diverse shortest paths (also called alternative paths) in road networks has been extensively studied, to the best of our knowledge, we are the first to formally study alternative pathfinding in game maps which are typically represented as Euclidean planes containing polygonal obstacles. First, we adapt the existing techniques designed for road networks to find alternative paths in the game maps. Then, we design a web-based system that allows the users to visualise the alternative paths generated by these existing approaches in different maps. Finally, we use this web-based system to conduct a user study that shows that the existing road network approaches generate high-quality alternative paths when adapted for the game maps. Furthermore, we also evaluate the quality of alternative paths returned by existing approaches using some well-known quantitative measures on a widely used game maps benchmark.

Keywords: Diverse shortest paths · Alternative pathfinding · Game maps

1 Introduction

Given a source s and a target t, a shortest path query requires finding the path from s to t with the minimal total cost. Finding shortest paths is a very well-studied problem and numerous techniques exist to find shortest paths in

© The Author(s), under exclusive license to Springer Nature Switzerland AG 2022
W. Hua et al. (Eds.): ADC 2022, LNCS 13459, pp. 76–88, 2022.
https://doi.org/10.1007/978-3-031-15512-3_6

different settings such as in road networks [1], general graphs (i.e., social net-works) [14], indoor venues [3], game maps [7] etc. In many applications, it is desirable to return not only the shortest path to the users/agents but also some alternative paths so that they can choose a path of their choice. Intuitively, these alternative paths must be short and sufficiently different from each other (i.e., diverse). Modern navigation systems such as Google Maps return several paths from source to target and the user can choose a path of their choice to travel on.

Inspired by the applications, computing alternative paths in road networks has received significant research attention, e.g., see [8,13,16] and references therein. However, to the best of our knowledge, computing alternative paths in game maps has received no research attention despite its applications. Typi-cally game characters take shortest paths to reach the target location. However, in many cases, it is desirable to have more than one paths for the characters to choose from. For example, in real-time strategy (RTS) games, if the opponent character always takes the shortest path to the target, their movement/plan may become predictable. Therefore, it may be better to compute alternative paths and randomly assign one of the alternative paths to the character. Many RTS games allow the users to choose a waypoint to allow them choosing a path different from the shortest path. In such games, the users may be shown sev-eral alternative paths and asked to select a path of their choice. Computing alternative paths also has applications in indoor venues which are also typically modeled as Euclidean plane containing obstacles. For example, an indoor navi-gation system may show multiple alternative paths to the target location so that the user can choose a path of their choice. Figure 1 shows two examples where four alternative paths are reported on two different game maps.

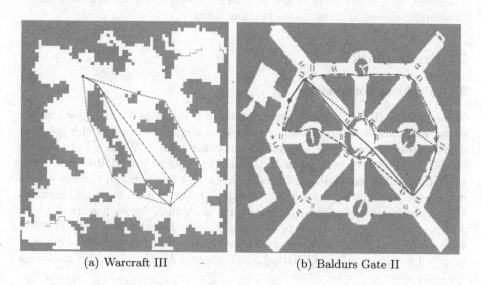

(a) Warcraft III   (b) Baldurs Gate II

Fig. 1. Four alternative paths on two different game maps.

Although some open-source game development projects[1] have included support for computing alternative paths in game maps, the efficiency and effectiveness of the proposed alternative pathfinding algorithms are not clear. In this paper, we fill this gap and formally study alternative pathfinding in game maps. We make the following contributions.

To the best of our knowledge, we are the first to study alternative pathfinding in game maps. First, we adapt some of the most well-known techniques for computing alternative paths on road networks (namely Penalty [2,4,11], Plateaus [9] and Dissimilarity [6,15]) for the game maps. However, it is not clear whether these techniques generate alternative paths of good quality when extended for the game maps. To this end, we created a web-based demonstration system and conducted a user-study on 9 diverse game maps selected from a widely used game maps benchmark. In total, we received 472 responses and the user study shows that the three approaches generate high-quality alternative paths in game maps as perceived by the users. We have made the source code[2] of the web-based demonstration system publicly available so that it can be reused and/or extended as needed. Furthermore, we also evaluate the quality of alternative paths returned by these algorithms on a widely used game maps benchmark using some well-known quantitative measures such as *path similarity*, *bounded stretch* and *local optimality* [10]. Our experimental study shows the paths returned by the existing approaches are comparable to each other in terms of quality metrics. However, the results show that the computation cost of these approaches is up to two orders of magnitude higher than the computation cost of the state-of-the-art shortest path algorithm, Polyanya [7], which computes only the shortest path, i.e., the overhead to compute alternative path is too high. Therefore, as a future work, there is a need for developing efficient techniques to compute diverse shortest paths in game maps.

2 Preliminaries

2.1 Problem Formulation

We assume a 2D Euclidean plane containing a set of polygonal obstacles. A **convex vertex** is a vertex that is located at a convex corner of the polygon. A **non-convex vertex** is located at a concave corner. We use V to denote the set of all convex vertices in the plane. Two points are **visible** from each other (also called **co-visible**) if there is a straight line between the two points not passing through any obstacle. A **path** P between a source s and a target t is an ordered set of points $\langle p_1, p_2, \cdots, p_n \rangle$ such that, for each p_i $(i < n)$, p_i and p_{i+1} are co-visible where $p_1 = s$ and $p_n = t$. **Length** of a path P is the cumulative Euclidean distance between every successive pair of points, denoted as $|P|$, i.e., $|P| = \sum_{i=1}^{k-1} EDist(p_i, p_{i+1})$ where $EDist(x, y)$ is the Euclidean

---

[1] For example, see a game development project with Unity3D at https://arongranberg. com/astar/docs/alternativepath.html.

[2] https://bitbucket.org/lingxiao29/customized/src/master/.

distance between x and y. The shortest path $sp(s,t)$ is a path between s and t with the minimum length. The shortest distance between s and t is denoted as $d(s,t)$, i.e., $d(s,t) = |sp(s,t)|$.

Given a positive integer k, we are interested in finding k **alternative paths** (including the shortest path $sp(s,t)$) between s and t such that each alternative path is no longer than $d(s,t) \times \epsilon$ where $\epsilon \geq 1$ is a user-defined parameter. Intuitively, the k alternative paths must be diverse (e.g., should have small overlap with each other) and each path must be a "reasonable" path, e.g., should not contain unnecessary detours and loops etc. Diversity can be quantified by defining a similarity function based on the overlap between paths and requiring the paths to have similarity with each other less than a given threshold. The previous works in road networks (e.g., see [10]) have defined several measures to quantify whether a set of alternative paths is "reasonable" or not. We formally define these measures in the Experiments section.

2.2 Related Work

While finding shortest paths in game maps has been extensively studied (e.g., see [7,18] and references therein), alternative pathfinding has only been studied in road networks. Below, we briefly describe three of the most popular approaches to compute alternative paths in road networks (we assume undirected road networks for simplicity).

Penalty: This approach [2,4,11] iteratively computes the shortest paths from s to t and, after each iteration, it applies a penalty to each edge on the shortest path found in the previous iteration by increasing its edge weight by a certain penalty factor (e.g., by multiplying the current edge weight with 1.5). Since the edge weights on the shortest path are increased, the approach is likely to choose a significantly different shortest path in the next iteration. The algorithm stops when k unique paths are found by the algorithm or when the length of the shortest path found in this iteration is longer than $d(s,t) \times \epsilon$.

Plateaus: This approach [9] was designed by Cotares Limited for their routing engine Choice Routing. First, two shortest path trees T_s and T_t are computed rooted at s and t, respectively. Then, the two tree are *joined* and common branches in the two trees are found. Each common branch is called a plateau. More formally, given a branch $\langle s, \cdots, u_1, u_2, \cdots, u_n, \cdots, y \rangle$ in T_s and a branch $\langle t, \cdots u_n, u_{n-1}, \cdots, u_1, \cdots, x \rangle$ in T_t, the common part of the two branches $\langle u_1, \cdots, u_n \rangle$ is a plateau, denoted as $pl(u_1, u_n)$. Note that the shortest path between s and t is a plateau with length $d(s,t)$. Let $pl(u,v)$ be a plateau such that u is the end closer to s and v is the end closer to t. The plateau is used to obtain an alternative path $sp(s,u) \oplus pl(u,v) \oplus sp(v,t)$ where $\oplus$ is the concatenation operation. It was observed in [9] that longer plateaus typically generate better alternative paths. Thus, the algorithm selects k longest plateaus and generates alternative paths for each of the plateaus. We show an example of how Plateaus computes alternative paths in game maps in the next subsection.

Dissimilarity: Techniques in this category specifically define a function that computes dissimilarity between two paths. Given a dissimilarity threshold θ, the goal is to return the shortest alternative paths such that the dissimilarity between any pair of returned paths is at least θ. It was shown that this problem is NP-hard [6]. Therefore, several approximate algorithms [6,15] have been proposed in the past. Below, we describe an algorithm [5] which was shown in [13] to generate high-quality alternative paths in road networks.

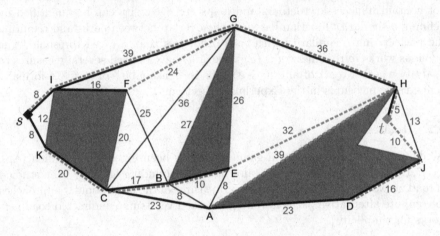

Fig. 2. Three alternative paths generated by Plateaus are $\langle s, I, G, H, t\rangle$, $\langle s, K, C, B, E, H, t\rangle$ and $\langle s, K, C, A, D, J, t\rangle$ with lengths 88, 92 and 100, respectively.

For a vertex v on the road network, a via-path passing through v is $sp(s, v) \oplus sp(v, t)$. Similar to the Plateaus approach, two shortest path trees T_s and T_t are computed and $d(s, v)$ and $d(v, t)$ are stored for each vertex v on the trees. Given these trees, the via-paths and their lengths can be efficiently computed. The algorithm iteratively accesses vertices on the road network in ascending order of the lengths of their via-paths. An accessed via-path is added to the set of alternative paths if its dissimilarity to the already added alternative paths is at least θ. The algorithm stops when k alternative paths are found or when the current via-path is longer than $d(s, t) \times \epsilon$.

3   Adapting Existing Techniques for Game Maps

We adapt Penalty, Dissimilarity and Plateaus for the game maps as follows. We create a visibility graph $G = \{V, E\}$ where V is the set of convex vertices in the game map and E is the set of edges connecting each pair of co-visible vertices (u, v) with edge weight corresponding to the Euclidean distance between them $EDist(u, v)$. For a given query, s and t are added to G by adding edges between s (resp. t) and the vertices visible from s (resp. t). Consider the example of Fig. 2 containing three grey polygonal obstacles. The visibility graph G consists of all the edges shown in the figure. Once G is constructed, each of the approach described earlier can then be applied on G to generate the alternative paths. We prune every *non-taut* path explored by these approaches. A taut path is a path which, when treated as a string, cannot be made "tighter" by pulling on its ends [17], e.g., the path $\langle s, I, F, G \rangle$ is non-taut because string-pulling results in a shorter path $\langle s, I, G \rangle$. We use Dijkstra's algorithm to compute the shortest path trees.

Example 1. Figure 2 shows an example of the paths generated by Plateaus. The convex vertices are A to K. The source and target are connected to their respective visible convex vertices (I and K for s and H and J for t). Plateaus then computes two shortest path trees T_s rooted at s (see the tree shown in blue edges) and T_t rooted at t (see the pink edges shown in broken lines). The common branches in the two trees are the plateaus. The three longest plateaus are $\langle s, I, G, H, t \rangle$, $\langle K, C, B, E \rangle$ and $\langle D, J \rangle$ with lengths 88, 47 and 16, respectively. Thus, three alternative paths are generated connecting s and t to the end of each plateau closer to them. The three alternative paths are $\langle s, I, G, H, t \rangle$, $\langle s, K, C, B, E, H, t \rangle$ and $\langle s, K, C, A, D, J, t \rangle$ with lengths 88, 92 and 100, respectively.

4   User Study

A recent work [13] presented a user study conducted on Melbourne, Dhaka and Copenhagen road networks which shows that Penalty, Dissimilarity and Plateaus generate alternative paths comparable to those generated by Google Maps. To compute alternative paths in game maps, we adapt these existing techniques originally designed for road networks as described in the previous section. However, the first question we ask ourselves is whether these techniques are able to generate high-quality alternative paths in game maps? To answer this, we conducted a user study and present the details in this section.

Based on our previous work [12], we developed a web-based system containing 9 diverse game maps selected from a widely used benchmark[3]. We created a webpage[4] containing the instructions for the participants and the links to the web-based system. The participants were asked to complete two types of surveys:

- **Pre-selected:** They were shown 3 pairs of pre-selected source-target pairs for each of the 9 game maps.
- **User-selected:** For each of the 9 maps, the participants could select any source-target pair of their choice by clicking on the map (they could select as many source-target pairs as they wanted but at least one for each map).

Once the source and target are selected, the system generates up to 4 alternative paths by each approach which can be viewed by clicking the radio button

---

[3] https://movingai.com/benchmarks/grids.html.
[4] http://aamircheema.com/paths_games/.

next to the approach's name. In the system, Plateaus, Dissimilarity and Penalty are named A, B and C, respectively, to avoid any potential preconceived biases. The participants were asked to enter a rating for each approach from 1–5 (higher the better). The participants were given a brief background on the alternative paths in road networks and game maps along with some applications. They were asked to rate the alternative paths generated by each approach based on how good they thought the paths generated by the approach were considering that the alternative routes should be significantly different from each other but meaningful/natural. People are used to see alternative paths in road networks (due to popular navigation applications), but they most likely have not seen alternative paths in game maps. Therefore, we selected the participants who were familiar with computer games or had research background either in pathfinding on game maps or alternative pathfinding in road networks.

Table 1. Results of the user study: average rating, average and maximum $Sim(T)$, and average path length for Plateaus, Dissimilarity (shown as Dissim.) and Penalty. Best values for each category are shown in bold.

	#Responses	Average rating		
		Plateaus	Dissimilarity	Penalty
All	472	**4.028**	3.998	3.852
Pre-selected	243	4.016	**4.025**	3.938
User-selected	229	**4.039**	3.969	3.760

Table 1 shows the results of the user study. We received 472 responses from 9 participants. The results indicate that, on average, the three approaches received overall quite similar ratings and the participants rated the alternative paths quite highly (rated at around 4 on a scale of 1–5). We also conducted one-way repeated measures ANOVA test. Given a null hypothesis of no statistically significant difference in mean ratings of the three approaches, the results suggest that, at $p < 0.05$ level, there is no evidence that the null hypothesis is false, i.e., there is no credible evidence that the three approaches received different ratings on average. Next, we present a detailed experimental study comparing these approaches using some well-known quantitative measures.

5   Experiments

5.1   Settings

Similar to the existing studies on shortest pathfinding in game maps [7,18], we conduct experiments on the widely used grid map benchmarks[5], described in [19]. On a total of 298 game maps, 67 maps from Dragon Age II (DA), 156

---

[5] https://github.com/nathansttt/hog2.

maps from Dragon Age Origins (DAO) and 75 maps from Baldur's Gate II (BG) (see Table 2).

We compare Plateaus, Dissimilarity and Penalty shown as Pla, Dissim, and Pen in the results, respectively. For Penalty, the penalty factor was set to 1.4 and the dissimilarity threshold θ for Dissimilarity was set to 0.6 (we tried various penalty factors and dissimilarity thresholds and chose the best values). ϵ was set to 1.5 for each approach.

Table 2. Benchmark stats include total number of maps and total number of queries in each benchmark, and average number of vertices and convex vertices per map.

Game	Benchmark stats			
	#Maps	#Queries	#Vertices	#Convex vertices
Dragon Age 2 (DA)	67	68K	1183	611
Dragon Age: Origins (DAO)	156	159K	1728	927
Baldurs Gate (BG)	75	93K	1295	668

We also include Polyanya [7] (shown as Poly) which is the state-of-the-art online algorithm for finding shortest paths in game maps. Although Polyanya only finds the shortest path, we compare against it to show the additional costs the alternative pathfinding algorithms pay to generate the alternative paths. We use the implementation of Polyanya provided by its authors[6]. For all algorithms except Polyanya, we vary k from 1 to 5 and the default value of k is 3.

5.2 Evaluation Measures

We evaluate the algorithms considering query processing time and quality of the alternative paths returned. To evaluate the quality of a set of alternative paths $\mathcal{P}$, we use bounded stretch, local optimality and similarity defined below.

Let $P = \langle p_1, p_2, \cdots, p_n \rangle$ be an alternative path between s and t such that $p_1 = s$, $p_n = t$, each p_i $(1 < i < n)$ is a vertex of an obstacle and for each p_i $(i < n)$, p_i and p_{i+1} are visible from each other. We use $P_{x,y}$ where $x < y$ to denote the subpath $\langle p_x, \cdots, p_y \rangle$ of P and denote its length as $d^P(p_x, p_y)$, i.e., $d^P(p_x, p_y) = \sum_{i=x}^{y-1} EDist(p_i, p_{i+1})$. Hereafter, whenever we use x and y, assume $x < y$.

Bounded Stretch [10]. Stretch of a path defines how long is the path compared to the shortest path. Formally, stretch of a subpath $P_{x,y}$ is defined as $S(P_{x,y}) = d^P(p_x, p_y)/d(p_x, p_y)$. For an alternative path P, its bounded stretch is the maximum stretch of any of its subpaths.

Given an alternative path P, we define its bounded stretch as follows.

$$BS(P) = \max_{\forall (x,y)} \frac{d^P(p_x, p_y)}{d(p_x, p_y)} \qquad (1)$$

---

[6] https://bitbucket.org/mlcui1/polyanya.

Consider a path P which has a bounded stretch 1.20, i.e., the maximum stretch of any of its subpath is 1.20. This means that there is no subpath of P which is more than 20% longer than the shortest distance between its end points. Note that an alternative path P with smaller bounded stretch is better. Also, if P is a shortest path, its bounded stretch is 1. Let $\mathcal{P}$ be a set of alternative paths returned by an algorithm. The bounded stretch of $\mathcal{P}$ is the maximum bounded stretch of any of the paths in $\mathcal{P}$, i.e., $BS(\mathcal{P}) = max_{\forall P \in \mathcal{P}} BS(P)$.

Local Optimality [10]. We say that a subpath $P_{x,y}$ is suboptimal if it is longer than the shortest distance between p_x and p_y, i.e., $d^P(p_x, p_y) > d(p_x, p_y)$. Given an alternative path P between s and t, we use $minL(P)$ to denote the length of the shortest suboptimal subpath of P (if all subpaths are optimal, $minL(P)$ is assumed to be $d(s,t)$). Note that any subpath of P which is shorter than $minL(P)$ must be optimal. Thus, $minL(P)$ is a measure of optimality. The local optimality $LO(P)$ normalises this measure w.r.t. the shortest distance $d(s,t)$ between s and t.

Given an alternative path P, we define its local optimality as follows.

$$LO(P) = \frac{minL(P)}{d(s,t)} = \min_{\forall(x,y):d^P(p_x,p_y)>d(p_x,p_y)} \frac{d^P(p_x,p_y)}{d(s,t)} \qquad (2)$$

Consider an alternative path P between s and t and assume that its shortest suboptimal path has length 20 and $d(s,t) = 100$. Its local suboptimality is $20/100 = 0.2$. This implies that every subpath of P which is shorter than 20% of the shortest path between s and t is guaranteed to be an optimal path. A path P with higher local optimality is better. Also, if P is a shortest path, its local optimality is 1. Let $\mathcal{P}$ be a set of alternative paths returned by an algorithm. The local optimality of $\mathcal{P}$ is $LO(\mathcal{P}) = min_{\forall P \in \mathcal{P}} LO(P)$.

Similarity [13]. Similarity $Sim(\mathcal{P})$ of a set of alternative paths $\mathcal{P}$ is

$$Sim(\mathcal{P}) = \max_{\forall(P_i,P_j)\in\mathcal{P}\times\mathcal{P}:i\neq j} \frac{|P_i \cap P_j|}{|P_i \cup P_j|} \qquad (3)$$

where $|P_i \cap P_j|$ (resp. $|P_i \cup P_j|$) denotes the total length of the overlap (resp. union) of two paths P_i and P_j.

In our experiments, we compute $BS(\mathcal{P})$, $LO(\mathcal{P})$ and $Sim(\mathcal{P})$ for each query and report average values. We also report the maximum of $BS(\mathcal{P})$ and $Sim(\mathcal{P})$ across all queries which correspond to the worst-case bounded stretch and similarity for an algorithm across all queries. We also report minimum of $LO(\mathcal{P})$ across all queries representing the worst-case for local optimality. If an approach is only able to generate less than k alternative paths, it may get better quantitative scores which is unfair (e.g., if an approach only returns the shortest path, it will receive the best possible score). Therefore, we only consider the queries where each approach generates exactly k alternative paths.

5.3   Results

Query Runtimes: Figure 3 shows query runtimes for different algorithms on DA, DAO and BG maps. Similar to the existing works on shortest pathfinding [7,18], we sort the queries by the number of nodes expansion required by the standard A* search to solve them (which is a proxy for how challenging a query is) and the x-axis corresponds to the percentile ranks of queries in this order. Figure 3 shows that Plateaus and Dissimilarity have almost the same query times as they both need to generate two shortest path trees which is the dominant cost. The penalty is more expensive as it needs to iteratively compute the shortest paths until k unique paths have been found. Polyanya is about two orders of magnitude faster than all three alternative pathfinding algorithms.

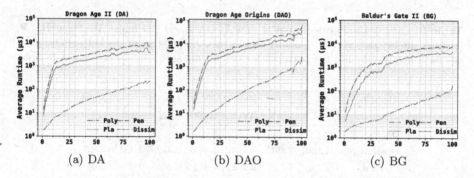

(a) DA   (b) DAO   (c) BG

Fig. 3. x-axis shows the percentile ranks of queries in number of node expansions needed by A* search to solve them.

Varying K: Figures 4(a), (b) and (c) show the result for varying k for the DA, DAO and BG maps, respectively. The cost of Plateaus and Dissimilarity do not change with k because they compute forward and backward shortest path trees regardless of the value of k which is the dominant cost. The cost of Penalty increases with increasing k because the algorithm needs to compute the results in at least k iterations. Polyanya was run only for $k = 1$ as it only generates the shortest path.

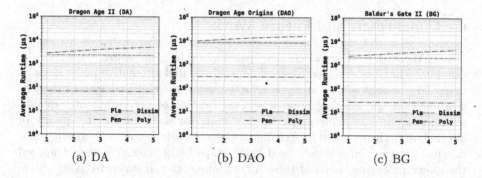

(a) DA   (b) DAO   (c) BG

Fig. 4. Effect of varying k.

Quality of Alternative Paths: Table 3 evaluates the quality of alternative paths generated by different algorithms. Regarding query runtimes, Plateaus and Dissimilarity are about two times faster than the Penalty approach. However, the Penalty method generates alternative paths with quality comparable to the Dissimilarity approach and better than Plateaus. The average bounded stretch of the Dissimilarity approach is better than Plateaus and Penalty. In terms of average similarity, Penalty performs the best. However, Penalty performs quite poorly in terms of the worst-case (i.e., max) similarity (with maximum similarity around 0.9), whereas Dissimilarity guarantees that the maximum similarity is no more than 0.4 (recall dissimilarity threshold $\theta = 0.6$). Dissimilarity is comparable to Penalty, which outperforms the Plateaus in terms of local optimality. Dissimilarity is the best approach in terms of average path length.

Table 3. Quality of alternative paths on DA, DAO and BG maps. We show $BS(\mathcal{P})$ (smaller the better), $Sim(\mathcal{P})$ (smaller the better), $LO(\mathcal{P})$ (larger the better) and average path length (smaller the better). Best values for each column are shown in bold.

Algorithm	$BS(\mathcal{P})$		$Sim(\mathcal{P})$		$LO(\mathcal{P})$		Length
	AVG	MAX	AVG	MAX	AVG	MIN	
DA							
Dissimilarity	**1.086**	**2.087**	0.188	**0.400**	0.352	0.008	**121.5**
Plateau	1.216	3.335	0.232	0.882	0.261	0.008	125.4
Penalty	1.157	7.000	**0.129**	0.953	**0.354**	0.008	124.1
DAO							
Dissimilarity	**1.050**	**3.481**	0.162	**0.400**	**0.336**	0.005	**124.9**
Plateau	1.207	6.859	0.184	0.931	0.190	0.005	132.7
Penalty	1.103	19.00	**0.083**	0.931	0.335	0.005	126.9
BG							
Dissimilarity	1.092	**2.903**	0.136	**0.400**	0.342	0.009	**282.1**
Plateau	1.224	4.454	0.137	0.876	0.252	0.009	298.0
Penalty	**1.088**	5.333	**0.089**	0.831	**0.343**	0.009	286.7

6   Conclusions and Future Work

We are the first to study alternative pathfinding in game maps. We adapt the existing techniques designed for road networks to find alternative paths in game maps. We present a user study conducted using a web-based system demonstrating that the existing approaches are capable of generating high-quality alternative paths in game maps. Furthermore, we also evaluate the quality of alternative paths returned by existing approaches using some well-known quantitative measures on a widely used game maps benchmark. We also compared the query processing costs of these algorithms with the state-of-the-art shortest path algorithm, Polyanya. The results show that Polyanya is almost two orders of magnitude faster than the existing alternative pathfinding techniques in terms of the query processing times. This implies that the overhead paid by these algorithms to compute alternative paths is quite high. Thus, there is a need to develop techniques to efficiently compute diverse shortest paths in game maps.

Acknowledgements. Muhammad Aamir Cheema is supported by ARC FT18010 0140.

References

1. Abraham, I., Delling, D., Goldberg, A.V., Werneck, R.F.: A hub-based labeling algorithm for shortest paths in road networks. In: Pardalos, P.M., Rebennack, S. (eds.) SEA 2011. LNCS, vol. 6630, pp. 230–241. Springer, Heidelberg (2011). https://doi.org/10.1007/978-3-642-20662-7_20
2. Akgün, V., Erkut, E., Batta, R.: On finding dissimilar paths. Eur. J. Oper. Res. **121**(2), 232–246 (2000)
3. Cheema, M.A.: Indoor location-based services: challenges and opportunities. SIGSPATIAL Spec. **10**(2), 10–17 (2018)
4. Chen, Y., Bell, M.G., Bogenberger, K.: Reliable pretrip multipath planning and dynamic adaptation for a centralized road navigation system. IEEE Trans. Intell. Transp. Syst. **8**, 14–20 (2007)
5. Chondrogiannis, T., Bouros, P., Gamper, J., Leser, U., Blumenthal, D.B.: Finding k-dissimilar paths with minimum collective length. In: SIGSPATIAL (2018)
6. Chondrogiannis, T., Bouros, P., Gamper, J., Leser, U., Blumenthal, D.B.: Finding k-shortest paths with limited overlap. VLDB J. **29**(5), 1023–1047 (2020)
7. Cui, M., Harabor, D.D., Grastien, A.: Compromise-free pathfinding on a navigation mesh. In: IJCAI.,pp. 496–502 (2017)
8. Häcker, C., Bouros, P., Chondrogiannis, T., Althaus, E.: Most diverse near-shortest paths. In: SIGSPATIAL, pp. 229–239 (2021)
9. Jones, A.H.: Method of and apparatus for generating routes. US Patent 8,249,810, 21 Aug 2012
10. Kobitzsch, M.: An alternative approach to alternative routes: HiDAR. In: Bodlaender, H.L., Italiano, G.F. (eds.) ESA 2013. LNCS, vol. 8125, pp. 613–624. Springer, Heidelberg (2013). https://doi.org/10.1007/978-3-642-40450-4_52
11. Kobitzsch, M., Radermacher, M., Schieferdecker, D.: Evolution and evaluation of the penalty method for alternative graphs. In: ATMOS, vol. 33, pp. 94–107 (2013)
12. Li, L., Cheema, M.A.: Alternative pathfinding in game maps and indoor venues. In: ICAPS (2021)
13. Li, L., Cheema, M.A., Lu, H., Ali, M.E., Toosi, A.N.: Comparing alternative route planning techniques: a comparative user study on Melbourne. Dhaka and Copenhagen road networks. IEEE TKDE (2021)
14. Li, Y., Yiu, M.L., Kou, N.M., et al.: An experimental study on hub labeling based shortest path algorithms. PVLDB **11**(4), 445–457 (2017)
15. Liu, H., Jin, C., Yang, B., Zhou, A.: Finding top-k shortest paths with diversity. IEEE Trans. Knowl. Data Eng. **30**, 488–502 (2017)
16. Moghanni, A., Pascoal, M., Godinho, M.T.: Finding shortest and dissimilar paths. Int. Trans. Oper. Res. **29**(3), 1573–1601 (2022)

17. Oh, S., Leong, H.W.: Edge n-level sparse visibility graphs: fast optimal any-angle pathfinding using hierarchical taut paths. In: SoCS, pp. 64–72 (2017)
18. Shen, B., Cheema, M.A., Harabor, D.D., Stuckey, P.J.: Euclidean pathfinding with compressed path databases. In: IJCAI, pp. 4229–4235 (2021)
19. Sturtevant, N.R.: Benchmarks for grid-based pathfinding. IEEE Trans. Comput. Intell. AI Games 4(2), 144–148 (2012)

Predicting Taxi Hotspots in Dynamic Conditions Using Graph Neural Network

Saurabh Mishra and Sonia Khetarpaul(✉)

Shiv Nadar University, NCR Campus, Gautam Buddha Nagar, Kalavakkam, India
{sm609,sonia.khetarpaul}@snu.edu.in

Abstract. Demand and supply are crucial elements of the ride-hailing business. After the evolution of the GPS supported mobile-based ride-hailing systems, hotspots detection in a spatial region is one of the most discussed topics among the urban planners and researchers. Due to the high non-linearity and complexity of traffic flow, traditional methods cannot satisfy the requirements of prediction tasks and often they neglect the dynamic constraint of a spatial region. To address this issue, this research considered the road network graph and transform hotspots detection problem into a node-wise decision-making problem and extracted subgraphs as hotspots. In this paper, the authors propose a graph neural networks enable reinforcement learning agents to learn the dynamic behaviour of a road network graph and use it for a subgraph extraction in a road network graph. The Graph Neural Networks (GNNs) can extract node features like the pickup requests and events in the city and generate the subgraphs by stacking multiple neural network layers. Experiments show that the proposed model effectively captures comprehensive spatio-temporal correlations and outperforms state-of-the-art approaches on real-world taxi datasets.

Keywords: Taxi demand · Hotspots prediction · Prediction model · Graph Neural Network · Reinforcement learning

1 Introduction

As per the United Nation's report on Urbanization, the global urban population is projected to reach sixty percent of the world population by 2030 [1]. This will bring new challenges to the urban infrastructure, mobility and city planning. Private cars are recognised as an unsustainable solution for mobility. The GPS based mobile application based ride-hailing systems (Ex. Uber, Ola) have become a part of the day-today life of the urban population. In the case of the ride-hailing system, an insufficient distribution of taxis leads to longer waiting times and longer distances to pick up the customer, leading to repetitive cancellations by the drivers. Predicting the potential customer in a spatial region or finding the next customer after completing a ride is a challenging and complex task for any taxi driver. Considering the scenario, the authors have chosen the problem of hotspots prediction in ride-hailing systems with dynamic environments, i.e., in the changing scenarios.

W. Hua et al. (Eds.): ADC 2022, LNCS 13459, pp. 89–102, 2022.
https://doi.org/10.1007/978-3-031-15512-3_7

Many researchers focused on identification and extraction of "taxi hot-spots" that typically has high demand of taxi pick up requests [2–6]. Researchers have adopted various clustering algorithms to cluster the area with high taxi demands and classify them as hotspots, e.g., *K-means* [2,3], clustering large application (CLARA) algorithm [4], and DBSCAN algorithm [3,5,6], and density-based hierarchical clustering (DBH-CLUS) method.

In recent years many researcher used neural network [7–11] and machine learning [12] based approaches to predict the hotspots in a spatio-temporal region. In [7], the Traffic Graph Convolutional Long Short-Term Memory Neural Network (TGC-LSTM) is used to learn the interactions among the roadways in the traffic network and recognize the most influential road segments in real-world traffic networks. The authors in [10] integrated the clustering models and deep learning approaches to learn and extract the network-wide taxi hotspots in both temporal and spatial dimensions. The authors in [12] have used a reinforcement learning-based approach to predict the taxi demand and order delivery in a spatio-temporal space.

1.1 Motivation

Most of the existing research focused on the static feature of the spatiotemporal region, ignoring new events happening in the city, such as sports events or music concerts. Compared to the existing approach, this research aims to develop a model based on the Graph Neural network (**GNN**) and the Reinforcement Learning (**RL**) agent that recommends the hotspots to drivers, such that the distance and time between them and the next customer is minimized. Each node has an associated two-dimensional feature vector that takes care of the event happening in the city. Since adding more constraints like events (Ex. Weekly Markets, Concerts, sports matches, etc.) makes a spatio-temporal road network graph a complex data structure, the proposed solution is necessary.

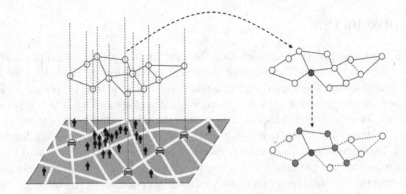

Fig. 1. The proposed framework to predict hotspots

Example. Figure 1 represents the prototype of the proposed model, in which road segments represent the edges and nodes is the intersection of the road segments. Each node has a node feature vector representing the number of taxi requests and events nearby (further explained in Sect. 3). After labelling different influential nodes in a road network graph, a reinforcement learning policy-based connected subgraph is generated; this extracted subgraph will work as a hotspot for mobile applications based ride-hailing systems.

Considering the research gaps and limitations of the existing research, the main contributions of this work are as follows:

- This research focused on hotspots extraction and prediction for idle drivers in a dynamic environment, such that the revenue of the system is maximized.
- The research devised a novel GNN based solution for spatio-temporal road networks like a complex graph that employs the Reinforcement Learning (RL) policy-based decision-making strategy. It integrates the sensing and recommendation components into a single system.
- We performed extensive benchmarking on real datasets from New York and verified the adaptability of the proposed model to changing scenarios, demand anomalies, and traffic variation during the different times of the day. The predictions have a high accuracy (up to 95%) and are significantly better than the state of the art methods.

The rest of the paper is organised as follows. Section 2 briefly discusses the related research works whereas Sect. 3 describes the preliminaries. Section 4 describes the problem statement. Section 5 that describes the proposed hotspots detection method. The evaluation results are presented in Sect. 6, and the conclusions and suggestions for future work are given in the Sect. 7.

2   Literature Review

Identification of taxi hotspots is relatively a recent and upcoming field of research [13–15]. Many researchers have been working on identifying the taxi hotspots. Li et al. [15] proposed a simple Dijkstra-based algorithm for approachable kNN query on moving objects for the ride-hailing service, which considers the occupation of objects. They further improved its efficiency by applying a grid-based Destination-Oriented index for occupied and non-occupied moving objects.

In many of the existing approaches, the researchers have applied various clustering algorithms, like K-means [16], DBSCAN algorithm [14,17–19], fuzzy clustering [20] or taxi-data mining algorithms, such as the density-based hierarchical clustering method to identify taxi pickup locations and spatial clustering [21]. Those clustering-based models mainly focused on spatial features of historical data to understand the taxi requirements. In order to understand the taxi demands more accurately, many researchers have explored the temporal properties [20,22,27]. Chang et al. [3] mined historical data to predict the demand distributions concerning different contexts of time, weather, and taxi location for predicting the taxi demand hotspots.

Predicting traffic states is challenging since traffic networks are dynamic and have complex dependencies. Cui et al. [7] combine GNNs and LSTMs to capture both spatial and temporal dependencies. STGCN [23] constructs ST-Conv blocks with spatial and temporal convolution layers, and applies residual connection with bottleneck strategies. [8,9] both incorporate attention mechanism to better model spatio-temporal correlation. Yu et al. [10] applied DBSTCAN and LSTM-CGAN models to process the large-scaled geo-coded taxi pick-up data into time-varying historical hotspots information. Zang et al. [24] applied a gated localized diffusion network (GLDNet) based model for network-based predictive mapping of sparse spatio-temporal events. Yang et al. [25] use a fuzzy set method based on adaptive kernel density estimation and dual temporal gated multi-graph convolution network to predict the future taxi demand. Xia et al. [11] proposed a parallel Grid-Search-based Support Vector Machine (GS-SVM) optimization algorithm on Spark, to provide an efficient method for searching for passengers in a complex urban traffic network quickly. Liu et al. [12] proposed a context-aware taxi dispatching approach that incorporates rich contexts into DRL modelling for more efficient taxi reallocations.

Our problem falls in the hotspot prediction category, where the goal is to find the nearest point for the taxi drivers, which has the potential to find the next customer. Comparing to the existing approaches, this research includes the dynamic environment, i.e., hotspot detection based on the event happening in the city, using reinforcement learning and graph neural networks based approach.

3   Preliminaries

3.1   Road Network Graph

The road network graph $G(V, E)$ is a planar graph, with node set $V = v_1, v_2, ... v_N$ and edge set $E \in VXV$. The twenty-four hours of a day are divided into four slots of six hours each as it is observed from the datasets that for each six hours slots, there are slightly increase or decrease in demand. Each node in V could be associated with feature vector χ; these feature vectors cannot directly handle geometric features of the road network and need to be manually

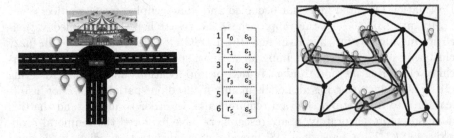

Fig. 2. (a) Snapshot of taxi request on a node (b) Node features (c) Sub-graph generation based on node classification

designed using a neural network structure, e.g., links between layers. Each node v_i of graph G has a feature vector.

$$\chi(v_i) = [\{r_1, r_2, r_3, r_4, r_5, r_6\}, \{\epsilon_1, \epsilon_2, \epsilon_3, \epsilon_4, \epsilon_5, \epsilon_6\}]$$

where, $\{r_1, r_2, r_3, r_4, r_5, r_6\}$ are the number of requests on each node during the six-hour timeslot as shown in Fig. 2. The values they will take can be any natural number between [0,m], where the m=maximum number of request. The set $\{\epsilon_1, \epsilon_2, \epsilon_3, \epsilon_4, \epsilon_5, \epsilon_6\}$ represents the occurrence of an event near that node. It will be 1 if an event occurs under a ten hop distance from that node and 0 otherwise.

3.2 GNN and Message Passing

Given an input graph G and node features χ, a GNN model $f(G, \chi)$ learns node representations [29]. The proposed GNN model utilizes graph feature vector and graph topology in a message-passing scheme and aggregates information from node neighbours. As shown in the Fig. 3, at each layer l, a node v aggregates all the messages in the $(l-1)^{th}$ layer from all its neighbours to generate its embedding:

$$h_v^l = \mathbf{update}(\sum\nolimits_{w \in N(v)} \mathbf{message}(h_v^{l-1}, h_w^{l-1})), h_v^{l-1}$$

where $N(v)$ is the neighbor set of node v. To facilitate understanding, we show an example of each layer's output with a three-layered GNN with a graph in Fig. 3. The **locator** selects the seed node and feeds it as input into the **generator**. The generator then propagates, adds up the most appropriate node to the sub-graph by further layers, generates the sub-graph and obtains the final cost function from the environment. The cost function is further used as feedback to update and optimize the generator and locator for better results.

4 Problem Definition

Given a road network graph $G = (V,E)$, and node features(historical taxi dataset and event dataset). Proposed model aims to generate a sub-graph (hotspots) $S = (V_S, E_S)$ where $V_S \subset V, E_S \subset E$. The goal is to maximize overall revenue for the taxi drivers available in the region (G) by recommending them to move to the nearest hotspot in case of no pick-up request in the region they dropped a customer.

5 Methodology: RL Based Hotspots (Sub-graphs) Selection Using GNN

Hotspot forecasting is a typical time-series prediction problem, i.e., the objective is to predict the area/subgraph which has the chance to get customer requests in the next 'n' hours. These number of requests can be computed from the historical data. We explore how the RL agent understands the topology produced by GNNs and generates subgraphs, optimizing the objective. The three main stages of this method are as follows:

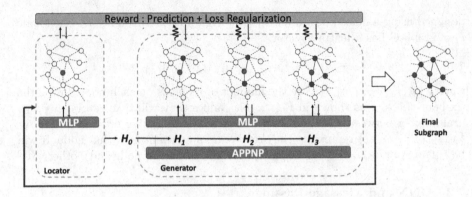

Fig. 3. An illustration of proposed approach for graph classification

5.1   Initial Influential Node Selection

In this problem to classify nodes and generate a connected sub-graph $S = (v_0, v_1, ...v_n)$, it need a starting node v_0. It is a complex task to select the starting point. The natural choice is to choose the nodes that are the most influential nodes of the graph, using historical information from the available datasets. We utilized an existing method; a dominating set based approach [26] to find the most influential nodes of a road network graph. Algorithm 1 returns the set of *top-k* most influential nodes.

Algorithm 1 depicts the *k-hop Dominating Set* formation based on number of requests originating on each node. It initiates an empty list '*DS*' and a empty dictionary *freq*. In this algorithm, dictionary *freq* stores nodes as keys and the number of requests on the respective node as value. In lines 3–5, *freq* appends each node with the respective 'total number of requests originating on that node calculated using historical data. Line 6–15 uses this data from *freq* to find the node with maximum request originating and selects this node along with its neighbours up to *k-hop* distance using *NeighbourSearch*. At each iteration, a node with a maximum value gets selected. The selected node and its neighbours get deleted from *freq*. When *freq* get empty, we get the dominating set *DS* for the graph. The complexity of this algorithm is $O(V^2)$, as for each element in the dominating set, function *NeighbourSearch* is called, and each neighbour is checked to be deleted or not. The complexity of this textitNeighbourSearch method is $O(V)$ as this algorithm uses a BFS search method. The insight details of this algorithm is available in the related publication [26].

5.2   Sub-graph Generation

To generate a connected sub-graph $S = (v_0, v_1, ...v_n)$, it need a starting node v_0, from there it selected one node at each layer during graph generation process. If a starting point v_0, the proposed model will generate a connected sub-graph $S = (v_0, v_1, ...v_n)$, where we select one node in at each step and n are the total number of steps. At the ith step, the current partial solution defined as $S_i = (v_0, v_1, ...v_{i-1})$. Next node v_i will be selected from the ring of nodes

---

Algorithm 1: Algorithm for finding Locator (most influential nodes) in a road network

---

Input: (a) Road Network Graph $G(V,E)$ (b) Taxi request data history
Output: List of most influential nodes of the graph $'DS'$
1: list DS = [ ]   //*an array list for adding dominating set node at each iteration*
2: dictionary freq = { } //*an empty dictionary data structure*
3: **for** every vertex v of Graph G **do**
4:     calculate no. of request $freq(v)$ on vertex v and add $(v, freq(v))$ in a dict $freq$
5: **end for**
6: **while** freq is not empty **do**
7:     maxnode = select node with maximum value from freq
8:     add maxnode to DS
9:     nbr = NeighbourSearch(G, maxnode, k value)
10:    **for** j in nbr **do**
11:        **if** j in freq **then**
12:            delete freq(j)
13:        **end if**
14:    **end for**
15: **end while**
16: return DS

δS_{i-1}, (i.e., the one hop neighbour of each boundary node of partial subgraph S_i) and the subgraph $S_i = S_{i-1} \cup v_i$. The state is defined as the combined representation of both v_0 and S_{i-1}. The action space is the ring of nodes $\delta S_{i-1} = \cup_{v \in S_{i-1}} N(v) \backslash S_{i-1}$ (neighbours of each node excluding subgraph). We further associate the solution with a cost function value.

State. In the proposed model, at i^{th} step, form the ring on nodes of current partial subgraph, one node is selected and that nodes added up the information of node feature vector of the current node and the current partial subgraph. For each node v in S_{i-1} or δS_{i-1}, the values of node feature vector x_v concatenates:

$$x'_v = [x_v, \mathbb{1}_{(v \in \{v_0\})}, \mathbb{1}_{(v \in S_{i-1})}], \quad X'_i = [x'_v]_{\forall v \in S_{i-1} \cup \delta S_{i-1}}$$

where $\mathbb{1}$ is the indicator function and $\mathbb{1}_{(v \in S)} = 1$ if $v \in S$ and otherwise 0. The concatenation of the node feature vector obtains the initial state representation X'_i. The subgraph further combines the information from the current neighbourhood. We used some existing GNN method [28,29] to achieve this; this method is highly efficient and defined the equation as:

$$H_i^{(0)} = \theta_1 X'_i, H_i^{l+1} = (1 - \alpha)\hat{A}H_i^l + \alpha H_i^{(0)}$$

where θ_1 is a trainable weight matrix, $\hat{A}$ is a symmetric adjacency matrix, α is a hyperparameter used to control weight, and H_i^L is node representation after L layers.

Action. Since the connectivity of the generated subgraph is required, we take δS_{i-1} as the action space at the ith step.

$$a_i(v) = \frac{exp(\theta_3^N \bar{H}_i(v))}{\sum\limits_{u \in \delta S_{i-1}} exp(\theta_3^N \bar{H}_i(u))}, v \in \delta S_{i-1}$$

where θ_3 is a trainable parameter vector.

Algorithm 2: Learning phase

Input: Road network graph $G(V,E)$, taxi request and event data history
Output: Sub-graphs(Hotspots) with maximum reward
1: **repeat**
2:    Initialise the reward for each subgraph (seed node) s_i to zero
3:    **for** each sub graph seed s_i **do**
4:        **for** Set N $(s_i) \in$ ring of neighbours **do**
5:            Aggregate the node features $\langle s_{ui}, r_i \rangle$
6:            **repeat**
7:                Generate taxi request
8:                **for** each neighbour **do**
9:                    **if** s_{ui} has a request **then**
10:                        $r_i = r_i + reward$
11:                    **end if**
12:                **end for**
13:                update the reward for each neighbour
14:            **until** end of timeslot
15:        **end for**
16:    **end for**
17:    Add the neighbour with maximum reward of the sub graph
18:    this
19: **until** no updation takes place

Reward and Objective. Hotspot detection aims to minimize the waiting time and distance travelled by all the drivers (taxis) in the city. However, the reward can be total travel time, but it cannot be calculated instantaneous at each step. We use the whole wait time and distance travelled as a reward:

$$W_t = \sum_{j \in T} w_{j,t},$$

$$D_t = \sum_{j \in T} d_{j,t}$$

where T is the total number of drivers/taxis available in the city, and W_t and D_t is the whole wait time and total distance travelled by a driver from dropping off a customer to picking up the next customer. The final goal is to maximize reward R where:

$$R(S_t) = (-\lambda_1 W_t) + (-\lambda_2 D_t)$$

where λ is a hyperparameter to control the term importance, the final objective is to minimize the waiting time and distance covered to pick up the next customer. So the reward is the negative of the objective functions W_t and D_t for each subgraph S_t.

Learning Phase. This work uses historical data to estimate the cost for a resultant hotspot (subgraph). In the process of subgraph generation, first, the GNN based model learns from the historical data using the road network graph and

---

Algorithm 3: Recommendation phase

Input: Road network graph $G(V,E)$, sub-graph(Hotspots), and taxi requests
Output: Updated expected reward for each hotspot

1: Generate the drivers randomly and taxi request from historical data
2: **for** each driver: **do**
3:   **if** divers are idle **then**
4:     Recommend them nearest hotspot(subgraph)
5:     Generate taxi request
6:     **if** Driver found a cutomer in τ minutes **then**
7:       Add reward to the sub-hraph
8:     **end if**
9:     Update the rewards for each sub-graph(hotspot)
10:   **end if**
11: **end for**

---

the node feature vectors, and then in the next phase, i.e., the recommendation phase, it gets verified.

Algorithm 2 presents the pseudo-code of learning the expected rewards of all subgraphs in the network. After selecting the seed node for each subgraph, its reward is initialized to zero. We choose each subgraph as the hotspot and generate taxi requests from historical data to calculate the reward by the subgraph (lines 3–15). For each subgraph, pull the node based on the policy function from the ring of neighbourhood nodes. The reward will be added to the subgraph if a driver gets the pick-up request, i.e., finds a customer. Notice that a node accumulates rewards when it is selected as the query location and when it is part of a chosen subgraph.

Recommendation Phase. Algorithm 3 presents the pseudocode of our online recommendation algorithm. In this phase, we not only recommend hotspots but also update the model based on the success or failure of our recommendations. The basic idea of recommending hotspots by iterative adding a sequence of nodes from the road network remains intact. In the recommendation phase, nearby drivers are recommended to move to the hotspot. If a driver gets the request in a time τ, the reward is added to the subgraph.

5.3 Sub-graph Completion Criteria

The proposed model learns the stopping criteria to judge the goodness of the current generated subgraph. The stopping criteria is the condition where adding a new node to the subgraph does not add any value to the subgraph, defined as:

$$\bar{H}_i(v)(STOP) = \begin{cases} 0, & \text{if } \forall\ v_i\ \in\ \delta S_{i-1}\ \textit{contribute no reward} \\ 1, & \text{otherwise} \end{cases}$$

6 Performance Analysis

In this section, we first introduce our experimental setup. After a brief study of related research, this work compares the proposed model in qualitative and quantitative evaluations based on different performance matrices. Further, we evaluate the performance of our method in comparing with other states of the art methods for hotspot prediction. The performance matrices that we selected are the most relevant in estimating the revenue in a ride-hailing system. In a ride-hailing system, **revenue** is directly proportional to the total number of trips a driver gets and inversely proportional to waiting time and distance covered.

Data Description. In our experiments, we have used NY city road network graph [30] and NY taxi dataset [31]. We cleaned the road map data, and in the NY-city road map, we had 20,700 nodes and 33,000 edges. The NY-city taxi dataset has attributes: date-time, pickup location, and drop-off location. The events data is collected from NYC OpenData [32], has attributes: event_id, event_name, start date-time, end date-time, event type, location, etc.

Metrics. To evaluate the performance of our proposed model, we considered three primary parameters: (a) The number of drivers who get at least one trip. (b) The total number of taxi pick up requests that were completed. (c) And, the distance covered by the driver to pick up the next customer is our primary metric. We considered these three parameters the most critical parameters for drivers and taxi service companies. Considering the temporal effects on the prediction of dominating set and the mentioned parameters.

6.1 Qualitative Evaluation

The proposed methods classify and generate the subgraphs of a road network graph, termed hotspots. Therefore, the hotspot prediction problem can be formalized as a binary classification task, where node features are the feature vectors used for ground truth, labelling them as a part of hotspots. We start with the most influential nodes for node classification and generate a subgraph from that most influential node. With the subgraphs generated by the proposed GNN mode, for train and test purposes, **loss and accuracy** can be computed as quantitative evaluation.

Loss is a value that represents the summation of errors in our model. It measures how well (or bad) our model is doing. If the errors are high, the loss will be increased, which means the model does not do a good job. Otherwise, the lower it is, the better our model works. Accuracy measures how well our model predicts by comparing the model predictions with the true values in terms of percentage.

Figure 4 represents the loss and accuracy of train and test scores in the case of classification for hotspot prediction. We divided the train and test data in the ratio of 70:30. We are getting over **90%** accuracy, performing the experiments on real-world datasets. The graph classification task uses a locator to find the most influential nodes of the graph to construct the subgraph. We also test the

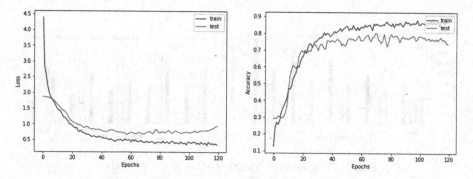

Fig. 4. Quantitative (loss and accuracy) analysis

performance of the locator and found that the locator selects 75 to 85% accurate 'influential nodes' for the experimental datasets.

6.2   Quantitative Evaluation

In this sub-section, the performance of the proposed model, GNN based hotspot prediction, is evaluated. This section studied how proposed methods effecting, i.e., Total number of trips, Waiting time, and distance covered to pick up the next customer. The analysis is done by varying the number of drivers using the proposed method and without using proposed methods to study how the proposed model is affecting metrics, as above mentioned. Figure 5 depicts the performance of the proposed model for different metrics.

Effect on Number of Trips: Figure 5(a) represents the total trips completed by all the drivers using the proposed method with the varying number of drivers. It can be observed from the obtained results that using the proposed method, the number of trips significantly increases with the increase in the number of drivers (as it varies during the different time slots of the day) as compared to the scenario in which drivers search the customers randomly without any strategy. The proposed method recommends the hotspot (subgraph of connected nodes), the area to which a driver can move, and it also increases the probability for a driver to find the next customer in the area.

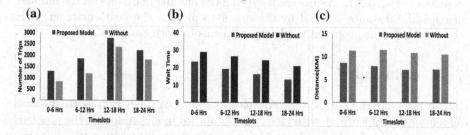

Fig. 5. (a) Total number of trips (b) Wait time and (c) Distance covered to pick next customer

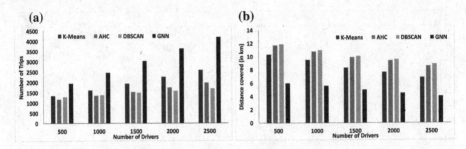

Fig. 6. Comparison with other state of art methods

Effect on Wait Time: Figure 5(b) shows the waiting time of drivers after dropping off the first customer and picking up the next customer. It can be observed from the figure that using the proposed approaches, the waiting time of the drivers to pick up the next customer is reduced significantly using the proposed system as the driver moves to the nearest hotspot after dropping off the previous customer. We have compared the proposed method with the random movement of the drivers when they are idle. The probability of picking the next customer also increases for each driver, as each hotspot node is a connected subgraph with the prediction of getting more requests.

Effect on the Distance Covered to Pick Next Customer: Figure 5(c) represents the distance covered by a driver to pick up the very next customer during the different time slots of the day using the proposed model. As it can be observed from Fig. 5(c) that the distance covered to pick up the next customer is reduced using the proposed model. For all the time slots, it is way less than compared to the strategy that the driver moves randomly.

6.3   Comparison with Other State of Art Methods

The present section compares the proposed method with the well-known clustering methods, viz. K-means, Agglomerative hierarchical clustering (AHC) and Density-Based Spatial Clustering of Applications with Noise (DBSCAN) algorithm, used in Chang et al. [3] for hotspot detection in a city. The results are depicted in Fig. 6. The results show varying the number of drivers on the number of trips and distance covered by the driver to pick up the next customer. It is observed that our proposed model outperforms in both cases.

7   Conclusion

In this research, the authors have developed a hotspot prediction method based on reinforcement learning with GNN. The proposed model addresses the problem of hotspot identification and extraction in a metropolitan city with changing conditions, using advanced neural networks and learning techniques.

We numerically evaluated the proposed method on different performance metrics using the road network, taxi request and event datasets. Each node is assigned a feature vector based on taxi requests and events near that node. The proposed methods introduce the RL based policy for detecting subgraphs in a spatiotemporal road network graph, with taxi requests and event features extracted for each node using the GNNs without manually designed features. Experiments show that our model outperforms other state-of-art methods using real-world datasets, indicating its great potential in exploring spatio-temporal features in a constantly changing environment. Moreover, the proposed framework can be applied to other dynamically changing spatio-temporal scenarios for traffic forecasting, route recommendation and other recommendation systems used in cab-booking and delivery applications.

References

1. United Nations: World urbanization prospects: The 2014 revision. Technical report, United Nations (2014)
2. Lee, J., Shin, I., Park, G.-L.: Analysis of the passenger pick-up pattern for taxi location recommendation. In: 2008 Fourth International Conference on Networked Computing and Advanced Information Management Analysis, pp. 199–204 (2008)
3. Chang, H.W., Tai, Y.C., Hsu, J.Y.J.: Context-aware taxi demand hotspots prediction. Int. J. Bus. Intell. Data Mining **5**(1), 3–18 (2010)
4. Verma, N., Baliyan, N.: PAM clustering based taxi hotspot detection for informed driving. In: Proceedings of the 8th International Conference on Computing, Communication and Networking Technologies, pp. 1–7 (2001)
5. Tang, J., Liu, F., Wang, Y., Wang, H.: Uncovering urban human mobility from large scale taxi GPS data. Phys. A **438**, 140–153 (2015)
6. Ester, M., Kriegel, H.-P., Sander, J., Xu, X.: A density-based algorithm for discovering clusters in large spatial databases with noise. In: Proceedings of the Second International Conference on Knowledge Discovery and Data Mining, pp. 226–231 (1996)
7. Cui, Z., Henrickson, K., Ke, R., Wang, Y.: Traffic graph convolutional recurrent neural network: a deep learning framework for network-scale traffic learning and forecasting, arXiv preprint arXiv:1802.07007 (2018)
8. Zheng, C., Fan, X., Wang, C., Qi, J., GMAN: a graph multi-attention network for traffic prediction. Proc. AAAI **34**, 1234–1241 (2020)
9. Guo, S., Lin, Y., Feng, N., Song, C., Wan, H.: Attention based spatial-temporal graph convolutional networks for traffic flow forecasting. Proc. AAAI **33**, 922–929 (2019)
10. Yu, H., Li, Z., Zhang, G., Liu, P., Wang, J.: Extracting and predicting taxi hotspots in spatiotemporal dimensions using conditional generative adversarial neural networks. IEEE Trans. Veh. Technol. **69**(4), 3680–3692 (2020)
11. Xia, D., et al.: A parallel grid-search-based SVM optimization algorithm on Spark for passenger hotspot prediction. Multim. Tools Appl. **88**, 1–27 (2022)
12. Liu, Z., Li, J., Wu, K.: Context-aware taxi dispatching at city-scale using deep reinforcement learning. IEEE Trans. Intell. Transp. Syst. **23**, 1996–2009 (2020)
13. Dwork, C., Kumar, R., Naor, M., Sivakumar, D.: Rank aggregation methods for the web. In: Proceedings of the 10th International Conference on World Wide Web, pp. 613–622 (2001)

14. Bohm, C., Ooi, B.C., Plant, C., Yan, Y.: Efficiently processing continuous k-NN queries on data streams. In: ICDE, pp. 156–165 (2007)

15. Li, M., He, D., Zhou, X.: Efficient kNN search with occupation in large-scale on-demand ride-hailing. In: Borovica-Gajic, R., Qi, J., Wang, W. (eds.) ADC 2020. LNCS, vol. 12008, pp. 29–41. Springer, Cham (2020). https://doi.org/10.1007/978-3-030-39469-1_3

16. Shekhar, S., Feiner, S.K., Aref, W.G.: Spatial computing. Comm. ACM **59**(1), 72–81 (2016)

17. Ailon, N., Charikar, M., Newman, A.: Aggregating inconsistent information: ranking and clustering. J. ACM **55**(5), 23 (2008)

18. Korn, F., Muthukrishnan, S., Srivastava, D.: Reverse nearest neighbor aggregates over data streams. In: PVLDB, pp. 814–825 (2002)

19. Li, C., Gu, Y., Qi, J., Yu, G., Zhang, R., Yi, W.: Processing moving kNN queries using influential neighbor sets. Proc. VLDB Endow. **8**(2), 113–124 (2014)

20. Khetarpaul, S., Gupta, S.K., Malhotra, S., Subramaniam, L.V.: Bus arrival time prediction using a modified amalgamation of fuzzy clustering and neural network on spatio-temporal data. In: Sharaf, M.A., Cheema, M.A., Qi, J. (eds.) ADC 2015. LNCS, vol. 9093, pp. 142–154. Springer, Cham (2015). https://doi.org/10.1007/978-3-319-19548-3_12

21. Li, M., Bao, Z., Sellis, T., Yan, S.: Visualization-aided exploration of the real estate data. In: Cheema, M.A., Zhang, W., Chang, L. (eds.) ADC 2016. LNCS, vol. 9877, pp. 435–439. Springer, Cham (2016). https://doi.org/10.1007/978-3-319-46922-5_34

22. Cheema, M., Zhang, W., Lin, X., Zhang, Y., Li, X.: Continuous reverse k nearest neighbors queries in Euclidean space and in spatial networks. VLDB J. **21**(1), 69–95 (2012)

23. Yu, B., Yin, H., Zhu, Z.: Spatio-temporal graph convolutional networks: a deep learning framework for traffic forecasting. In: Proceedings of IJCAI, pp. 3634–3640 (2018)

24. Zhang, Y., Cheng, T.: Graph deep learning model for network-based predictive hotspot mapping of sparse spatio-temporal events. Comput. Environ. Urban Syst. **79**, 101403 (2020)

25. Yang, T., Tang, X., Liu, R.: Dual temporal gated multi-graph convolution network for taxi demand prediction. Neural Comput. Appl. 1–16 (2021). https://doi.org/10.1007/s00521-021-06092-6

26. Mishra, S., Khetarpaul, S.: Optimal placement of taxis in a city using dominating set problem. In: Qiao, M., Vossen, G., Wang, S., Li, L. (eds.) ADC 2021. LNCS, vol. 12610, pp. 111–124. Springer, Cham (2021). https://doi.org/10.1007/978-3-030-69377-0_10

27. Xia, T., Zhang, D., Kanoulas, E., Du, Y.: On computing top-t most influential spatial sites. In: PVLDB, pp. 946–957 (2005)

28. Klicpera, J., Bojchevski, A., Günnemann, S.: Predict then propagate: graph neural networks meet personalized pagerank. arXiv preprint. arXiv:1810.05997 (2018)

29. Shan, C., Shen, Y., Zhang, Y., Li, X., Li, D.: Reinforcement learning enhanced explainer for graph neural networks. Adv. Neural Inf. Process. Syst. **34** (2021)

30. http://users.diag.uniroma1.it/challenge9/download.shtml

31. https://www1.nyc.gov/site/tlc/about/tlc-trip-record-data.page

32. https://data.cityofnewyork.us/City-Government/NYC-Permitted-Event-Information-Historical/bkfu-528j

Analysing Big Brain Signal Data for Advanced Brain Computer Interface System

Taslima Khanam(✉) ⓘ, Siuly Siuly, and Hua Wang

Institute for Sustainable Industries and Liveable Cities, Victoria University,
Melbourne, VIC, Australia
taslima.khanam@live.vu.edu.au

Abstract. The modern commercial industry is increasingly dependent on the analysis of vast data records. Analysing big electroencephalogram (EEG) signal data (called brain signal data) plays an important role in a wide variety of applications such as healthcare practices, brain computer interface (BCI) systems, innovative education, privacy and security, and biometrics. The key objective of this paper is to establish a methodological framework for identifying communicative intentions of motor disabled people from EEG data for application in BCI systems. The proposed framework is designed based on common spatial pattern (CSP) data method and optimized ensemble (OE) machine learning method for the application of BCI technologies. The CSP method is used for discovering important features from EEG data and finally the extracted features are fed as an input to optimized ensemble (OE) method. The proposed method was tested on BCI Competition III dataset IVa, which contains motor imagery-based EEG signal data. The experimental results show that our proposed method can handle brain signal big data for identifying communicative intentions for an advanced BCI system. We compared the performance of our proposed method with several other existing methods. In comparison with other established methods, our method achieves higher classification accuracy performance. This research assists the experts in processing and analysing EEG signals for BCI applications. It also supports technologists to create a new EEG data analyser for BCI systems.

Keywords: Electroencephalography · Brain computer interface · Common spatial pattern · Machine learning

1 Introduction

Electroencephalography (EEG) signal data called brain signals data plays an essential role in biomedical science and brain computer interface systems (BCI) [2,3,29]. This EEG records are used to monitoring and recording electrical activity in the brain using electrodes placed on the scalp. Traditional scanning and analysis of EEGs is time-consuming since these records may last hours or days. Therefore, high performing automated analysis of EEGs can lower time to diagnosis and develop real-time applications by identifying mental states for brain computer interface application (BCI) [9].

A BCI, sometimes called a brain-machine interface (BMI), is a direct communication pathway between the brain's electrical activity and an external device, most commonly a computer or robotic limb. A BCI is a computer-based system that receives brain signals, analyses them, and converts them into commands that are conveyed to an output device to carry out the desired action (see Fig. 1) [7]. The primary purpose of BCI research is to generate a new communication pathway permitting direct transmission of communications from the brain by evaluating the brain's mental imagery task for those who are suffering from severe neuromuscular disabilities [21].

The big challenge of BCI systems is the identification of motor imagery (MI) task-based EEG for discovering the communicative intentions of motor disabled people [4,28]. So, our research problem is how to develop more accurate and robust methodological framework to identify communicative intentions from motor imagery BCI brain signal data. Hence, we are interested in developing a method which would be capable of executing a computationally complex machine learning algorithm on big data platforms with high speed and accuracy.

The transition of brain activities into EEG signals in BCI systems involves a robust and accurate classification to create a communication system for motor immobilized people [23]. Although BCI techniques have been improving quickly in recent years, there exists a number of unsolved challenges related to MI signal classification, which is still unable to achieve 100% accuracy [10]. Now we are presenting some recent studies which have been worked on mental state identification for BCI application. Chaudhry et al. [6] deployed a machine learning method using the common spatial pattern (CSP) and dynamic weighted majority (DWM) based classifier. The author's employed procedure reached 85.6% accuracy, which is not satisfactory. Another author Miao et al. [14] established a framework termed common time-frequency-spatial patterns (CTFSP) with multiple support vector machine (SVM) machine learning algorithm. The accuracy was achieved 85% in this study. The drawback of this procedure is various signal processing and classification techniques have been used in low-frequency movement-related cortical potential (MRCP) detection involving locality preserving projection (LPP). Tiwari and Chaturvedi, Cherloo et al. and Inbarani et al. [8,20,30] gained less than 90% accuracy by using several machine learning methods. Rashid et al. [19] accomplished 89.64% and 88.56% accuracy by using CSP-SVM, CSP-KNN machine learning methods, respectively. Siuly et al. [27] established a novel cross-correlation based machine learning technique with a least square support vector machine (LS-SVM) for two-class MI signals recognition. The LS-SVM classifier produced average accuracy performance of 88.32%. The drawback of that method was that they did not select the parameters optimally through any method. They manually selected the parameters for the LS-SVM method.

The above-mentioned existing literatures show that most of the methods are very complex for practical application and also their performance is not satisfactory for identifying mental states in BCI signal output. Hence, an automatic analysis robust classification method needs to be designed to resolve the weaknesses faced in this research. In line with the literature gap, we proposed an algorithm of CSP for feature extraction and OE for classification of the obtained features for getting closer to 100% accuracy for identifying mental states in the development of BCI systems.

2 Proposed Framework

This research represents a scheme based on data mining and machine learning methods for analysis of big EEG signal data [24,34]. Figure 1 show a diagram of the proposed plan that can be used for handling big amount of brain signal data (for example, EEG data). This figure is an example of how EEG signal data are processed for analysis in the proposed plan for each subject. The proposed methodology is divided into several parts such as signal pre-processing, feature extraction and classification. The detail of each part is provided in the following sections.

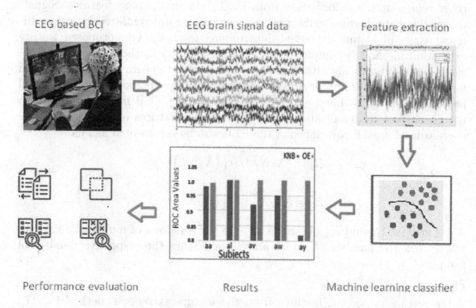

Fig. 1. Proposed methodological diagram for the analysis of big brain signal data

Signal Pre-processing: EEG signal is more often contaminated with noises or unwanted signal. The most common noises in EEG signals are the eye movement or blinking, power line or interference with other device and muscle. These noises are overlapping each other [16]. To overcome these noises from the brain signal EEG data, we applied Butterworth filter. Butterworth filter is a type of electronic filter, which was first designed by British engineer Stephen Butterworth (1930). There are two advantages of Butterworth filter: one is the frequency response curve in the pass band is flat to the maximum extent and the other one is selecting a higher order filter will then have a steeper attenuation slope near the cut-off frequency each time the order of the filter is increased. Hence, we used Butterworth filter considering low frequency 0.1 Hz, high 4 Hz and 5th order derivatives in order to getting a noise free EEG signal data. Thus from the raw data we get the noise removed filtered data [1].

Butterworth filter can be defined with the first 2n-1 derivatives response of

$$|H(JW)| = \frac{1}{\sqrt{1 + \left(\frac{\omega}{\omega_c}\right)^{2n}}}$$

where, ω_c is the filter cut-off frequency and n is the filter order. At low frequencies, we can obtain a gain closer to one, and as the frequency increases, the gain decreases [1].

Feature Extraction: After getting noise free data, the next step is to discover representative information from EEG data that acts as features. Signals undertaking the feature extraction process will be differentiated by using different types of feature extracted data mining methods. Our proposed feature extraction method is common spatial pattern (CSP) method. This is an efficient spatial filtering algorithm and has been proven to be an effective algorithm for the binary motor imagery tasks classification. This method examines spatial patterns of imagined hand and foot movements [32]. CSP method depends on the concurrent diagonalization of the covariance matrices of two classes. The standardized spatial covariance of the EEG can be represented as follows:

$$R_1 = (X_1 X_1^T)/(t_1 (X_1 X_1^T))$$

$$R_2 = (X_2 X_2^T)/(t_2 (X_2 X_2^T))$$

X_1 of size (n, t_1) and X_2 of size (n, t_2) are two windows of multivariate signal, where n is the number of signal and t_1 and t_2 are the respective number of samples.

Classification

After getting important features from the feature extraction method [12,17], our next step is to conduct classification of the features data. In this study, we used two classification methods. One is naive bayes classifier and the other one is ensemble classifier. Naïve bayes is one of the simple and most effective classification algorithms which helps in building the fast machine learning models that can make quick predictions. It is a probabilistic classifier, which means it predicts based on the probability of an object. It is highly scalable with the number of predictors and data points. It is fast and can be used to make real-time predictions [25]. Since a naive bayes text classifier is based on the Bayes's theorem, which helps us compute the conditional probabilities of occurrence of two classes (right hand and right foot) based on the probabilities of occurrence of each individual event, encoding those probabilities is extremely useful. The classifier can be expressed as below:

$$P(A/B) = \frac{P(B/A)P(A)}{P(B)}$$

where,

P(A): The probability of hypothesis H being true. This is known as the prior probability, P(B): The probability of the evidence.

P(A|B): The probability of the evidence given that hypothesis is true, P(B|A): The probability of the hypothesis given that the evidence is true.

The reason of choosing naïve bayes classifier because it is easy and fast to predict the class of the test data set. It also performs well in binary-class prediction. When assumption of independence holds, a naive bayes classifier performs better compared to other models like logistic regression and we need less training data [31].

In order to evaluate the performance of the obtained features, we use another machine learning model called ensemble learning. Ensemble learning is a general meta-approach to machine learning that seeks better predictive performance by combining the predictions from multiple models. Each classifier in the ensemble is a decision tree classifier and is generated using a random selection of attributes at each node to determine the split. During classification, each tree votes and the most popular class is returned. The reason of choosing this classifier is it's better performance and robustness. An ensemble can make better predictions and achieve better performance than any single contributing model and ensemble reduces the spread or dispersion of the predictions and model performance [5].

3   Experimental Data

Our proposed method will be tested on publicly available EEG databases from BCI Competition III dataset IVa (https://drive.google.com/u/0/open-BCI-data-file.) This dataset was recorded from five healthy subjects (labelled aa, al, av, aw, ay) who performed right hand (class1) and right foot (class 2) MI tasks. Subjects sat in a comfortable chair with arms resting on armrests. This data set contains MI EEG data from the four initial sessions without feedback. EEG signals were recorded from 118 electrodes according to the international 10/20 system. There were 280 trials for each subject, namely 140 trials for each task per subject. During each trial, the subject was required to perform either of the two (right hand and right foot) MI tasks for 3.5 s. Among 280 trials, 168, 224, 84, 56 and 28 trials composed the training set for subject aa, al, av, aw and ay respectively and the remaining trials composed the test set.

4   Results and Discussions

In this section, we provide the experimental results of our proposed method for BCI Competition III, IVa dataset. For removing unexpected signal, we used Butterworth filter and then we applied CSP method for feature extraction. In this dataset, there are five healthy subjects each subject accomplished two tasks. Task one is imagination of right-hand movement and task two is imagination of right-foot movement. Each task or effort is counted as a class of EEG data. Figure 2 shows the box plots of the data after feature extraction of all subjects considering two classes: right hand and right foot. To assess the consistency of the proposed method, this study applied a 10-fold cross-validation method. 10-fold cross-validation process estimates the models by distributing the original feature vector into ten sub features, where only one is computed as the testing set and the rest of the nine are the training set applying for the classifier. Figure 3 represents the comparison of training and testing classification accuracy of the individual subject by kernel naïve bayes and optimized ensemble machine learning model.

Table 1 shows the classification outcomes of the classifier kernel naïve bayes and optimized ensemble. It gives information about accuracy, sensitivity and specificity for each subject. From Table 1, it is very clear that optimizable Ensemble machine learning algorithm achieves higher classification results comparing to the Kernel naïve bayes machine learning algorithm for each of the subject. From this observation, we may conclude that optimizable Ensemble classifier is more accurate to classify EEG based motor imagery tasks.

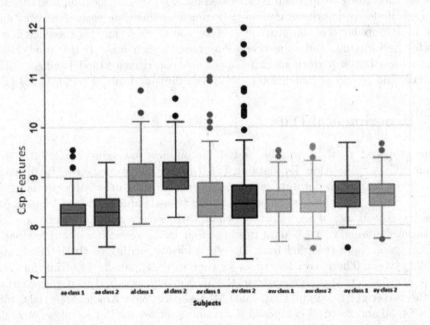

Fig. 2. Boxplot shows the feature extraction of all subjects considering two classes

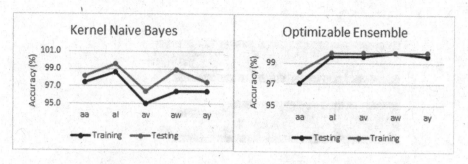

Fig. 3. Comparison of training and testing classification accuracy of the individual subject among Kernel naïve bayes and optimizable ensemble

Figure 4 shows the F-1 score comparison for KNB and OE classifiers by subjects. Here error bars show the standard error. From the figure it is clear that in case of OE classifier, F-1 score is closer to 1 for all the subjects. So, OE is a better model than KNB. Kappa Statistic is used to measure the level of agreement between two raters or judges who each classify items into mutually exclusive categories. We know that kappa of >0.81 represents excellent agreement. From Fig. 5, we found that both the classifier's score is good.

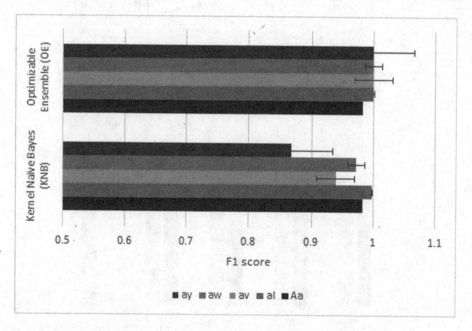

Fig. 4. F1 score comparison for KNB and OE classifiers by subjects. Error bars show the standard error.

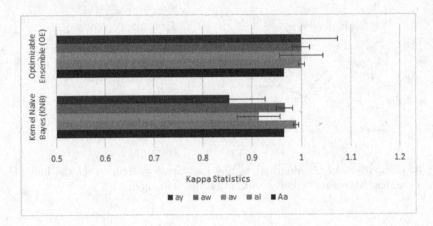

Fig. 5. Kappa comparison for KNB and OE classifiers by subjects. Error bars show the standard error.

Table 1. Overall accuracy, sensitivity and specificity using 10-fold cross validation for individual subjects

Subjects	Kernel naïve bayes machine learning algorithm			Optimizable ensemble machine learning algorithm		
	Accuracy (%)	Sensitivity (%)	Specificity (%)	Accuracy (%)	Sensitivity (%)	Specificity (%)
Aa	98.20	97.86	98.57	98.20	97.86	98.57
Al	99.60	100.00	98.25	100.00	100.00	100.00
Av	96.40	91.67	98.47	100.00	100.00	100.00
Aw	98.90	94.64	100.00	100.00	94.92	100.00
Ay	97.50	82.14	99.21	100.00	100.00	100.00
Average	98.12	93.26	98.90	99.64	98.55	99.71

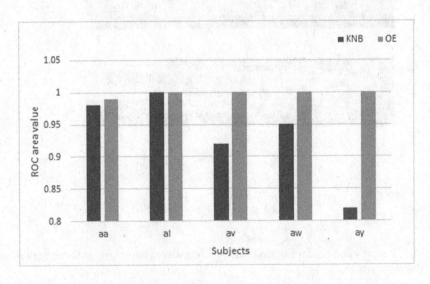

Fig. 6. ROC area for KNB and OE classifiers by subjects

Figure 6 depicts the ROC areas for the KNB and OE classifiers for each of the individual subject. An ROC curve (receiver operating characteristic curve) is a graph shows the performance of a classification model at all classification thresholds. We know, ROC area 0.8 to 0.9 is considered excellent, and more than 0.9 is considered outstanding. So from this experimental result it is clear that OE classifier is better than KNB.

Table 2 shows the performance comparison between our proposed method based on OE classifier and eleven existing machine learning algorithm considering individual subject's classification accuracy and overall classification accuracy for EEG dataset. Our proposed method achieved 99.64% overall performance. This is the highest performance achievement among the other existing methods. In this study, for subject aa, CA rate is 98.2%, all other subject's (al, av, aw and ay) CA rate is 100%. The overall classification accuracy of MSPCA based LR [22], OA+NB [28], CS+SVM [11], CC+LS-SVM [27], ISSPL [33] and Clustering with LS-SVM [13] are 97.7%, 96.36%, 96%, 95.72%, 94.21% and 88.32% respectively. Some other studies average classification accuracy Z-LDA [36], SSFO [35], R-AdaBoost [15], FBCSP-LSSVM [18] and CSP +AM-BA-SVM [26] are 81.1%, 73.50%, 80.6%, 86.73% and 85.01% respectively. So, the overall results show that our proposed method succeeds by 1.24% to 26.14% improvements comparing with the eleven existing machine learning algorithm considering overall classification accuracy in the identification of mental states for BCI application.

Table 2. Comparison between the results of our proposed methods with some reported research outcome.

Author	Method	Classification accuracy (%)					
		Aa	Al	Av	Aw	Ay	Average
Proposed method	Common spatial pattern based optimized ensemble	98.20	100.00	100.00	100.00	100.00	99.64
Sadiq et al. [22]	Multiscale principal component analysis based linear regression	97.80	98.80	98.90	100.00	93.20	97.70
Siuly et al. [28]	Optimal allocation based Naïve Bayes algorithm	97.92	97.88	98.26	94.47	93.26	96.36
Ince et al. [11]	Class separability-based support vector method	95.06	99.70	90.50	98.40	95.70	96.00
Siuly et al. [27]	Cross correlation based least square support vector machine	97.88	99.17	98.75	93.43	89.36	95.72
Wu et al. [33]	Iterative spatio-spectral patterns learning algorithm	93.57	100.00	79.29	99.64	98.57	94.21
Siuly et al. [13]	Clustering with least square support vector machine	92.63	84.99	90.77	86.50	86.73	88.32
Zhang et al. [36]	Z score linear discriminant analysis	77.70	100.00	68.40	99.60	59.90	81.10
Yong et al. [35]	Sparse spatial filter optimization based linear discriminant analysis	57.50	86.90	54.40	84.40	84.30	73.50
Y Miao et al. [15]	Regularized common spatial pattern based on Adaboost algorithm	79.60	93.90	53.20	87.90	88.20	80.60
Park and Chung [18]	Filter bank common spatial pattern based on least square support vector machine	92.85	89.28	71.43	83.04	94.05	86.73
Selim et al. [26]	Common spatial pattern with bat optimization algorithm based on support vector machine	86.61	100.00	66.84	90.63	80.95	85.01

5　Conclusion

In this study, we proposed a CSP method-based OE method for exploring big EEG signal data for the application of BCI systems. For analytical purposes we used some important statistical characteristics to establish design of the distribution. We applied CSP method for feature extraction and OE as a machine learning model, which was tested on EEG brain signal data BCI Competition III dataset IVa. Our experimental results show that our proposed method is capable of handling big brain signal data for identifying communicative intentions for advance BCI system. We compared the performance of classification accuracy of our proposed method with several other existing methods. In comparison with other established method our method achieves higher performance of classification accuracy. This research assists the experts to process and analyse EEG signals for BCI applications. It also supports technologist to create a new EEG data analyser for BCI systems.

References

1. AlHinai, N.: Introduction to biomedical signal processing and artificial intelligence. In: Biomedical Signal Processing and Artificial Intelligence in Healthcare, pp. 1–28. Elsevier (2020)
2. Alvi, A.M., Siuly, S., Wang, H.: Developing a deep learning based approach for anomalies detection from EEG data. In: Zhang, W., Zou, L., Maamar, Z., Chen, L. (eds.) WISE 2021. LNCS, vol. 13080, pp. 591–602. Springer, Cham (2021). https://doi.org/10.1007/978-3-030-90888-1_45
3. Alvi, A.M., Siuly, S., Wang, H.: A long short-term memory based framework for early detection of mild cognitive impairment from EEG signals. In: IEEE Transactions on Emerging Topics in Computational Intelligence (2022)
4. Alvi, A.M., Siuly, S., Wang, H., Wang, K., Whittaker, F.: A deep learning based framework for diagnosis of mild cognitive impairment. Knowl. Based Syst. **248**, 108815 (2022)
5. Chatterjee, R., Datta, A., Sanyal, D.K.: Ensemble learning approach to motor imagery EEG signal classification. In: Machine Learning in Bio-Signal Analysis and Diagnostic Imaging, pp. 183–208. Elsevier (2019)
6. Chaudhary, P., Agrawal, R.: Sensory motor imagery EEG classification based on non-dyadic wavelets using dynamic weighted majority ensemble classification. Intell. Decis. Technol. **15**(1), 33–43 (2021)
7. Chaudhary, S., Taran, S., Bajaj, V., Siuly, S.: A flexible analytic wavelet transform based approach for motor-imagery tasks classification in BCI applications. Comput. Methods Programs Biomed. **187**, 105325 (2020)
8. Cherloo, M.N., Amiri, H.K., Daliri, M.R.: Ensemble regularized common spatio-spectral pattern (ensemble RCSSP) model for motor imagery-based EEG signal classification. Comput. Biol. Med. **135**, 104546 (2021)
9. Golmohammadi, M., Torbati, A.H.H.N., de Diego, S.L., Obeid, I., Picone, J.: Automatic analysis of EEGS using big data and hybrid deep learning architectures. Front. Human Neurosci. **13**, 76 (2019)
10. Graham, S., et al.: Artificial intelligence for mental health and mental illnesses: an overview. Current Psych. Rep. **21**(11), 1–18 (2019)

11. Ince, N.F., Goksu, F., Tewfik, A.H., Arica, S.: Adapting subject specific motor imagery EEG patterns in space-time-frequency for a brain computer interface. Biomed. Signal Process. Control **4**(3), 236–246 (2009)
12. Li, J.-Y., Du, K.-J., Zhan, Z.-H., Wang, H., Zhang, J.: Distributed differential evolution with adaptive resource allocation. IEEE Trans. Cybern. (2022)
13. Li, Y., et al.: Clustering technique-based least square support vector machine for EEG signal classification. Comput. Methods Programs Biomed. **104**(3), 358–372 (2011)
14. Miao, Y., et al.: Learning common time-frequency-spatial patterns for motor imagery classification. IEEE Trans. Neural Syst. Rehabil. Eng. **29**, 699–707 (2021)
15. Miao, Y., Yin, F., Zuo, C., Wang, X., Jin, J.: Improved RCSP and adaboost-based classification for motor-imagery BCI. In: 2019 IEEE International Conference on Computational Intelligence and Virtual Environments for Measurement Systems and Applications (CIVEMSA), pp. 1–5. IEEE (2019)
16. Milne, E.: Increased intra-participant variability in children with autistic spectrum disorders: evidence from single-trial analysis of evoked EEG. Front. Psychol. **2**, 51 (2011)
17. Pandey, D., Wang, H., Yin, X., Wang, K., Zhang, Y., Shen, J.: Automatic breast lesion segmentation in phase preserved DCE-MRIS. Health Inf. Sci. Syst. **10**(1), 1–19 (2022)
18. Park, Y., Chung, W.: Optimal channel selection using covariance matrix and cross-combining region in EEG-based BCI. In: 2019 7th International Winter Conference on Brain-Computer Interface (BCI), pp. 1–4. IEEE (2019)
19. Rashid, M., et al.: The classification of motor imagery response: an accuracy enhancement through the ensemble of random subspace K-NN. Peer J. Comput. Sci. **7**, e374 (2021)
20. Renuga Devi, K., Hannah Inbarani, H.: Neighborhood based decision theoretic rough set under dynamic granulation for BCI motor imagery classification. J. Multimod. User Interfaces **15**(3), 301–321 (2021)
21. Sadiq, M.T., et al.: Exploiting pretrained CNN models for the development of an EEG-based robust BCI framework. Comput. Biol. Med. **143**, 105242 (2022)
22. Sadiq, M.T., Siuly, S., Ur Rehman, A.: Evaluation of power spectral and machine learning techniques for the development of subject-specific BCI. In: Artificial Intelligence-Based Brain-Computer Interface, pp. 99–120. Elsevier (2022)
23. Sadiq, M.T., Yu, X., Yuan, Z., Aziz, M.Z., Siuly, S., Ding, W.: Toward the development of versatile brain-computer interfaces. IEEE Trans. Artif. Intell. **2**(4), 314–328 (2021)
24. Sarki, R., Ahmed, K., Wang, H., Zhang, Y., Wang, K.: Automated detection of COVID-19 through convolutional neural network using chest x-ray images. PLOS ONE **17**(1), e0262052 (2022)
25. Sarki, R., Ahmed, K., Wang, H., Zhang, Y.,Wang, K.: Convolutional neural network for multi-class classification of diabetic eye disease. EAI Endorsed Trans. Scalab. Inf. Syst. p. e15 (2022)
26. Selim, S., Tantawi, M.M., Shedeed, H.A., Badr, A.: A CSP\AM-BA-SVM approach for motor imagery BCI system. IEEE Access. **6**, 49192–49208 (2018)
27. Siuly, S., Li, Y.: Improving the separability of motor imagery EEG signals using a cross correlation-based least square support vector machine for brain-computer interface. IEEE Trans. Neural Syst. Rehabil. Eng. **20**(4), 526–538 (2012)
28. Siuly, S., Li, Y.: Discriminating the brain activities for brain-computer interface applications through the optimal allocation-based approach. Neural Comput. App. **26**(4), 799–811 (2015)

29. Siuly, S., Li, Y., Zhang, Y.: EEG signal analysis and classification. IEEE Trans. Neural Syst. Rehabil. Eng. **11**, 141–144 (2016)
30. Tiwari, A., Chaturvedi, A.: A novel channel selection method for BCI classification using dynamic channel relevance. IEEE Access **9**, 126698–126716 (2021)
31. Wang, H., Zhang, Y., et al.: Detection of motor imagery EEG signals employing Naïve Bayes based learning process. Measurement **86**, 148–158 (2016)
32. Wang, Y., Gao, S., Gao, X.: Common spatial pattern method for channel selection in motor imagery based brain-computer interface. In: 2005 IEEE Engineering in Medicine and Biology 27th Annual Conference, pp. 5392–5395. IEEE (2006)
33. Wei, W., Gao, X., Hong, B., Gao, S.: Classifying single-trial EEG during motor imagery by iterative spatio-spectral patterns learning (ISSPL). IEEE Trans. Biomed. Eng. **55**(6), 1733–1743 (2008)
34. Yin, J., Tang, M.J., Cao, J., Wang, H., You, M., Lin, Y.: Vulnerability exploitation time prediction: an integrated framework for dynamic imbalanced learning. World Wide Web **25**(1), 401–423 (2022)
35. Yong, X., Ward, R.K., Birch, G.E.: Sparse spatial filter optimization for EEG channel reduction in brain-computer interface. In: 2008 IEEE International Conference on Acoustics, Speech and Signal Processing, pp. 417–420. IEEE (2008)
36. Zhang, R., Peng, X., Guo, L., Zhang, Y., Li, P., Yao, D.: Z-score linear discriminant analysis for EEG based brain-computer interfaces. PLOS ONE **8**(9), e74433 (2013)

Hop-Constrained $s\text{-}t$ Simple Path Enumeration in Large Uncertain Graphs

Xia Li[✉], Kongzhang Hao, Zhengyi Yang, Xin Cao, and Wenjie Zhang

The University of New South Wales, Sydney, NSW 2052, Australia
{xia.li,k.hao,zhengyi.yang,xin.cao,wenjie.zhang}@unsw.edu.au

Abstract. Uncertain graphs are graphs where each edge is assigned with a probability of existence. In this paper, we study the problem of hop-constrained $s\text{-}t$ simple path enumeration in large uncertain graphs. To the best of our knowledge, we are the first to study this problem in the literature. Specifically, we propose a light-weight index to prune candidate paths by adopting the concept of probability-constrained distance. An efficient enumeration algorithm is designed based on the index structure. Experiment results on real-world datasets show that our proposed methods significantly outperform the baseline methods by up to 6 times.

Keywords: Graph · Uncertain graph · Path enumeration

1 Introduction

Uncertain graphs are graphs where each edge is assigned with a probability of existence. Compared with normal graphs (i.e., deterministic graphs), uncertain graphs can represent the uncertainties in many real-world applications due to noise, incompleteness and inaccuracy. For example, in bioinformatics, protein-protein interaction (PPI) networks obtained through error-prone laboratory experiments are noisy – they may contain interactions that do not really exist and at the same time they may miss real interactions. It is thus more natural to represent a PPI network as an uncertain graph [8] where vertices (proteins) are connected by uncertain edges which indicate the possibility of interaction between the proteins. Other examples of uncertain graphs include social networks with inferred influence [4] and sensor networks with uncertain connectivity links [2].

With the proliferation of graph applications, extensive research efforts have been devoted to many fundamental problems in analyzing graphs. Among them, the problem of *hop-constrained $s\text{-}t$ simple path* (HC-s-t path) enumeration receives considerable attention in the literature [1,5–7,9]. However, while all of the existing algorithms for HC-s-t path enumeration focus on deterministic graphs, the problem of HC-s-t path enumeration in uncertain graphs remains unexplored.

© The Author(s), under exclusive license to Springer Nature Switzerland AG 2022
W. Hua et al. (Eds.): ADC 2022, LNCS 13459, pp. 115–127, 2022.
https://doi.org/10.1007/978-3-031-15512-3_9

Motivated by this, in this paper, we study the problem of HC-s-t path enumeration in uncertain graphs (referred to as UHC-s-t path enumeration). Specifically, given a source vertex s and a destination vertex t in an uncertain graph G, UHC-s-t path enumeration finds all *simple paths* from s to t within k hops, where the product of probabilities of all edges in the path is larger or equal to a given threshold γ. An example of UHC-s-t path enumeration is shown in Fig. 1, with $s = v_0$, $t = v_9$, $k = 5$ and $\gamma = 0.3$. Only one path is found in this example, namely (v_0, v_5, v_7, v_9).

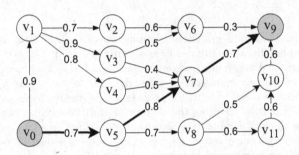

Fig. 1. Example of UHC-s-t path Enumeration

Applications. Below are three representative real-life applications of UHC-s-t path enumeration in uncertain graphs.

Biological Networks. Pathway queries are essential in biological networks analytics [3], which are usually represented as uncertain graphs as mentioned above. UHC-s-t path enumeration can be used to find the chains of interactions between two substances in a PPI network.

Social Networks. In a social network, edge probabilities may represent the likelihood of two users are friend. In this case, UHC-s-t path can be used for link-prediction [4]. Namely, the more paths can be enumerated for a person to another person, the more likely they know each other.

Wireless Sensor Network. Path planning is one of the most important problems in wireless sensor network. However, since the wireless connection may not be stable between two sensors, it can represent them as uncertain edges when modelling [2]. To plan route in such networks, we can use UHC-s-t path enumeration to list all promising paths to achieve high availability.

Challenges. The naive method of UHC-s-t path enumeration in uncertain graphs would be applying a two-step search and verify approach. In the first step of searching, we apply the state-of-the-art HC-s-t path enumeration algorithm for deterministic graphs (i.e., BaseEnum in [9]). Then in the second step of verification, we remove the invalid results that violate the probability constraints. The two main drawbacks of such naive approach are presented as follows.

1. *Large Search Space.* As BaseEnum is designed for deterministic graphs, it does not take edge probability into account. This results in an unsatisfactory pruning power for uncertain graphs, and therefore a large search space.
2. *High Verification Cost.* The naive approach verifies all possible candidates. The extra step of verifying is time-consuming and further limits the efficiency of UHC-s-t path enumeration in large uncertain graphs.

Our Solution and Contributions. In this paper, we propose efficient algorithms for UHC-s-t path enumeration in large uncertain graphs. To the best of our knowledge, we are the first to study this problem in the literature. Specifically, we make the following contributions.

1. *An Efficient* UHC-s-t path *Enumeration Algorithm.* To reduce the search space and verification cost, we propose a light-weight index to prune candidate paths, by adopting the concept of *probability-constrained distance.* An efficient algorithm for UHC-s-t path enumeration is designed based on our index structure.
2. *Extensive Experimental Evaluation on Billion-scale Uncertain Graphs.* We conduct extensive experiments on 4 real-world datasets up to billion scale. Experiment results show that our proposed methods of UHC-s-t path enumeration significantly outperform the baseline approach by up to 6 times.

Paper Organization. The rest of the paper is organized as follows. Section 2 introduces preliminaries. Section 3 discusses related work. We describe our baseline solution in Sect. 4. Our new approach is presented in Sect. 5. Experimental evaluations are demonstrated in Sect. 6, followed by conclusion in Sect. 7.

2 Preliminary

Let $G = (V, E, \delta)$ denote a directed uncertain graph, where $V(G)$ is the set of vertices, $E(G)$ is a set of directed edges, and δ is the function that assigns each edge $e \in E(G)$ a probability $0 < \delta(e) \leq 1$. For a vertex $v \in V(G)$, we use $G.\text{nbr}^-(v)/G.\text{nbr}^+(v)$ to denote the in-neighbors/out-neighbors of v in G. We omit G in the notations when the context is self-evident. Given a graph G, the reverse graph of G, denoted by $G_r = (V, E_r)$, is the graph generated by reversing the direction of all edges in G.

A path from vertex u to vertex v, denoted by $p(u, v)$, is a sequence of vertices $\{u = v_0, v_1, ..., v_h = v\}$ such that $(v_{i-1}, v_i) \in E(G)$ for every $1 \leq i < h$. Given two paths p_A and p_B, p_A is a partial path of p_B if p_A makes up part of P_B, denoted by $p_A \subseteq p_B$. A simple path is a loop-free path where there are no repetitions of vertices and edges. By $|p|$ and $p[i]$, we denote the length of path p and the ith vertex of p, respectively. We define the probability of p as $\theta(p)$, which is the product of the probability of all its edges. We call the intermediate path of a query during its enumeration as its *prefix.* Given two vertices u and v, the shortest distance from u to v, denoted by $\text{dist}_G(u, v)$, is the length (i.e., the number of hops in this paper) of the shortest path from u to v on G, we omit G in the notations when the context is self-evident. Given a pre-defined hop constraint k, we say a simple path p is a HC-s-t path if $|p| \leq k$. Additionally, p is called a UHC-s-t path if $\theta(p)$ is greater than or equal to the given threshold γ. The results of a query q are denoted as $P(q)$.

3   Related Work

HC-s-t path enumeration is a fundamental problem in graph analysis and several algorithms have been proposed [1,5–7,9] for this problem. We divided them into two categories, which are *pruning-based algorithms* [1,5,7] and *index-based algorithms* [9]. We discuss each category in the following.

Pruning-Based Algorithms. Pruning-based algorithms typically adopt a backtracking strategy based on a depth-first search based framework. During the enumeration, [7] and [1] dynamically compute the shortest path distance from v to t and prunes v if it is unreachable to t, while [5] dynamically maintains a lower bound of hops to the target vertex t for the vertices visited and prunes v if the current remaining hop budget is smaller than the lower bound of hops required.

Index-Based Algorithm. [9] finds that the pruning-based algorithms typically suffer from severe performance issues caused by the costly pruning operations during enumeration. Therefore, BaseEnum builds a light-weight index to reduce the number of edges involved in the enumeration. Thanks to the index structure, BaseEnum significantly outperform pruning-based algorithms as demonstrated in [9]. Hence, we also adopt the index-based approach in UHC-s-t path enumeration in this paper.

4   The Baseline Solution

In this section, we introduce the state-of-the-art algorithm, BaseEnum [9], for HC-s-t path enumeration query, as well as a baseline solution for UHC-s-t path query processing based on BaseEnum. Given a HC-s-t path query q from s to t with hop constraint k, the fundamental idea of BaseEnum is to prune every vertex v visited during the enumeration if the shortest distance $dist(v, t)$ from v to t is larger than the remaining hop budget.

The straightforward approach for UHC-s-t path query processing based on BaseEnum is as follows: because the paths computed by BaseEnum contains all the valid results for UHC-s-t path enumeration, it is immediately clear that all UHC-s-t paths for q can be accurately enumerated by ruling out the HC-s-t paths whose probability are larger than the given threshold. Algorithm 1 demonstrates the baseline solution BaseEnum for UHC-s-t path query processing.

Given a graph G and a UHC-s-t path query q, BaseEnum computes the shortest distance between t and every vertex in G by executing a BFS (line 1). Then the enumeration for UHC-s-t paths is performed on G (line 2). The paths obtained

---

Algorithm 1: BaseEnum(G, q, γ)

---

1 Find dist$_{G_r}(q.t, v)$ for each $v \in V(G)$ by a BFS;
2 Search$(G, P, (q.s), q)$;
3 $P \leftarrow$ Verify(P, q);
4 **foreach** $p \in P$ **do**
5 $\quad$ Output p;
6 **Procedure** Search(G, P, p, q)
7 $\quad v' \leftarrow p[|p|]$;
8 $\quad$ **if** $|p| = q.k$ **then** P.add(p); **return**;
9 $\quad$ **foreach** $v'' \in$ nbr$^+(v')$ $s.t.$ $|p| +$ dist$_{G_r}(q.t, v'') < k$ **do**
10 $\quad\quad$ **if** $v'' \notin p$ **then** Search$(G, P, p\bigcup\{v''\}, q)$;
11 **Procedure** Verify(P, q)
12 $\quad P' \leftarrow \emptyset$;
13 $\quad$ **foreach** $p \in P$ **do**
14 $\quad\quad$ **if** $\theta(p) \geq \gamma$ **then**
15 $\quad\quad\quad P'$.add(p);
16 $\quad$ **return** P';

---

by the search are then verified to ensure that only paths with probability greater or equal to the threshold will be considered as valid and output (lines 3–5). Recursively, the procedure Search enumerates the paths with a hop constraint of k (lines 6–10). Specifically, if a path p with length k is found, p is added into P (line 11). Otherwise, for the out-neighbor v'' of v' which follows the hop constraint and has not been added in p, BaseEnum extends v'' in p and continues the search (line 9–10). In procedure Verify, the paths found by Search are examined in a row, such that any path that contains invalid labels are filtered and the rest are returned as the final results for q (lines 11–18).

Remark. As shown in [9], searching bidirectionally could potentially enhance the overall enumeration performance as the common computation can be shared. As this optimization is orthogonal to our probability constraint and can be applied seamlessly to our solution, we follow the single direction search when introducing BaseEnum and our approach in Sect. 5. In Sect. 6, both of these methods are evaluated in the experiments.

5 Our Approach

In this section, we discuss our approach of UHC-s-t path enumeration. As mentioned before, our method adopts the index-based approach.

5.1 Overview

Although BaseEnum can enumerate all UHC-s-t paths correctly, it contains a huge amount of unnecessary computation during its enumeration procedure, which can be potentially avoided. Considering the example in Fig. 2, which aims

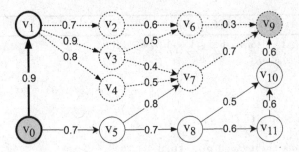

Fig. 2. Main observation of our approach

to enumerate all UHC-s-t paths from v_0 to v_9 with a hop constraint of 5 and a probability threshold of 0.3.

When the search starts from v_0 and explores v_1, the current enumeration prefix is $p_0 = \{v_0, v_1\}$, which is shown using the bold lines in Fig. 2. Subsequently, the search will explore the out-neighbors of v_1, with a remaining hop budget of 4. As all the out-neighbors of v_1, namely v_2, v_3 and v_4, are promising regarding to their shortest distance to v_9 which is smaller than the remaining hop constraint, all of them will be explored, resulting in the search prefixes $p_1 = \{v_0, v_1, v_2\}$, $p_2 = \{v_0, v_1, v_3\}$ and $p_3 = \{v_0, v_1, v_4\}$. After this, p_1 and p_2 will explore v_6, and p_2 and p_3 will explore v_7. This is because both v_6 and v_7 are considered fruitful regarding to their shortest distance to v_9. Finally, v_9 is added to all prefixes, which leads to a total of 4 valid HC-s-t paths. However, during the verification stage, it is obvious that all these paths have a probability that is smaller than the given threshold. Therefore, none of the found paths are valid as a UHC-s-t path and thus their corresponding computation is unnecessary, which is demonstrated by the dashed part in Fig. 2.

In accordance with the above observation, it is obvious that there exists a huge amount of fruitless computation by BaseEnum regarding the enumeration of UHC-s-t paths. We aim to avoid them to reduce the amount of overall computation, and thus improve the whole performance. To achieve the goal, we first devise a light-weight index that is computed *online* for each query. The index identifies the fruitless computation during the actual enumeration. Then, we propose an efficient UHC-s-t path enumeration algorithm that effectively uses the constructed index to reduce the search space. We describe each of them in the following subsections.

5.2   Light-Weight Index for Pruning

On the one hand, as discussed in Sect. 5.1, pruning the unnecessary computation that computes paths violating the probability constraint can considerably improve the enumeration performance; on the other hand, the goal cannot be trivially achieved by dynamically pruning the search based on the probability of explored edges.

Reconsider the same example in Fig. 2. Starting from the source vertex v_0, the search will normally explore v_1 as v_1 satisfies the hop constraint and the probability of edge (v_0, v_1) has a greater probability than the probability threshold of 0.3. Nevertheless, as discussed in Sect. 5.1, it is already clear that all the computation following v_1 will be fruitless, and hence v_1 should be excluded from the search. According to this contradicted example, it is obvious that dynamically pruning the search based on the probability of explored edges cannot effectively reduce the unnecessary computation attributed to the probability constraint. As a result, the following question arises: is it possible to design an algorithm such that the fruitless exploration caused by the probability constraint can be effectively identified and pruned? In this section, we aim to answer this questions and introduce our approach to prune the unpromising search in UHC-s-t path enumeration.

Looking back at the example in Fig. 2, it can be easily derived that the reason why the search following $\{v_0, v_1\}$ is fruitless is because there does not exist a valid path from v_1 to v_9 that follows the hop and probability constraint at the same time. As a result, if we can identify such property before actually proceeding the enumeration, the unpromising search can be well-pruned. Following this idea, we define:

Definition 1. *(**Probability-constrained Distance** UDist) Given a graph G, two vertices v_0, v_1 and a probability γ, the probability-constrained distance from v_0 to v_1 with probability threshold γ, denoted by $\mathsf{UDist}_G(v_0, v_1, \gamma)$, is the length of the shortest path from v_0 to v_1 on G whose probability is greater than or equal to γ. G is omitted in the notation when the context is self-evident.*

Based on the definition of probability-constrained distance, we then prove the following lemma on which our index is based:

Lemma 1. *Given a uncertain graph G, a UHC-s-t path query q and a vertex $v \in V(G)$, if there exists a path p from s to t with $|p| \leq k$ and $\theta(p) \geq \gamma$, then for any $p[i] = v$ where $0 \leq i < |p|$, $\mathsf{UDist}_G(s, v, \gamma) \leq i$ and $\mathsf{UDist}_{G_r}(t, v, \gamma) \leq k - i$.*

Proof. Based on the definition of UHC-s-t path, if $0 \leq i < |p|$, then there should exist a path p_0 from s to $p[i]$ where $|p_0| \leq i$ and $\theta(p_0) \geq \gamma$. There should also exist a path p_1 from $p[i]$ to t where $|p_1| \leq |p| - i$ and $\theta(p_1) \geq \gamma$. Moreover, given that $\theta(p) \geq \gamma$, $\theta(p_0)$ and $\theta(p_1)$ must also be greater or equal to γ. $\qquad\square$

According to Lemma 1, we further prove the following theorems to demonstrate how the vertices can be pruned during the search to reduce unnecessary computation:

Theorem 1. *Given a graph G, a vertex $v \in V(G)$ and a UHC-s-t path query q, if $\mathsf{UDist}_G(q.\mathsf{s}, v, q.\gamma) + \mathsf{UDist}_{G_r}(q.\mathsf{t}, v, q.\gamma) > q.k$, then $\nexists p \in P(q)$ s.t. $v \in p$.*

Proof. Based on Lemma 1, if $\mathsf{UDist}_G(q.\mathsf{s}, v, q.\gamma) + \mathsf{UDist}_{G_r}(q.\mathsf{t}, v, q.\gamma) > q.k$, then when v exists in a UHC-s-t path p from s to t, the length $|p|$ of p must be larger than $q.k$, thus p obviously cannot be a valid result for q, which proves $\nexists p \in P(q)$ s.t. $v \in p$. $\qquad\square$

Algorithm 2: ConstructIndex(G, q, γ)

---

1 $S_v \leftarrow \{(q.s, 1)\}$; $end \leftarrow$ False;
2 UDist $\leftarrow \emptyset$; UDist($q.s, q.s, q\gamma$) $= 0$;
3 **while** $|S_v| \neq 0$ and $!end$ **do**
4     $(v, prob) \leftarrow S_v[0]$; S_v.remove(v);
5   **foreach** $v' \in$ nbr$^+_G(v)$ $s.t.$ $prob * \delta((v, v')) \geq \gamma$ **do**
6   **if** $(q.s, v', q.\gamma) \notin$ UDist **then**
7   **if** $q.k <$ UDist($q.s, v, q.\gamma$) $+ 1$ **then**
8              $end =$ True; **break**;
9   UDist($q.s, v', q.\gamma$) $=$ UDist($q.s, v, q.\gamma$) $+ 1$;
10   S_v.add($(v', prob * \delta((v, v')))$);
11 **return** UDist;

According to Theorem 1, given a UHC-s-t path query q, it is clear that for any vertex $v \in V(G)$, if UDist$_G(q.s, v, q.\gamma) +$ UDist$_{G_r}(q.t, v, q.\gamma) > q.k$, then vertex v can never appear in a valid UHC-s-t path and thus does not need to be explored at all during the enumeration, which can be removed from $V(G)$ before the enumeration begins. Moreover, the pruning can also take place during the enumeration, as shown in the following lemma:

Theorem 2. *Given a graph G, a prefix p' and a* UHC-s-t path *query q, if $|p'| +$* UDist$_{G_r}(q.t, p'[|p'|], q.\gamma) > q.k$, *then $\nexists p \in P(q)$ s.t. $p' \subseteq p$.*

Proof. Based on Lemma 1, if $|p'| +$ UDist$_{G_r}(q.t, p'[|p'|], q.\gamma) > q.k$, then p' requires at least $q.k - |p'| + 1$ hops to explore $q.t$, which obviously exceeds the hop budget left. As a result, $\nexists p \in P(q)$ s.t. $p' \subseteq p$. □

According to Theorem 2, given a UHC-s-t path query q and a prefix p', if $|p'| +$ UDist$_{G_r}(q.t, p'[|p'|], q.\gamma) > q.k$, then p' requires to proceed more hops to reach $q.t$ than its remaining hop budget. Hence the enumeration procedure following p' is fruitless and can be directly pruned.

Based on the observations, given a graph G and a UHC-s-t path query q, in order to reduce unnecessary computation during the enumeration, we want to build an index to support instant lookup on both UDist$_G(q.s, v, q.\gamma)$ and UDist$_{G_r}(q.t, v, q.\gamma)$ for $v \in V(G)$, which gives rise to our index construction algorithm ConstructIndex.

Algorithm. Algorithm 2 illustrates the procedure of the index construction on G, as the same procedure on G_r can be achieved similarly. Given a graph G and a UHC-s-t path query q, ConstructIndex performs a BFS exploration on G while updating the probability-constrained distance UDist from $q.s$ to each visited vertex.

In particular, ConstructIndex first creates a queue S_v to store the current set of (vertices, probability) pairs $(v, prob)$, where the out-neighbors of v need to be explored. Initially, S_v only contains $q.s$. Meanwhile, end is created to indicate whether the index construction needs to terminate (line 1). Subsequently, UDist

---

Algorithm 3: UncertainEnum(G, q)

---

1 UDist ← ConstructIndex$(G/G_r, q)$;
2 Prune1(G, q, UDist); $P \leftarrow \emptyset$;
3 Prune2$(G, P, (q.s), q)$;
4 **foreach** $p \in P$ **do**
5   Output p;
6 **Procedure** Prune1(G, q, UDist)
7   **foreach** $v \in V(G)$ **do**
8   **if** $\text{UDist}_G(q.s, v, q.L) + \text{UDist}_{G_r}(q.t, v, q.L) > q.k$ **then**
9            $V(G)$.remove(v);
10   **foreach** $e \in E(G)$ *s.t.* $v \in e$ **do**
11              $E(G)$.remove(e);
12 **Procedure** Prune2(G, P, p, q)
13     $v' \leftarrow p[||p||]$;
14   **if** $|p| = q.k$ **then** P.add(p); **return**;
15   **foreach** $v'' \in \text{nbr}^+(v')$ *s.t.* $|p| + \text{UDist}_{G_r}(q.t, v') < k$ **do**
16   **if** $v'' \notin p$ and $\theta(p \bigcup \{v''\}) \geq q.\gamma$ **then** Prune2$(G, P, p \bigcup \{v''\}, q)$;

---

is created to record the probability-constrained shortest, with $\text{UDist}(q.s, q.s, q.\gamma)$ set to 0 (line 2). After this, ConstructIndex keeps exploring the graph in a BFS order until the hop budget has been fully used (lines 3–10). Initially, the first $(v, prob)$ pair is popped out from S_v, whose out-neighbors v' that follows the probability constraint is visited (lines 4–5). If the current distance from $q.s$ to v' has increased over the hop constraint, the search is fruitless and ConstructIndex terminates (lines 7–8). Otherwise, $\text{UDist}(q.s, v', q.\gamma)$ is set to $\text{UDist}(q.s, v, q.\gamma) + 1$ (line 9). The neighbor v' with new probability value is added to S_v for further exploration (line 10). Finally, UDist is returned (line 11).

Theorem 3. *The time complexity of* ConstructIndex *is* $O(|V(G)| + |E(G)|)$.

Proof. The time complexity of ConstructIndex is $O(|V(G)| + |E(G)|)$ because a breadth-first search is performed during the construction procedure, which visits each vertex and edge in G once. □

5.3   UHC-*s-t* path Enumeration

Given a graph G and a UHC-*s-t* path query q, after constructing the index on the probability-constrained distances from $q.s/q.t$ to each $v \in V(G)$, we can prune the unnecessary exploration during the enumeration according to the pruning rules Theorem 1 and Theorem 2, and thus significantly improve the performance of UHC-*s-t* path query processing.

Algorithm. Our final algorithm UncertainEnum is shown in Algorithm 3. For a UHC-*s-t* path query q, UncertainEnum first constructs the index on both G and G_r, which computes $\text{UDist}_G(q.s, v)$ and $\text{UDist}_{G_r}(q.t, v)$ for all $v \in V(G)$ (line 1).

Then, UncertainEnum removes unpromising vertices from the graph by following Theorem 1 (line 2). After this, the enumeration is performed in a recursive manner while avoiding any fruitless search following Theorem 2 (line 3). Each UHC-s-t path found is directly output (lines 4–5). In procedure Prune1, each vertex $v \in V(G)$ is examined. If sum of the probability-constrained distances from q.s to v and from v to q.t is larger than q.k, it is immediate that v will never appear in a valid UHC-s-t path, and v is thus removed from $V(G)$ (lines 6–11). In procedure Prune2, the search keeps exploring the out-neighbors of v' that meets the hop and probability constraint at the same time, and stores the path p if $|p| = q$.k (lines 12–16).

6   Experimental Evaluation

In this section, we evaluate the efficiency of the proposed algorithms. All the experiments are performed on a machine with one 20-core Intel Xeon CPU E5-2698 and 512 GB main memory running Red Hat Linux 7.3, 64 bit.

Table 1. Statistics of the datasets

Dataset	Name	$|V|$	$|E|$	d_{avg}	d_{max}
Epinsion	EP	75K	508K	13.4	3,079
LiveJournal	LJ	4M	69M	17.9	20,333
Twitter-2010	TW	42M	1.46B	70.5	2,997,487
Friendster	FS	65M	1.81B	27.5	5,214

Datasets. We evaluate our algorithms on four real-world graphs, which are shown in Table 1. Among them, Twitter-2010 is downloaded from LAW[1] and the rest are downloaded from SNAP[2]. We randomly generate the probability for all edges in each graph, which varies from 0.5 to 1.

Algorithms. We compare the following algorithms:

- BaseEnum: Algorithm 1 where PathEnum runs in a single direction (Sect. 4).
- BaseEnum$^+$: Algorithm 1 where PathEnum runs with an optimized bidirectional search order (Sect. 4).
- UncertainEnum: Algorithm 3 (Sect. 5.3).
- UncertainEnum$^+$: UncertainEnum with an optimized bidirectional search order introduced by BaseEnum$^+$ (Sect. 4).

All the algorithms are implemented in Rust 1.43. In the experiments, we measure the wall-clock time elapsed during the program's execution.

---

[1] https://law.di.unimi.it/index.php.
[2] https://snap.stanford.edu/data/.

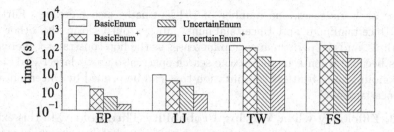

Fig. 3. Processing time on all datasets

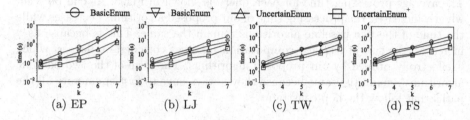

Fig. 4. Processing time when varying k

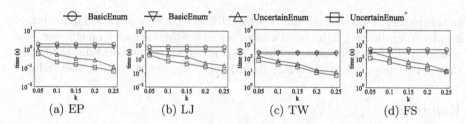

Fig. 5. Processing time when varying γ

Exp-1: Efficiency on Different Datasets. In this experiment, we evaluate the processing time of four algorithms (i.e. BaseEnum, BaseEnum$^+$, UncertainEnum, UncertainEnum$^+$) on all four graphs. We randomly generate 100 random UHC-s-t path query $q(s,t,k,\gamma)$ on each graph where source vertex s could reach target vertex t in k hops with the probability threshold γ. We set $k = 6$ and $\gamma = 0.1$ by default. The results are reported in Fig. 3. As can be seen in Fig. 3, our proposed UHC-s-t path enumeration algorithms UncertainEnum and UncertainEnum$^+$ always outperform the other two algorithms on all of the graphs. This is because the devised index used in our proposed algorithms can significantly reduce the fruitless exploration regarding to the probability constraint.

Exp-2: Efficiency when Varying Hop Constraint k. In this experiment, we evaluate the efficiency when varying hop constraint k from 3 to 7. For each hop constraint k, we randomly generate 50 queries. The average processing time for each query is shown in Fig. 4. As reported, when the hop constraint k increases, the processing time of all algorithms increases as well. This is because as k increases, the number of UHC-s-t paths also increases. Furthermore, UncertainEnum and UncertainEnum$^+$ always outperform the other two algorithms, and the performance gap increases as the hop constraint k increases. This is because when k increases, the search space also grows larger and therefore, contains more fruitless computation that can be pruned by UncertainEnum and UncertainEnum$^+$.

Exp-3: Efficiency when Varying Probability Threshold γ. In this experiment, we evaluate the efficiency when varying the probability threshold γ from 0.05 to 0.25. For each probability threshold γ, we randomly generate 50 queries. The average processing time for each query is shown in Fig. 5. As can be seen, when γ increases, the processing time of our proposed algorithms decreases while the time of the two baseline algorithms remain the same. This is because as γ increases, the size of fruitless computation becomes considerably larger, which is effectively pruned by our proposed algorithms. The time of the two baseline algorithms remain the same because they always have to first enumerate all the paths that follow the hop constraint.

7   Conclusion

In this paper, we present the first work of UHC-s-t path enumeration in uncertain graphs. We propose a light-weight index structure together with an efficient enumeration algorithm for this problem. Experiments on real-world datasets show that our proposed algorithms significantly outperform the baseline methods.

References

1. Grossi, R., Marino, A., Versari, L.: Efficient algorithms for listing k disjoint st-paths in graphs. In: Bender, M.A., Farach-Colton, M., Mosteiro, M.A. (eds.) LATIN 2018. LNCS, vol. 10807, pp. 544–557. Springer, Cham (2018). https://doi.org/10.1007/978-3-319-77404-6_40
2. Kawahigashi, H., Terashima, Y., Miyauchi, N., Nakakawaji, T.: Modeling ad hoc sensor networks using random graph theory. In: Second IEEE Consumer Communications and Networking Conference, CCNC 2005, pp. 104–109 (2005). https://doi.org/10.1109/CCNC.2005.1405152
3. Leser, U.: A query language for biological networks. In: ECCB/JBI'05 Proceedings, Fourth European Conference on Computational Biology/Sixth Meeting of the Spanish Bioinformatics Network (Jornadas de BioInformática), Palacio de Congresos, Madrid, Spain, 28 September–1 October 2005, p. 39 (2005). https://doi.org/10.1093/bioinformatics/bti1105
4. Liben-Nowell, D., Kleinberg, J.: The link prediction problem for social networks. In: Proceedings of the Twelfth International Conference on Information and Knowledge Management, CIKM 2003, pp. 556–559. Association for Computing Machinery, New York (2003)
5. Peng, Y., Zhang, Y., Lin, X., Zhang, W., Qin, L., Zhou, J.: Hop-constrained s-t simple path enumeration: towards bridging theory and practice. Proc. VLDB Endow. **13**(4), 463–476 (2019)

6. Qiu, X., et al.: Real-time constrained cycle detection in large dynamic graphs. Proc. VLDB Endow. **11**(12), 1876–1888 (2018). https://doi.org/10.14778/3229863. 3229874

7. Rizzi, R., Sacomoto, G., Sagot, M.-F.: Efficiently listing bounded length st-paths. In: Kratochvíl, J., Miller, M., Froncek, D. (eds.) IWOCA 2014. LNCS, vol. 8986, pp. 318–329. Springer, Cham (2015). https://doi.org/10.1007/978-3-319-19315-1_28

8. Sevon, P., Eronen, L., Hintsanen, P., Kulovesi, K., Toivonen, H.: Link discovery in graphs derived from biological databases. In: Leser, U., Naumann, F., Eckman, B. (eds.) DILS 2006. LNCS, vol. 4075, pp. 35–49. Springer, Heidelberg (2006). https://doi.org/10.1007/11799511_5

9. Sun, S., Chen, Y., He, B., Hooi, B.: Pathenum: towards real-time hop-constrained s-t path enumeration. In: Proceedings of SIGMOD, pp. 1758–1770 (2021)

Improving Eco-Friendly Routing Considering Detailed Mobility Profiles, Driving Behavior and Vehicle Type

Ahmed Fahmin[1]([envelope]), Shenyi Zhang[1], Muhammad Aamir Cheema[1],
Adel N. Toosi[1], and Hesham A. Rakha[2]

[1] Faculty of Information Technology, Monash University, Melbourne, Australia
{ahmed.fahmin,aamir.cheema,adel.n.toosi}@monash.edu,
szha0177@student.monash.edu
[2] Charles E. Via, Jr. Department of Civil and Environmental Engineering,
Virginia Tech, Blacksburg, USA
hrakha@vt.edu

Abstract. Traditional vehicle routing algorithms aim to find the fastest or shortest route, whereas eco-friendly routing algorithms aim to find the route that minimizes vehicle fuel consumption or greenhouse gas (GHG) emissions. To accurately estimate fuel consumption and emissions along a route, a detailed mobility profile of the vehicle traveling on the route is needed including acceleration/deceleration and idling time. However, the existing techniques that aim to find eco-friendly routes make a simplistic assumption by assigning each road segment of the road network an average speed or average fuel consumption along the road, ignoring detailed mobility profiles and driving behavior (e.g., aggressive or moderate) altogether. This simplistic treatment leads to sub-optimal route choices because such representation fails to capture driving behaviors and detailed mobility profiles of the candidate routes resulting in poor quality estimates. Furthermore, many of the existing techniques employ a one-size-fits-all approach ignoring that different vehicles (e.g., truck vs car) and drivers exhibit different behaviors, thus, the most eco-friendly route may be significantly different for different types of vehicles and/or drivers. This paper addresses these limitations and presents an eco-routing algorithm that computes the most fuel economical route considering the detailed mobility profiles, driving behavior, and vehicle type. We conduct an extensive experimental study on a real road network considering different vehicles and driving behaviors and show that our algorithm generates routes that reduce fuel consumption by up to 35%.

Keywords: Eco-routing · Navigation systems · Mobility profile · Microscopic simulation · Intelligent transportation systems

W. Hua et al. (Eds.): ADC 2022, LNCS 13459, pp. 128–140, 2022.
https://doi.org/10.1007/978-3-031-15512-3_10

1   Introduction

Road transport is a major contributor to greenhouse gas (GHG) emissions. In 2013–2014, domestic transport accounted for around 17% of Australia's GHG emissions, with approximately 60% of this attributable to light vehicles. From 2013–2014 to 2029–2030, transport emissions are projected to increase by 25% [1]. Reports from various other countries also show that the road transport accounts for 16% to 20% of the total global GHG emissions [2]. Various studies show that eco-friendly navigation strategies can significantly reduce fuel consumption and GHG emissions. For example, it was shown that approximately 12%–33% of fuel can be saved by using the most fuel economical route instead of selecting the fastest or shortest route [11]. Similarly, our previous work [5] also showed that 18%–23% of fuel could be saved by choosing a longer route that has better traffic conditions for the same origin-destination pair. Another study [11] validated the actual effects of different routes on fuel consumption, showing that the fuel consumption could be reduced by up to 33% at the expense of a 3% increase in trip-time. Inspired by this, many existing studies have focused on designing eco-friendly routing algorithms with a focus on minimizing fuel consumption and GHG emissions. Note that fuel consumption is directly proportional to GHG emissions and the techniques designed to minimize fuel consumption can be easily extended to minimize GHG emissions, and vice versa [20]. In the rest of the paper, we focus on minimising the fuel consumption (and our techniques can be immediately applied to minimise emissions by using the emission models instead of fuel consumption models).

Accurately estimating a route's fuel consumption is the key to developing an effective eco-routing algorithm. A large body of work has focused on developing models to estimate fuel consumption and emissions for different types of vehicles (see [30] for a comprehensive survey). Microscopic models such as VT-CPFM [23] are the most accurate fuel consumption models. However, these models require detailed mobility profiles (e.g., instantaneous speed, acceleration/deceleration, idling time) as well as parameters specific to vehicles (e.g., vehicle mass, engine details) and driving behaviors (e.g., hard brake vs soft brake). However, almost all existing eco-routing algorithms make simplistic assumptions. For example, they assume that the vehicles travel along an edge with a constant speed (e.g., at average link speed) [8,11] ignoring the detailed mobility profile such as acceleration, deceleration, etc. Some works [13,22] create a weighted graph where each road segment (i.e., edge) is assigned a fuel consumption cost which is estimated based on the fuel consumption cost of other vehicles that traveled along this road (e.g., using historical or real-time data). This simplistic treatment compromises accuracy as the average values also fail to capture the detailed mobility profiles and do not take into account different vehicle types (cars vs trucks) and driving behaviors (aggressive vs moderate driving). Consequently, such simplistic treatment leads to sub-optimal route choices resulting in poor quality estimates (up to 40% inaccurate [30]). Furthermore, most of these techniques employ a one-size-fits-all approach ignoring that different vehicles (e.g., truck vs car) and drivers exhibit different behaviors; thus, the most eco-friendly route may be significantly different for different types of vehicles and/or drivers [20].

One of our earlier works [26] addressed the limitations mentioned above. However, the solution proposed in [26] assumes a connected vehicles environment where the server receives up-to-date travel information from the vehicles in real-time (e.g., each vehicle traveling on an edge sends its instantaneous speed, acceleration, deceleration etc. to the server which uses this information for accurate fuel consumption estimation in the navigation algorithm). While this strategy provides more accurate fuel consumption estimates, the assumption that the vehicles can send their detailed travel information for each edge to the server may not always hold, e.g., there may not be any (or enough) connected vehicle(s) on the road, the vehicles may not want to share their travel information due to privacy reasons, etc. In this paper, we remove this assumption and provide an eco-routing algorithm that does not rely on vehicles sharing their travel information with the server. Instead, we rely on the input road network graph where edge weights correspond to the speed on the edge (which can be obtained based on the current or historical traffic data). We create the mobility profile of a vehicle on-the-fly considering the maximum possible edge speed, traffic lights, vehicle type, and driving behavior.

We make the following contributions in this paper: (i) to the best of our knowledge, we are the first to propose an eco-friendly routing algorithm that uses highly accurate microscopic fuel consumption models and does not rely on vehicles sharing their travel information; (ii) we conduct an exhaustive evaluation of the proposed algorithm using a real-world road network considering three different types of vehicles and different driving behaviors; and (iii) we compare our proposed eco-routing algorithm with other routing strategies, including the shortest path algorithm, fastest path algorithm, and a recent work that estimates fuel consumption considering average speed. The results demonstrate that our approach generates routes that save up to 35% fuel at the expense of around 10% longer travel time or distance.

The rest of the paper is organized as follows. In Sect. 2, we formally define the problem and discuss related works. In Sect. 3, we present our proposed eco-friendly routing algorithm. In Sect. 4, we present our experimental study. Finally, Sect. 5 concludes the paper and presents directions for future work.

2 Preliminaries

2.1 Problem Formulation

A road traffic network is represented as a directed graph $G = (V, E)$ that consists of a set of nodes/vertices V and a set of edges/links E. Each edge $e = (u, v) \in E$ is a directed edge from vertex $u \in V$ to vertex $v \in V$ and is associated with its length e^l (i.e., the length of the road segment connecting vertex u to vertex v) and the maximum speed on this edge e^s (e.g., the speed limit of the edge or the maximum possible speed based on the current traffic). A path from a source $s \in V$ to a target $t \in V$ is a path on the graph G defined as a sequential list of edges: $(s, u), \ldots, (v, t)$. The input to the routing algorithm is the graph G, source s, target t, the vehicle type the user is driving (e.g., Honda Accord 2022), and the driving behavior (typical acceleration, deceleration values for the driver). Fuel consumption of a path is the total fuel consumed by the user traveling on the path on the specified vehicle following the given driving behavior. The problem is to return the path from s to t that has the minimum fuel consumption among all paths from s to t in G.

2.2   Related Work

There are two key components of an eco-friendly navigation system. First, it requires models to accurately estimate fuel consumption or emissions. Second, it requires a routing algorithm that can compute the most eco-friendly route. A large body of work has focused on developing models to estimate fuel consumption and emissions for different types of vehicles (see [30] for a comprehensive survey). Microscopic models such as VT-CPFM [23] are the most accurate fuel consumption models. We employ the VT-CPFM model in this paper (see details in Sect. 3.2). These models require detailed mobility profiles (e.g., instantaneous speed, acceleration/deceleration, idling time) as well as parameters specific to vehicles (e.g., vehicle mass, engine details) and driving behaviors (e.g., hard brake vs soft brake). Next, we discuss the existing work on routing algorithms.

Routing algorithms have received significant research attention in the past couple of decades [6,14,17,18,21,28]. Dijkstra's algorithm [12] and A*-search are among the most fundamental algorithms that do not rely on any specific pre-processing on the graph. A large body of work has focused on developing routing algorithms that build indexes on the graph in a pre-processing phase and significantly improve the query performance, e.g., see contraction hierarchies [14,24], hub-labeling [4,6,19] etc. However, these more efficient algorithms are not typically suitable for eco-friendly routing because the fuel-consumption is typically computed on-the-fly and, therefore, pre-processing may not be possible. For this reason, most existing algorithms [7,11,25,26] including this work use Dijkstra's or A*-search. Guo et al. [15] presented a Mesoscopic model for eco-routing and further integrated it with Dijkstra's algorithm to select eco-friendly routes. Boriboonsomsin et al. [9] use the Dijkstra algorithm with the binary heap priority queue to calculate routes for their eco-routing navigation system. Users' route preferences, such as favoring freeways or avoiding toll roads, are taken into account in their path building approach. When it comes to electric vehicles, De Nunzi et al. [10] propose a novel macroscopic energy consumption model and a novel eco-routing strategy based on Bellman-Ford's algorithm. All existing routing algorithms suffer from the limitations discussed in Sect. 1 which are addressed by our work.

3   Methodology

3.1   Overview

We adapt Dijkstra's algorithm [12] for computing the route with the minimum fuel consumption cost (see Algorithm 1). The key difference compared to Dijkstra's algorithm is that the fuel consumption costs are calculated by generating mobility profiles on-the-fly. Specifically, when the algorithm extracts a vertex v, its adjacent edges are expanded as follows. Based on the road network G, vehicle parameters vp, and the driving behavior db, our algorithm generates a detailed mobility profile on-the-fly for each edge adjacent to v (line 10). A detailed description of how this mobility profile is generated on-the-fly is presented in Sect. 3.3. The algorithm then employs the VT-CPFM fuel consumption model to compute the fuel consumption cost for traveling on this edge while taking the mobility profile generated for the edge and the vehicle type into account (line 11). Then, similar to traditional Dijkstra's algorithm, each adjacent vertex u of v is inserted in the priority queue with minimum estimated fuel consumption cost to travel from s to u. The algorithm stops when the target t is expanded.

Algorithm 1: Proposed Eco-Friendly Routing Algorithm

    Input: $G = (V, E)$: road network; vp: vehicle parameters (Table 1) ; db: driver
           behavior (i.e., acceleration/deceleration values); s: source ; t: target
    Output: The most fuel economical route from s to t

1 **foreach** $v \in V$ **do**
2 | $fc[v] \leftarrow \infty$;   // `fc[v]` is fuel consumption to reach v
3 | $pred[v] \leftarrow null$;   // `pred[v]` stores predecessor of v on optimal path
4 insert s in a priority queue Q with $fc[s] = 0$;
5 **while** Q *is not empty* **do**
6 | $v \leftarrow$ vertex in Q with the minimum cost ;
7 | **if** v *is the target node* t **then**
8 | | extract path from s to t using $pred[]$ and **return** the path;
9 | **foreach** *neighbor* u *of* v **do**
10 | | $MP(v, u) \leftarrow getMobilityProfile(v, u, G, vp, db)$;   // Sect. 3.3
11 | | $edgeCost \leftarrow$ VT-CPFM$(G, vp, MP(u, v))$;   // Sect. 3.2
12 | | **if** $fc[v] + edgeCost < fc[u]$ **then**
13 | | | $fc[u] \leftarrow fc[v] + edgeCost$;
14 | | | $pred[u] \leftarrow v$;

3.2   VT-CPFM Fuel Consumption Model

In this research, we use VT-CPFM fuel consumption model [23] which is among the most accurate fuel consumption models. We remark that our proposed framework can easily employ other microscopic fuel consumption models if required. In VT-CPFM, fuel consumption at time t denoted as $FC(t)$ is computed as

$$FC(t) = \begin{cases} \alpha_0 + \alpha_1 P(t) + \alpha_2 P(t)^2, & \forall P(t) \geq 0 \\ \alpha_0, & \forall P(t) < 0 \end{cases} \quad (1)$$

where $P(t)$ denotes instantaneous vehicle power at the wheels (kW) at time t, and α_1, α_2 and α_0 denote vehicle-specific model coefficients. The instantaneous power of the vehicle $P(t)$ is computed as

$$P(t) = \left(ma(t) + mg\frac{C_r}{1000} (c_1 v(t) + c_2) + 0.5\rho_a A_f C_D v^2(t) + mg \cdot \tan(\theta) \right) \times \frac{v(t)}{1000\eta_d} \quad (2)$$

where m is the vehicle mass in kg, $a(t)$ is the value of acceleration in m/s^2 at t, g is the gravitational acceleration $(9.8066\,\text{m/s}^2)$, θ is the road inclination angle (assumed to be zero if unavailable), C_r, c_1, c_2 are the rolling coefficients (unit-less), $v(t)$ is the instantaneous vehicle speed in m/s at t, ρ_a is the air density at sea level $(1.2256\,\text{kg/m}^3)$, A_f is the frontal area (m^2) of the vehicle, C_D is the drag coefficient (unit-less), η_d is the driveline efficiency. For details of the VT-CPFM model and how the coefficients are calculated, please see [23,27].

3.3   Generating Detailed Mobility Profile

Recall that accurately estimating fuel consumption using VT-CPFM model requires instantaneous speed $v(t)$ and acceleration $a(t)$ at each t. To this end, we generate a mob]ility profile on-the-fly which contains instantaneous speed and acceleration information needed by the VT-CPFM model.

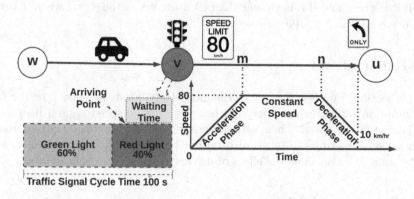

Fig. 1. Generating mobility profile

Assume that a vehicle is at vertex v and will travel on the adjacent edge $e = (v, u)$ (see Fig. 1 as an example). Let s^v be the initial speed of the vehicle at vertex v (e.g., if the vehicle had stopped at v due to a traffic light, then s^v is 0). Let s^e be the maximum possible speed for the edge (e.g., say 80 km/h is the speed limit for the road) and s^u be the speed at which the vehicle will arrive at u, e.g., if the vehicle needs to slow down to 10 km/h at u (say for a left turn), s^u will be 10 km/h. The mobility profile is generated in up to three phases: 1) in the acceleration phase, the vehicle accelerates until the speed reaches from s^v to s^e (or until the vehicle reaches at the end of the edge); 2) if the vehicle reaches the maximum possible speed of the edge s^e, it continues traveling at s^e until it is about to reach the end vertex u; and 3) when the vehicle is arriving at u, the vehicle decelerates such that the speed reduces to s^u when it reaches u. The acceleration and deceleration of the vehicles are set based on the driving behavior of the user and the vehicle type (which are inputs to the algorithm). Consider the example in Fig. 1. The mobility profile for the vehicle traveling from v to u is generated by accelerating the vehicle starting from v until the speed reaches from 0 km/h to 80 km/h at point m on the edge. The vehicle continues traveling at this speed on the edge until point n and then decelerates towards the end of the edge such that its speed reduces to 10 km/h when it arrives at u.

For a more accurate fuel consumption estimation, we also consider the idling time at traffic intersections. Figure 1 shows an example where a vehicle travels from vertex w to vertex v which has a traffic light. If the real-time traffic signal information is available (e.g., using vehicle-to-infrastructure communication), it can directly be used by our algorithm to compute idling time at the red light if any. Otherwise, we handle this as follows. Assume that the traffic light has a 100 s cycle (60 s green and 40 s red). Our algorithm computes the arriving time considering the mobility profile and then calculates the probability of meeting a red light when the vehicle arrives at vertex v. Specifically, the system generates a random number n between 1 to 100 and assumes that the vehicle reaches at v at time n in its cycle, e.g., if n is at most 60, the vehicle arrives at the light when it is green and if n is greater than 60 it arrives at the signal when it is red and needs to wait for $(100 - n)$ seconds.

4   Experiments

In this section, we present our experimental study. First, we show how the fuel consumption estimates are affected when the average speed is used instead of the instantaneous speed. Then, we compare the route generated by our approach with some competitors in terms of total fuel consumption, travel distance, and travel time. We also show the effect of driving behavior and vehicle types.

4.1   Experimental Setup

We downloaded the road network of Melbourne from OpenStreetMap [16] which includes length and speed for each edge as well as traffic signal information. The road network contains 784, 622 nodes and 862, 711 edges. We assume that each traffic signal cycle consists of 60% green time duration and 40% red time duration. We randomly generated 1 million source-target pairs in the road network. We computed the shortest distances between each pair and divided the queries based on these distances into 75 buckets (1 km–75 km). We ran each experiment on all the query buckets and took the average unless mentioned otherwise.

Table 1. Vehicle specific parameters

		Vehicle model		
		Honda Accord	Ford Expedition	Truck (International/9800 SBA)
Mass m (kg)		1469	2626	7239
Drag coefficient C_D		0.325	0.41	0.78
Frontal area A_f (m^2)		2.3	3.88	8.9
Rolling coefficients (unit-less)	C_r	1.75	1.75	1.75
	c_1	0.0328	0.0328	0.0328
	c_2	4.575	4.575	4.575
Acceleration a (m/s^2)		3.725	4.326	1.788

We use three different vehicles: *Honda Accord, Ford Expedition* and a *truck*. The vehicle-specific parameters are acquired from the U.S. Environmental Protection Agency (EPA) website [3]. Table 1 shows these parameters. The Honda Accord is representative of sedan passenger cars, and Ford Expedition is a full-size sport utility vehicle (SUV). We tested one of the truck models (International/9800 SBA) to characterize typical truck fuel consumption behavior. Many other studies [20,26,29] have also utilised these vehicles. The acceleration values for these vehicles were obtained from the manufacturer's website (for example, the Honda Accord takes 7.2 s to go from start to 60 mph). To explore the impact of driver behavior, we assume three types of driver profiles, e.g., aggressive, calm, and conservative. Drivers with a calm profile always accelerate as per the manufacturer's website. We assume that the aggressive drivers tend to accelerate 10% more than the calm drivers, and conservative drivers undercut by 15%. The default driving behavior is calm unless mentioned otherwise.

4.2 Competitors

We compare our algorithm (shown as "Mobility Profile" in experimental results) with three other competitors: 1) shortest path algorithm (shown as "Shortest") which returns the shortest path in terms of total distance; 2) fastest path algorithm (shown as "Fastest") which returns the shortest path in terms of travel time; 3) a recent vehicle path planning (VPP) method [15] (shown as "VPP") which computes the most eco-friendly route but considers average speed for each edge for fuel estimation instead of considering the detailed mobility profile. VT-CPFM fuel consumption model is among the most well-known and accurate models for estimating fuel consumption. Therefore, we use the VT-CPFM fuel consumption model to compute the actual fuel consumption for the route generated by each of the approaches.

4.3   Results

Effect of Using Average Speed Instead of Instantaneous Speed. Similar to the existing works that show that using average speed to estimate fuel consumption results in poor estimation, we also conduct experiments on how the fuel consumption estimates are affected when instantaneous speed (e.g., the speed at each time t) is used instead of average speed on the edge. We computed the shortest path (in terms of distance) for each query and then estimated the fuel consumption of this path using the VT-CPFM model and show the results in Fig. 2a. The results show that, as expected, using the average speed significantly underestimates the fuel consumption (up to 42%) as it ignores acceleration, deceleration, and idling time which are major contributors to fuel consumption. Figure 2b shows the effect on total travel time when the travel time is estimated, assuming that the vehicle moves on the edge with constant (average) speed compared with when instantaneous speed is taken into account. The results show that using the average speed significantly underestimates the travel time (by up to 34%) because it ignores idling time, acceleration, deceleration, etc.

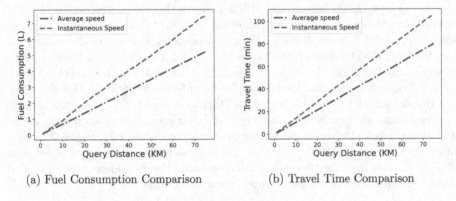

(a) Fuel Consumption Comparison   (b) Travel Time Comparison

Fig. 2. Effect of considering average speed and instantaneous speed on estimation of fuel consumption and travel time (Honda Accord)

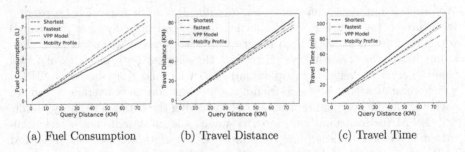

(a) Fuel Consumption   (b) Travel Distance   (c) Travel Time

Fig. 3. Performance comparison (Honda Accord)

Comparisons of Routes Generated by Different Algorithms. In this experiment, we run each algorithm to generate routes for each query and compare these routes on their total fuel consumption, total distance and total travel time. Figure 3 shows the results. Figure 3a shows that considering the detailed mobility profile significantly reduces the fuel consumption especially when the distance between source and target is bigger. However, Fig. 3b and Fig. 3c, that this saving in fuel consumption comes at the expense of routes that are slightly longer and take more travel time. Table 2 shows the average percentage increase or decrease of the competitors compared to our approach, e.g., assuming conservative driving, the shortest path consumes 33.4% more fuel compared to our approach, whereas its distance is 11.4% smaller. The results show that our approach significantly reduces fuel consumption at the expense of a somewhat longer route or more travel time.

Table 2. Percentage increase (↑) or decrease (↓) of competitors compared to our algorithm in terms of fuel consumption, distance and travel time

Driver behavior	Shortest path			Fastest path			VPP [15]		
	Fuel	Dist.	Time	Fuel	Dist.	Time	Fuel	Dist.	Time
Honda Accord									
Aggressive	19.2% ↑	12.3% ↓	3.7% ↓	25.3 ↑	3.1% ↓	9.2% ↓	8.9% ↑	7.2% ↓	5.5% ↓
Calm	26.9% ↑	11.2% ↓	4.6% ↓	31.2% ↑	3.4% ↓	10.6% ↓	12.7% ↑	7.8% ↓	6.7% ↓
Conservative	33.4% ↑	11.4% ↓	5.9% ↓	35.3% ↑	3.9% ↓	13.4% ↓	16.1% ↑	7.1% ↓	8.2% ↓
Ford Expedition									
Aggressive	17.3% ↑	10.1% ↓	4.1% ↓	19.5 ↑	3.5% ↓	9.6% ↓	7.8% ↑	6.9% ↓	6.3% ↓
Calm	23.7% ↑	10.4% ↓	5.2% ↓	27.5% ↑	2.7% ↓	11.5% ↓	10.9% ↑	7% ↓	7.8% ↓
Conservative	28.1% ↑	10.3% ↓	6.3% ↓	32.9% ↑	3.3% ↓	12.9% ↓	13.1% ↑	7.2% ↓	8.5% ↓
Truck (International/9800 SBA)									
Aggressive	10.4% ↑	10.2% ↓	3.4% ↓	17.1 ↑	2.2% ↓	12.2% ↓	5.2% ↑	6.9% ↓	6.8% ↓
Calm	15.5% ↑	9.8% ↓	4.2% ↓	22.4% ↑	2.9% ↓	14.3% ↓	7.9% ↑	6.3% ↓	7.9% ↓
Conservative	18.6% ↑	10.4% ↓	4.8% ↓	25.6% ↑	2.7% ↓	16.5% ↓	12.1% ↑	7.2% ↓	9.2% ↓

5   Conclusions and Future Work

Almost all existing eco-friendly routing algorithms make a simplistic assumption that the vehicles move with a constant speed on an edge ignoring the acceleration, deceleration, idling time etc. Consequently, this results in a poor estimate of the fuel consumption model which leads to poor quality eco-friendly routes. We addressed this limitation and considered detailed mobility profiles of the vehicles. We also considered the impact of traffic signals to include the idling time of the vehicles at red lights. Furthermore, we considered account vehicle type and driving behavior for more accurate fuel consumption estimates. Our experimental study on a real-world road network and three different vehicles showed that our proposed eco-routing algorithm returns routes with significantly lower fuel consumption.

Almost all existing works, including this work, rely on basic shortest path algorithms such as A*-search or Dijkstra's algorithm to compute the path with the lowest fuel consumption or emissions. However, these algorithms are not suitable for large graphs such as road networks as it may take several seconds for these algorithms to answer a single shortest path query. Hence, such approaches are unsuitable for large-scale deployment in real-world navigation systems that need to compute tens of thousands of routes per second. An interesting direction for future work is to design new data modeling, indexing, and query processing techniques to efficiently compute eco-friendly routes while considering detailed mobility profiles, driving behavior, and vehicle types. Another interesting direction for future work is to study more advanced eco-friendly routing queries such as travel time/distance constrained eco-friendly routes (e.g., find the most eco-friendly route such that the length of the route is no longer than 1.2 times of the shortest route), diverse eco-friendly routes or finding kNNs in terms of fuel consumption instead of distances. Also, in this work, we assumed 100-s traffic light cycle (green light 60% and red light 40%). In future work, we will also use a phase split and compute the green light times depending on which phase controls the link. Furthermore, micro-simulation of a network should also be used to compare our estimated fuel consumption to the actual fuel consumption.

References

1. Department of the Environment, Australian Government, Canberra. Australia's emissions projections 2014–15
2. International organization of motor vehicle manufacturers. https://www.oica.net/category/climate-change-and-co2/
3. U.S. environmental protection agency (EPA) (2021). https://www.fueleconomy.gov/
4. Abeywickrama, T., Cheema, M.A., Taniar, D.: k-nearest neighbors on road networks: a journey in experimentation and in-memory implementation. Proc. VLDB Endow. **9**(6) (2016)
5. Ahn, K., Rakha, H.: The effects of route choice decisions on vehicle energy consumption and emissions. Transp. Res. Part D: Transp. Environ. **13**(3), 151–167 (2008)
6. Akiba, T., Iwata, Y., Kawarabayashi, K.I., Kawata, Y.: Fast shortest-path distance queries on road networks by pruned highway labeling. In: ALENEX (2014)
7. Andersen, O., Jensen, C.S., Torp, K., Yang, B.: Ecotour: reducing the environmental footprint of vehicles using eco-routes. In: MDM (2013)
8. Barth, M., Boriboonsomsin, K., Vu, A.: Environmentally-friendly navigation. In: IEEE Intelligent Transportation Systems Conference (2007)
9. Boriboonsomsin, K., Barth, M.J., Zhu, W., Vu, A.: Eco-routing navigation system based on multisource historical and real-time traffic information. IEEE Trans. Intell. Transp. Syst. **13**(4), 1694–1704 (2012)
10. De Nunzio, G., Thibault, L., Sciarretta, A.: Model-based eco-routing strategy for electric vehicles in large urban Networks. In: Watzenig, D., Brandstätter, B. (eds.)

Comprehensive Energy Management – Eco Routing & Velocity Profiles. SAST, pp. 81–99. Springer, Cham (2017). https://doi.org/10.1007/978-3-319-53165-6_5

11. Dhaou, I.B.: Fuel estimation model for eco-driving and eco-routing. In: 2011 IEEE Intelligent Vehicles Symposium (IV), pp. 37–42. IEEE (2011)

12. Dijkstra, E.W., et al.: A note on two problems in connexion with graphs. Numer. Math. **1**(1), 269–271 (1959)

13. Elbery, A., Rakha, H., ElNainay, M.Y., Drira, W., Filali, F.: Eco-routing: an ant colony based approach. In: VEHITS, Rome, Italy, pp. 31–38 (2016)

14. Geisberger, R., Sanders, P., Schultes, D., Delling, D.: Contraction hierarchies: faster and simpler hierarchical routing in road networks. In: McGeoch, C.C. (ed.) WEA 2008. LNCS, vol. 5038, pp. 319–333. Springer, Heidelberg (2008). https://doi.org/10.1007/978-3-540-68552-4_24

15. Guo, D., et al.: A vehicle path planning method based on a dynamic traffic network that considers fuel consumption and emissions. Sci. Total Environ. **663**, 935–943 (2019)

16. Haklay, M., Weber, P.: Openstreetmap: user-generated street maps. IEEE Pervasive Comput. **7**(4), 12–18 (2008)

17. Li, L., Cheema, M.A., Ali, M.E., Lu, H., Taniar, D.: Continuously monitoring alternative shortest paths on road networks. Proc. VLDB Endow. **13**(12), 2243–2255 (2020)

18. Li, L., Cheema, M.A., Lu, H., Ali, M.E., Toosi, A.N.: Comparing alternative route planning techniques: a comparative user study on Melbourne, Dhaka and Copenhagen road networks. IEEE Trans. Knowl. Data Eng. (2021)

19. Li, Y., U, L.H., Yiu, M.L., Kou, N.M.: An experimental study on hub labeling based shortest path algorithms. Proc. VLDB Endow. **11**(4), 445–457 (2017)

20. Nie, Y.M., Li, Q.: An eco-routing model considering microscopic vehicle operating conditions. Transp. Res. Part B Methodol. **55**, 154–170 (2013)

21. Ouyang, D., Qin, L., Chang, L., Lin, X., Zhang, Y., Zhu, Q.: When hierarchy meets 2-hop-labeling: efficient shortest distance queries on road networks. In: Proceedings of the 2018 International Conference on Management of Data, pp. 709–724 (2018)

22. Rakha, H.A., Ahn, K., Moran, K.: Integration framework for modeling eco-routing strategies: logic and preliminary results. Int. J. Transp. Sci. Technol. **1**(3), 259–274 (2012)

23. Rakha, H.A., Ahn, K., Moran, K., Saerens, B., Van den Bulck, E.: Virginia tech comprehensive power-based fuel consumption model: model development and testing. Transp. Res. Part D: Transp. Environ. **16**(7), 492–503 (2011)

24. Shen, B., Cheema, M.A., Harabor, D.D., Stuckey, P.J.: Contracting and compressing shortest path databases. In: Proceedings of the International Conference on Automated Planning and Scheduling, vol. 31, pp. 322–330 (2021)

25. Sun, J., Liu, H.X.: Stochastic eco-routing in a signalized traffic network. Transp. Res. Procedia **7**, 110–128 (2015)

26. Wang, J., Elbery, A., Rakha, H.A.: A real-time vehicle-specific eco-routing model for on-board navigation applications capturing transient vehicle behavior. Transp. Res. Part C Emerg. Technol. **104**, 1–21 (2019)

27. Wang, J., Rakha, H.A.: Fuel consumption model for heavy duty diesel trucks: model development and testing. Transp. Res. Part D Transp. Environ. **55**, 127–141 (2017)

28. Zhang, M., Li, L., Hua, W., Mao, R., Chao, P., Zhou, X.: Dynamic hub labeling for road networks. In: 2021 IEEE 37th International Conference on Data Engineering (ICDE), pp. 336–347. IEEE (2021)

29. Zhao, Y., Yao, S., Liu, D., Shao, H., Liu, S.: Greenroute: a generalizable fuel-saving vehicular navigation service. In: 2019 IEEE International Conference on Autonomic Computing (ICAC), pp. 1–10. IEEE (2019)
30. Zhou, M., Jin, H., Wang, W.: A review of vehicle fuel consumption models to evaluate eco-driving and eco-routing. Transp. Res. Part D Transp. Environ. **49**, 203–218 (2016)

Real-Time Detection and Visualization of Traffic Conditions by Mining Twitter Data

Sonia Khetarpaul(✉) ⓘ, Dolly Sharma ⓘ, Jackson I. Jose ⓘ,
and Mohith Saragur ⓘ

Department of Computer Science and Engineering, Shiv Nadar University, NCR,
Greater Noida, India
{sonia.khetarpaul,dolly.sharma,jj779,ms207}@snu.edu.in

Abstract. There have been various attempts to leverage the massive amount of data generated from social media websites. The real-time nature of social media platforms can help detect events, especially in a metropolitan city. In this paper, a system is proposed, that detects traffic-related events and road conditions in real-time from tweets by using classification algorithms and custom-trained named entity recognition model (NER) to classify and extract contextual information and visualise it on a map to get an overall picture of the traffic conditions in a city. The proposed system is versatile and can be applied to other use cases such as detecting calamities, social unrest, etc.

Keywords: Social media mining · Text mining · Traffic analysis · Classification · Named entity recognition · Data visualization

1 Introduction

The ever-growing popularity of social networking websites like Facebook, Instagram, Twitter, etc. causes more and more people to use these networks to connect with others and as a source of information. These websites have become a very rich source of unstructured data. The users of these websites share real-time information on a variety of topics. These websites allow users to find more people with similar interests and help in the easy flow of information among their social groups/communities. Users can also share their personal or public experiences, express different ideas and thoughts, report different problems and events using these websites in real-time.

Twitter has more than 330 million active users and produces more than 500 million tweets each day. This makes it one of the largest social networking portals in the world, generating more than 12 terabytes of data every day. The sheer volume of data produced every day, if mined properly could prove to be a very constructive source of information. Twitter's question of "What's happening?" captures the primary objective of the portal very well, i.e., to share what's happening around you. In this paper, data generated by Twitter is used to detect

W. Hua et al. (Eds.): ADC 2022, LNCS 13459, pp. 141–152, 2022.
https://doi.org/10.1007/978-3-031-15512-3_11

events in real-time with a greater level of precision as compared to other studies. The study is limited to events related to traffic, such as congestion, accidents, diversions, etc.

Since tweets are highly unstructured, various text mining techniques like pre-processing, classification, named entity recognition are applied to transform it into structured information which can be used for further analysis. The main objective of this paper is to create a system, which consumes unstructured data to detect real-time events and produce visualisations on the city map, thus making the model usable in other domains as well.

1.1 Motivation

In most metropolitan cities, traffic is a serious issue. Many people travel to work using the same route every day and the traffic can get very severe during peak hours. Events like road blockage, diversions due to accidents, construction work, etc. adds on to the traffic. Detecting such events as they occur and notifying commuters can help save time, fuel and manpower. Google Maps detects real-time traffic but it does so based on the data it receives from mobile devices: the number of devices in a particular area and their speed is used to determine the density of the traffic. Suppose a road is obstructed and the amount of traffic in the road is also sparse or certain routes are blocked by the police on a particular day, Google Maps may fail to detect and provide an alternate route.

The proposed system will be useful in detecting traffic events and can be extrapolated to detect areas of stress in events such as civil unrest, calamities, etc.

1.2 Contributions

The following are the main contributions of the paper:

- After preprocessing, the tweets are classified based on whether they contains traffic related information with very high accuracy.
- Custom trained named entity recognition (NER) model to extract information such as event type, location, reason and advice is used.
- The extracted information is further processed and is converted into coordinates, which is then consumed by an application that visualizes the information.

2 Literature Review

Twitter activity increases during events of stress such as natural disasters, riots, wars, etc. In [3], the authors have described people as a social sensor. Their work provides the base for event detection on Twitter. They formed a system that detects and reports earthquakes by monitoring Twitter. This allowed them to detect an earthquake and then report it much quicker than traditional broadcast announcements in Japan.

Aya Ishino et al. in [4] proposed methods to retrieve transportation information and traffic problems from tweets written in Japanese and posted during a disaster. The data sets used by them were quite small, which reflected in the performance of the models they trained. They were able to obtain a precision of 77.7% and recall of 70.7% in identifying tweets with traffic-related content.

In [5], the authors analyzed tweets related to traffic in the city of Jeddah and found the most congested roads and time of the day. They monitored Tweets related to traffic in the city of Jeddah and using temporal information present in the tweets they identified which roads are generally congested at different hours of the day. In [1], authors classified traffic related tweets into point or link where link information is the traffic information that has all the attributes: Road, Start point and End point, and point information is the traffic information that has Road and Start or Stop point attribute or only Road or Start point attribute or Stop attribute.

In [6], the authors created a system that performs event classification and location prediction from tweets during disasters. They used Markov model to predict the location of the tweet when geolocation data was not present. They achieved a classification accuracy of 81% and predicted location with an accuracy of 87%. In [7] the authors propose a method for automatic detection of road traffic-related events. They also used big data technologies like Spark to perform analytics. Their system used multiple classifiers to detect various kinds of events like accidents, roadwork, road closure, road damage, etc. Their study is unique in the sense that they use big data technologies for event detection of road traffic events from tweets in Arabic.

In [15] the authors have developed a big data tool over Apache Spark for traffic-related event detection from Twitter data in Saudi Arabia. They have used 3 Machine Learning algorithms to build multiple classifiers that can detect 8 different types of events. In [14] the authors propose a technique, "Transaction-based Rule Change Mining" to extract hashtag keywords present in tweets. This provides a rule dynamics approach to event detection, they demonstrated its application in the domain of sports and politics to detect events.

Authors in [16] have used the text data from social multimedia websites like YouTube and Flickr (title, description, tags, time, location etc.), they have devised a clustering-based approach to detect sub-events or smaller events during a crisis. In [2], the authors broadly categorize events into Large-Scale events (e.g. - earthquakes, tornadoes etc.) and Small-Scale events (e.g. - traffic, accidents etc.). Detecting small scale events is difficult since there is a small number of tweets about them and they belong to a small geographic location. On the other hand, Large-Scale events have a large number of tweets and belong to a wider location. They performed classification to detect events belonging to both these categories.

3   Proposed Approach

In this section, first the high-level view of the proposed system is discussed followed by each component. It is important to note that all of the following components work on run time, i.e., dynamically, as our objective is to detect events as they happen and not at a later point in time.

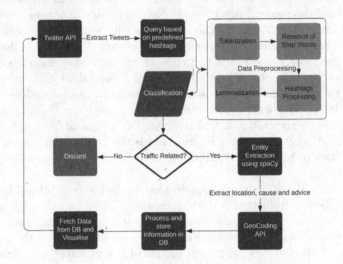

Fig. 1. The architecture of the proposed system

3.1   The Proposed Architecture

The architecture of the proposed model is shown in Fig. 1. The model starts with a Twitter streaming API, whenever a tweet satisfying certain conditions is found, it enters our pipeline. The first step in the process is to clean the tweets because the tweets are unstructured texts, they may contain abbreviations, misspelt words and sometimes grammatical errors. Twitter users commonly use trending slang, emoticons, shorthand, etc. If the tweets are not pre-processed, it would hamper the accuracy levels of our models. After this, the cleaned tweets are classified based on whether the tweet contains information related to traffic or not. If it is found to be a traffic-related, the tweet is sent to the next stage of the model. The next step is using a named entity recognition (NER) model to extract information such as event type, location, reason and advice. A table containing this information is created. The location information is then converted into coordinates and sent to a cloud database, which then gets consumed by an application that visualizes the retrieved information.

3.2   Data Collection

Two different data sets are used to build the models. The first one is obtained by crawling Twitter's publicly available API to query tweets. Tweets tweeted by the Delhi Traffic Police and certain other handles which regularly post updates related to traffic were queried, and then manually labelled to 0 or 1 depending on whether it had traffic related information or not. The second data set is from Mendeley Data [22]. This data set has tweets labelled in three classes, 0, 1 and 2. The label 0 represents tweets that are not related to traffic. Label 1 represents tweets that report non-recurring events which generate an abnormal increase in traffic demand or reduces transportation infrastructure's capacity. Label 2 represents the type of tweets that report traffic flow conditions such as daily rush hours, traffic congestion, traffic delays due to high traffic volume or jammed traffic. Classes 1 and 2 are combined since both of them contain traffic-related information. Both of these data sets are used in different combinations in different parts of the process.

The reason two data sets are used is to capture both types of tweets - those from organizations such as Delhi Traffic Police, whose tweets are structured and also those which are tweeted by individual users.

An example to demonstrate their difference:
Official Delhi Police Tweet:
"Traffic Alert Obstruction in traffic in the carriageway from Nangloi chowk towards Peera Garhi due to breakdown of a Cluster bus near Nangloi flyover. Kindly avoid the stretch".
User Tweet:
"Disabled vehicle, right lane blocked in #VanAlystneGraysonCo.Line on NB at County Line Rd, stop and go traffic back to FM- #DFWTraffic".

As evident, the tweet by Delhi Traffic Police is both formal and well structured, hence using both these data sets are necessary to train the models to capture information from both types of tweets. The data set included roughly 100k tweets. It was split in 80:20 ratio for training and testing sets. There was no class imbalance, both the classes were approximately equal in size, both in training and testing set.

3.3 Data Preprocessing

This is a very crucial step in the pipeline as the quality of the data plays an important role in improving the overall performance of machine learning models. Precision and recall are two important metrics for the evaluation of any model. If the recall becomes low the model would miss certain information which might have been useful, or if the precision becomes low the model might include irrelevant data points.

Once a tweet enters the system, the following steps are taken:

1. All user mentions are removed. User mention begins with '@', hence is easy to identify. They do not provide any useful information in this use case.
2. A common trend in most social networks is that people embed information in hashtags. For example consider these tweets "Accident cleared in #OxonHill on Beltway Local Lanes Outer Loop on Woodrow Wilson Memorial Brg,

jammed back to highway, delay of mins" and "Disabled Train Causes Rush-Hour NJ Transit Delays #NewYorkCity", both of these tweets have location information embedded in hashtags, which should not be disregarded. Hence while preprocessing hashtags are converted to proper words, "#OxonHill" is replaced by "Oxon Hill" and "#NewYorkCity" is replaced by "New York City".

3. All hyperlinks are removed from tweets as they also do not provide much useful information.
4. All stop words are removed and each word is lemmatized.
5. The tweet is deleted if its length becomes less than 3 tokens (words).

3.4 Classification of Tweets

Once a tweet enters into this part of the pipeline it gets classified into two classes depending on whether it contains information related to traffic or not. Existing machine learning models like Logistic Regression [8], Random Forest Classifier [9], Support Vector Machines [10] and Naive Bayes Classifier [11] are employed on our data set and their performance is compared.

Class 1 represents tweets with traffic-related information, and class 0 represents tweets without traffic-related information. The performance of each model employed is described and shown in Table 1, and comparison of **mean square error** is shown in Table 2.

Table 1. Performance comparison of different classifiers on the 2-class datasets

Classifier	Class	Precision	Recall	F1-score	Support
Logistic Regression	1	0.98	0.99	0.99	5239
	0	0.99	0.98	0.99	5250
Naive Bayes	1	0.98	0.98	0.98	5239
	0	0.98	0.98	0.98	5250
Support Vector Machine	1	0.99	0.99	0.99	5239
	0	0.99	0.98	0.99	5250
Random Forest Classifier	1	1	0.99	0.99	5239
	0	0.99	1	0.99	5250

The most notable performance was of Support Vector Machine and Random Forest Classifier with the mean squared error of just **0.0084** and **0.0056** respectively. Random Forest Classifier has low bias and moderate variance, this is due to each tree in the forest having low bias, and as the variance of each tree is averaged out, the overall variance turns out to be moderate. These characteristics, along with high accuracy scores made it the ideal choice. The tweets which get labelled as Class 1 are sent forward into the pipeline, the rest are discarded.

Table 2. Comparison of mean squared errors

Classifier	Mean squared error
Logistic Regression	0.0135
Naive Bayes	0.0226
Support Vector Machine	0.0084
Random Forest Classifier	0.0056

3.5   Named Entity Recognition

Named entity recognition (NER) [13] is a process where a sentence is parsed to find entities that can be categorized into names, locations, quantities, monetary values, places, etc. In the system, NER is being used to detect location, event, cause of the event, time and suggestions in a particular tweet. "spaCy" [12], an open-source software library with built in NER models was used. Users generally do not mention the time/date of the incident which they are tweeting about, but that is not a problem, as information related to time can be extracted from the tweet itself.

To create the data set for the NER, 100 dissimilar tweets which contained information related to traffic were identified. Then parts of the text which belonged to classes such as event type, location, reason and advice were marked in each tweet, and then the data set was supplied to train a blank NER model using spaCy.

Results of NER Extraction. The tweets which enter this part of the pipeline are cleaned and most probably (99% accuracy) contain traffic information. Some examples can be seen below. Examples of the output of the NER pipeline is shown in Table 3. The text shown is after preprocessing.

1. "Traffic is affected on Signature Bridge due to demonstration near Bhajanpura. Motorists are advised to use NH-24, Geeta Colony Flyover & NH-1 to cross Yamuna River."
2. "Traffic Alert Traffic be affect near Indraprastha Gas, Rohini due to water logging."
3. "Traffic Alert Traffic be slow near Kabutar Market, Please avoid the stretch"
4. "Traffic Alert Obstruction in traffic in the carriageway from Nangloi chowk towards Peera Garhi due to breakdown of a Cluster bus near Nangloi flyover. Kindly avoid the stretch."

The NER extracts these entities from each tweet in this pipeline which is then passed onto the next stage, Geocoding.

The evaluation of the custom trained NER is different from the way traditional models are measured. Entity level and token level evaluation are two different methods to measure a NER model. Entity level evaluation considers

Table 3. Output of NER

Tweet	Event/Reason	Locations	Advice
1	Demonstration	Signature Bridge	Use
		Bhajanpura	
		NH-24, Geeta Colony	
		Yamuma River	
2	Water logging	Indraprastha Gas, Rohini	
3		Kabutar Market	Avoid
4	Breakdown of cluster bus	Nangloi Chowk	Avoid
		Peera Garhi	
		Nanngloi Chowk	

Table 4. Performance of named entity recognition

Class	Precision	Recall	F1-score	Support
Location	0.80	0.85	0.83	39
Reason	0.73	0.58	0.65	19
Event	0.84	0.84	0.84	19
Advice	0.64	0.60	0.62	15
Other	0.84	0.84	0.84	87
Macro avg	0.81	0.79	0.80	179
Macro avg	0.80	0.79	0.80	179

Overall Accuracy : 88.42%

only the correctly labelled named entities. For example "Shaheen Bagh" is a location and it is considered as correctly labelled if the entire word is being marked as "LOCATION" (as one named entity). Token level evaluation checks the label of each token. For example "Shaheen Bagh" is treated as two tokens, and if both the tokens get marked as "LOCATION" it is treated as correctly labelled, but if one gets marked as "LOCATION" and the other does not, it is considered as a partial match. In this paper, entity level evaluation is used to evaluate the NER model as partial matches are not beneficial. Based on the number of correctly recognised named entities the accuracy score is calculated in Table 4.

3.6   GeoCoding

This part of the pipeline processes the location data, into a more manageable format, i.e., coordinates. The NER model identifies all the different locations in a tweet which needs to be converted into coordinates. Forward Geocoding is the process of taking input text, such as an address or the name of a place and returning a latitude/longitude. Forward GeoCoding is used to obtain the latitude and longitude of the locations found by the NER. Google's GeoCoding API is used for this.

3.7   Data Storage and Traffic Events Visualization

Firebase is popular backend support for modern applications, it can host websites, provide real-time databases, safe and secure authentication for mobile and web apps. Cloud Firestore, a flexible NoSql database is used to store the details of the events, like coordinates for all locations, the reason behind the event and advice for the public. This information is fetched by an application which then visualises it.

The application constantly scans the database for all the information posted and plots them on Google Maps. Single points of focus are depicted using a heat map surrounding that point. When a road or route is identified, it is then highlighted with red or green depending on whether to avoid the particular route or use it instead of some other route.

4   Results

The proposed system can detect, analyse extract information accurately, and visualize the information from tweets on a map. The information extracted could be useful to both traffic police operators who would be aided with the ease of use of this application which identifies stress locations and to travellers who can take alternate routes when their usual path is obstructed. Figure 2 contains plots made based on tweet 1 from Sect. 3.5, the NER identified four different locations, and corresponding to the second pair of locations, i.e., NH-24, "Geeta Colony" and "Yamuna River" found the "Advice" to be "use". Hence the second pair of locations has its route marked in the colour green, signifying an alternate route to cross the river.

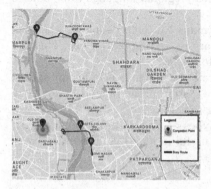

Fig. 2. Real-time visualization of advised routes

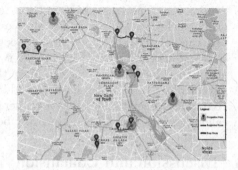

Fig. 3. Real-time visualization at a given point of time

When a tweet highlights a traffic problem in some specific location and not a route, a heat map is generated around that location. Figure 3 shows an overall view of all the information at a given point of time.

4.1 Comparison with Related Studies

In [2], the authors created a system that fetches tweets based on various search criteria, processes them by applying text mining techniques, and then performs classification on it. They solve a multi-class classification problem to determine what kind of event occurred. They obtained an accuracy value of 88.89% for the multi-class problem of detecting different kinds of events and 95.75% for the binary classification problem (traffic versus non-traffic tweet).

The system created has significant differences when compared with [2, 19–21]:

1. A higher accuracy is obtained in the binary classification problem (traffic versus non-traffic tweet). This improves the overall accuracy of the proposed system.
2. NER extracts exact contextual information from a tweet. The accuracy of the NER was 88.42%, which is comparable to the accuracy obtained in [2] (88.89%), which uses several different classification models to extract entities.
3. The proposed approach visualises and captures events that lead to traffic congestion, such as protests, social unrest in certain parts of the city or any other form of large scale event that can affect the traffic.

5   Future Work

The proposed end-to-end model is one of its kind. The system shows promising results which can be further extended into other domains. The following ideas can be considered in the future:

1. The NER also needs to understand the local/regional language to be able to detect locations better.
2. Adding real-time trusted information to maps can help people on the road avoid blocked/closed routes and unnecessary re-routing on the way. This feature can enhance the experience of Google Maps.
3. This service can be extended to user tweets too, so that people can update about their locality but this can make the system prone to a wide variety of adversarial attacks which has to be addressed [18].
4. Extrapolate the system to detect other types of events such as civil unrest, calamities, etc. which could especially be useful in identifying areas of stress.

6   Discussion and Conclusion

The ability to identify/detect traffic events in a metropolitan city can be of great use for the daily commuters and the authorities, saving time, fuel and manpower. Through this paper, we have used social platforms to detect traffic conditions and visualise them. This use case is not just limited to traffic events in the city but can also be used to identify others mass events that might need urgent attention from the authorities. This paper stands out in a number of ways compared to previous work in this area as mentioned in the above section. In the initial classification task (traffic vs non-traffic) random forest classifier was the most effect model. Next NER was able to detect 4 different entity classes with an accuracy of 88.42%. The visualisation was able to intuitively summarise all the extracted information on the map. The model can be used to help authorities better manage traffic by visualising all major traffic events on the map. By incorporating real-time information into maps, it can help users save time and fuel by avoiding congested or blocked routes.

In this paper, we demonstrated incorporating information extracted from Twitter data into internet services. The application of these techniques is countless, this study aimed to demonstrate one such use case which utilises the massive pool of data generated each day by social media.

References

1. Wanichayapong, N., Pruthipunyaskul, W., Pattara-Atikom, W., Chaovalit, P.: Social-based traffic information extraction and classification. In 2011 11th International Conference on ITS Telecommunications, pp. 107–112. IEEE, August 2011
2. D'Andrea, E., Ducange, P., Lazzerini, B., Marcelloni, F.: Real-time detection of traffic from twitter stream analysis. IEEE Trans. Intell. Transp. Syst. 16(4), 2269–2283 (2015)
3. Sakaki, T., Okazaki, M., Matsuo, Y.: Tweet analysis for real-time event detection and earthquake reporting system development. IEEE Trans. Knowl. Data Eng. 25(4), 919–931 (2012)
4. Ishino, A., Odawara, S., Nanba, H., Takezawa, T.: Extracting transportation information and traffic problems from tweets during a disaster. In: Proceedings of the Institute of Mathematics and Mechanic, pp. 91–96 (2012)
5. Alomari, E., Mehmood, R.: Analysis of tweets in Arabic language for detection of road traffic conditions. In: Mehmood, R., Bhaduri, B., Katib, I., Chlamtac, I. (eds.) SCITA 2017. LNICST, vol. 224, pp. 98–110. Springer, Cham (2018). https://doi.org/10.1007/978-3-319-94180-6_12
6. Singh, J.P., Dwivedi, Y.K., Rana, N.P., Kumar, A., Kapoor, K.K.: Event classification and location prediction from tweets during disasters. Ann. Oper. Res. 283(1), 737–757 (2019)
7. Alomari, E., Mehmood, R., Katib, I.: Road traffic event detection using twitter data, machine learning, and apache spark. In 2019 IEEE SmartWorld, Ubiquitous Intelligence & Computing, Advanced & Trusted Computing, Scalable Computing & Communications, Cloud & Big Data Computing, Internet of People and Smart City Innovation (SmartWorld/SCALCOM/UIC/ATC/CBDCom/IOP/SCI), pp. 1888–1895. IEEE, August 2019
8. Svensén, M., Bishop, C.M.: Pattern Recognition and Machine Learning, Springer, New York (2007)
9. Liaw, A., Wiener, M.: Classification and regression by randomForest. R. News 2(3), 18–22 (2002)

10. Tong, S., Koller, D.: Support vector machine active learning with applications to text classification. J. Mach. Learn. Res. **2**(Nov), 45–66 (2001)
11. Chen, J., Huang, H., Tian, S., Qu, Y.: Feature selection for text classification with Naïve Bayes. Exp. Syst. Appl. **36**(3), 5432–5435 (2009)
12. Partalidou, E., Spyromitros-Xioufis, E., Doropoulos, S., Vologiannidis, S., Diamantaras, K.I.: Design and implementation of an open source Greek POS Tagger and Entity Recognizer using spaCy. In: 2019 IEEE/WIC/ACM International Conference on Web Intelligence (WI), pp. 337–341. IEEE, October2019
13. Nadeau, D., Sekine, S.: A survey of named entity recognition and classification. Lingvis. Investig. **30**(1), 3–26 (2007)
14. Adedoyin-Olowe, M., Gaber, M.M., Dancausa, C.M., Stahl, F., Gomes, J.B.: A rule dynamics approach to event detection in twitter with its application to sports and politics. Exp. Syst. Appl. **55**, 351–360 (2016)
15. Alomari, E., Katib, I., Mehmood, R.: Iktishaf: a big data road-raffic event detection tool using Twitter and spark machine learning. Mob. Netw. Appl. **21**, 1–16 (2020)
16. Pohl, D., Bouchachia, A., Hellwagner, H.: Social media for crisis management: clustering approaches for sub-event detection. Multim. Tools Appl. **74**(11), 3901–3932 (2013). https://doi.org/10.1007/s11042-013-1804-2
17. Li, W.J., Yen, C., Lin, Y.S., Tung, S.C., Huang, S.: JustIoT Internet of Things based on the Firebase real-time database. In: 2018 IEEE International Conference on Smart Manufacturing, Industrial & Logistics Engineering (SMILE), pp. 43–47. IEEE, February 2018
18. Ravi, V., Alazab, M., Srinivasan, S., Arunachalam, A., Soman, K.P.: Adversarial defense: DGA-based botnets and DNS homographs detection through integrated deep learning. IEEE Trans. Eng. Manag. Early Access (2021)
19. Jones, A.S., Georgakis, P., Petalas, Y., Suresh, R.: Real-time traffic event detection using Twitter data. Infrastr. Asset Manag. **5**(3), 77–84 (2018)
20. Zulfikar, M.T.: Detection traffic congestion based on Twitter data using machine learning. Procedia Comput. Sci. **157**, 118–124 (2019)
21. Dabiri, S., Heaslip, K.: Twitter-based traffic information system based on vector representations for words. arXiv preprint arXiv:1812.01199 (2018)
22. Dabiri, S.: Tweets with traffic-related labels for developing a Twitter-based traffic information system. Mendeley Data V1 (2018). https://doi.org/10.17632/c3xvj5snvv.1. Accessed 15 Feb 2020.

FluMA: An Intelligent Platform
for Influenza Monitoring and Analysis

Xi Chen, Zhi Chen$^{(\boxtimes)}$, Zijian Wang, Ruihong Qiu, and Yadan Luo

The University of Queensland, Brisbane, Australia
zhi.chen@uq.edu.au

Abstract. Monitoring and analysing epidemic trends is essential for an early warning system to impend outbreaks that could become public health emergencies and help track progress towards specified goals. In this paper, we present an intelligent platform for influenza monitoring and analysis, which pipelines the process of utilising the raw surveillance data to visualise and model the graphical representations of the data. In particular, the platform involves data preparation, time series prediction and data visualisation components. Within the data visualisation component, we deliver statistical analysis that draws insights from the plain data. Further, the platform is capable of predicting future trends based on various machine learning models that are learned from previous years.

Keywords: Medical data analysis · Epidemiological modeling

1 Introduction

Influenza (flu) is a contagious disease occurring essentially in seasonal epidemics, which may cause mild to severe symptoms and even life-threatening complications [8,9,12]. Thus, it is necessary to continually monitor the spreading of influenza and make appropriate prevention to minimise pandemic risk. The Australian health department maintains annual reports providing a massive amount of raw information about influenza activities [2]. However, the plain data in itself is merely raw numbers, which hinders decision-makers from understanding the trends, outliers, patterns and further making data-driven decisions. Further, the Australia health departments have been continually curating more data. Yet, the discrete reports fail to reflect the time-series patterns. Therefore, it could be beneficial to develop a system to make the reports more accessible to the public and improve their prevention awareness.

This paper presents an intelligent platform for influenza monitoring and analysis, which provides accurate and insightful information for different stakeholders. Specifically, there are three components involved in the proposed platform, including data preparation, time series prediction and data visualisation. First, to prepare the dataset for analysing and monitoring, we collect, clean and normalise the raw surveillance and auxiliary datasets. Further, in the time series prediction step, we train and evaluate various machine learning models on the preprocessed datasets. Lastly, we present visualisation from the statistical and machine learning perspectives. The visualisation allows interactive manipulation and exploration of the graphical representations of the influenza data.

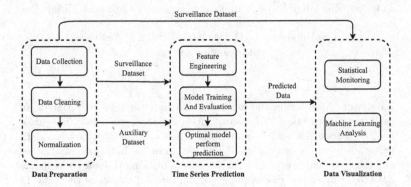

Fig. 1. An overview of proposed platform, which contains data preparation, time series prediction, and data visualisation.

2   System Overview

The system consists of three components: data preparation, time series prediction, and data visualisation. The data preparation component concentrates on collecting surveillance data and auxiliary data and removing the noise from the datasets. Time series prediction aims to reform the datasets and predict future trends with machine learning models. For data visualisation, we develop an interactive interface that presents the visualisation results derived from the datasets.

2.1   Data Preparation

The datasets used in this system consist of two parts: surveillance data and auxiliary data. The surveillance data [2] records information of each patient over the last decade, including diagnosed time, gender, age, indigenous status, and subtype. The auxiliary data consists of possible factors that may influence the spreading of influenza, including climate data [1] and census data [3]. The two sources of auxiliary data provide features during the prediction process in order to improve the prediction accuracy.

The data preparation step dedicates to removing the noise from the datasets in order to improve the quality of visualisation and prediction. There are two types of noise in the datasets: missing values and outliers. The missing values are filled by the most common feature value or the average feature value in its specific time period and location. Meanwhile, the outliers are removed from the datasets, as the number of outliers is much smaller than the size of the original dataset. The last step in this component is normalisation, as there are multiple auxiliary features spanning various ranges.

2.2   Time Series Prediction

This component dedicates to predicting future trends using machine learning models. To start with, we perform feature engineering on the preprocessed data by selecting and transforming the most relevant variables. The surveillance records information of each patient. Thus, the weekly diagnosed number can be derived from this dataset. This value is utilised as label and lag features. Lag features in this system indicate records from previous timestamps and differences from the previous two timestamps. In addition, auxiliary features can be generated by matching corresponding climate and census data based on time and geological information. For fair evaluation, the data is divided into 5 folds to perform cross-validation [6], which aims to find the optimal hyperparameters for training the sequence models. Specifically, we conduct experiments with four widely used machine learning models, including Long Short-term Memory (LSTM) [7], Multi-Layer Perceptron (MLP) [10], Linear Regression [11] and Random Forest [5]. To model the trends in the seven states of Australia, the entire Australia and the two serogroups, we independently train different models and take the hyperparameters from the best cross-validation results.

2.3   Data Visualisation

This component focuses on visualising surveillance data and prediction results to provide insights from different aspects. We leverage Tableau [4] to implement this dashboard, which contains two parts: statistic analysing and machine learning analysing. Statistical monitoring focuses on presenting visualisation that is directly derived from the surveillance data, whereas machine learning analysing focuses on presenting data generated by the four machine learning models. To facilitate the interaction, a control pad is provided to specify the conditions. The entire dashboard will present visualisation based on the corresponding control pad filtering.

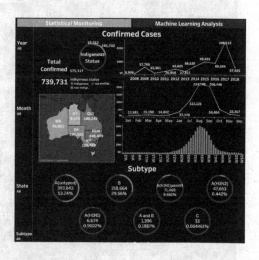

Fig. 2. The interactive visualisation for statistical monitoring.

Meanwhile, there is a navigation bar on the top of the dashboard that allows users to switch visualisation between statistical monitoring and machine learning analysis.

In statistic analysis, we present the confirmed cases, subtypes and the infection details, as shown in Figs. 2 and 3. The confirmed cases are presented with the number of patients in different time periods and locations. The map shows the total confirmed number over the entire country in the last decade. Meanwhile, the three charts on the right side illustrate the number of patients each year, month, and week respectively. In addition, we

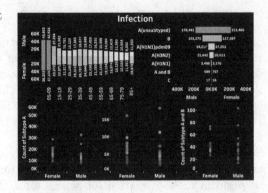

Fig. 3. Infection details in statistical monitoring.

show the proportional relations of the different subtypes. It is worth noting that serogroup A is the most contagious virus, followed by serogroup B, and C. Combining the information of serogroups, the high-risk group can be easily targeted.

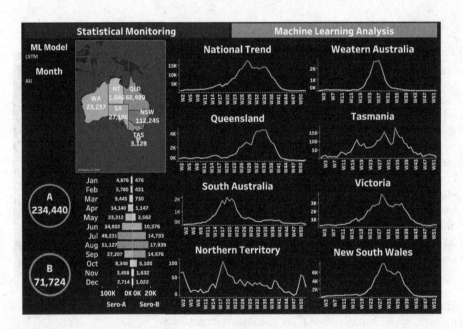

Fig. 4. The interactive visualisation for influenza data analysis with machine learning models.

The machine learning analysis results are delivered by the four types of machine learning models. The dashboard allows users to choose different model predictions. The map shows the predicted monthly confirmed cases for different states. The charts beneath the map are the distribution of two main subtypes. The two ring charts present the total number, and the divergent bar chart illustrates the monthly trends for the two serogroups. The line graphs on the right-hand side illustrate the weekly trends in Australia and each state. Different states will meet their influenza season at different times whereas mostly in the middle of the year.

3   Conclusion

In this paper, we present a platform that provides insights from different aspects to benefit different stakeholders. It is educational as it provides knowledge relevant to influenza. Meanwhile, it reveals the patterns and trends in the last decade and future trends in the next years. This platform not only improves the prevention awareness of the public but also supports health departments and policymakers to make data-driven decisions to improve public health.

References

1. Climate data online - Australian Bureau of Meteorology. https://www.bom.gov.au/climate/data/index.shtml?bookmark=200. Accessed 1 May 2020
2. Datasets for the national notifiable diseases surveillance system. https://www1.health.gov.au/internet/main/publishing.nsf/Content/ohp-pub-datasets.htm. Accessed 1 May 2022
3. National, State and Territory Population - Australian Bureau of Statistics. https://www.abs.gov.au/statistics/people/population/national-state-and-territory-population/dec-2020#data-download. Accessed 1 May 2020
4. Tableau software (2022). https://www.tableau.com
5. Breiman, L.: Random forests. Mach. Learn. **45**(1), 5–32 (2001)
6. Browne, M.W.: Cross-validation methods. J. Math. Psychol. **44**(1), 108–132 (2000)
7. Hochreiter, S., Schmidhuber, J.: Long short-term memory. Neural Comput. **9**(8), 1735–1780 (1997)
8. Palese, P.: Influenza: old and new threats. Nat. Med. **10**(12), S82–S87 (2004)
9. Potter, C.W.: A history of influenza. J. Appl. Microbiol. **91**(4), 572–579 (2001)
10. Ramchoun, H., Ghanou, Y., Ettaouil, M., Janati Idrissi, M.A.: Multilayer perceptron: architecture optimization and training. Int. J. Interact. Multim. Artif. Intell. **4**(1), 26–30 (2016)
11. Seber, G.A., Lee, A.J.: Linear Regression Analysis. John Wiley & Sons, New York (2012)
12. Stöhr, K.: Influenza-who cares. Lancet Infect. Dis. **2**(9), 517 (2002)

Short Research Papers

Brain Data Mining Framework Involving Entropy Topography and Deep Learning

Md. Nurul Ahad Tawhid[1]([⊠]), Siuly Siuly[1], Kate Wang[2], and Hua Wang[1]

[1] Institute for Sustainable Industries and Liveable Cities, Victoria University, Melbourne, Australia
md.tawhid1@live.vu.edu.au, {siuly.siuly,hua.wang}@vu.edu.au
[2] School of Health and Biomedical Sciences, RMIT University, Melbourne, Australia
kate.wang@rmit.edu.au

Abstract. Mining large scale brain signal data using artificial intelligence offers an unparalleled chance to investigate the dynamics of the brain in neurological disorders diagnosis. Electroencephalography (EEG) produces a multi-channel time-series large scale brain signal data recorded from scalp and visually analyzed by expert clinicians for abnormality detection. It is time-consuming, error-prone, subjective and has reliability issues. Thus, there is always a need of automated mining system for brain signal data to detect abnormality from those large volume data. This study presents an entropy topography with deep learning-based technique to solve the above mentioned issues. We have used shannon entropy to extract entropy values from EEG signal and plotted them to produce the topographic image. Then those images are trained and classified using our proposed convolutional neural network. We have tested it on two EEG datasets of schizophrenia disorder and the results showed that the proposed method can be used for brain signal data mining purposes.

Keywords: Brain signal data · EEG · Data mining · Topographic image · Shannon entropy · Deep learning

1 Introduction

Brain signal data is increasingly being used to assess brain activity, and it has a lot of potential for diagnosing and treating mental and brain diseases and disorders. EEG signal data is called as brain signal data. Worldwide, there is an increasing demand for efficient methods of interpretation of brain signal data for effective and inexpensive healthcare service. In biomedical research field, developing and adopting modern signal processing algorithms for EEG data analysis is crucial [12]. EEG captures the brain's spontaneous electrical activity as a huge volumes of time-series data with non-linear and non-stationary in nature and have patterns associated to the subject's mental health state. EEG data has been used for a variety of purposes, including developing brain computer interface [11], studying changes in the electrical activity of the brain in response to an external event or an inner mental process [12], and predicting a brain-related health condition [14,16]. Expert clinicians usually analyze the signal visually, which is often difficult to distinguish minor but essential changes in the EEG data. As a result, this opens up a new study field for biomedical engineers to develop and use innovative and efficient algorithms for identifying these changes. Data mining based techniques can extract essential biomarkers from brain signal data and use those markers to automatically categorize brain states into distinct categories of disorders by building a computer-aided diagnostic (CAD) system.

EEG technique has recently received a lot of attention for its accuracy in monitoring brain activity, however the raw signal is contaminated with artifacts and is complex due to its variance across time and space. Traditional manual feature extraction and selection from EEG data require specific domain knowledge. Moreover, cost of traditional feature selection process rises quadratically as the number of features grows [2]. In most studies, feature extraction process mostly focused on time domain [9] or frequency domain [1] or time-frequency domain [10], with only a few studies focusing on spatial domain but there is still room for improvement. This study aims to accurately identify abnormalities from EEG recordings by combining time, frequency, and spatial domains.

Several studies have been reported for mining large volume of EEG data in last decades [3,4,10,15]. Most of these studies used various statistical information as signal features and classified those features using various classifiers. However, for large data, conventional methods frequently fall short of identifying meaningful and distinctive traits. Moreover, statistical features of long-length signals may neglect the short-term traits, which are crucial for detecting abnormalities [16]. This problem can be resolved by visualizing the small signal segment entropy as a topographic image. Additionally, deep learning (DL) based models outperform machine learning (ML) based classifiers when the volume of data is huge, and also have the capacity to automatically learn features and conduct classification [16]. Nonetheless, the majority of studies in this area have only assessed their proposed methods on a single dataset, making their adaptability to other datasets questionable.

Therefore, detecting abnormality from this large scale EEG data, we have proposed a topographic image and DL based data mining framework. In topographic imaging process, waveform patterns are converted to images that show the electric landscape of brain activity at discrete moments or varied frequency content of recorded EEG signals for imaging purposes [13]. In the proposed method, at first, the signals are segmented into small time window to extract features from short signal segment. Then shannon entropy is used to extract the entropy values of those segments and generated the topographic images for those segments. After that, a DL based convolutional neural network (CNN) is developed to extract features and perform classification on those topographic images. Finally, the performance of the model is validated using two different EEG datasets of schizophrenia disease. These are the study's primary contributions:

1. Develop a data mining framework for brain signal data specially for EEG.
2. Introduce an entropy based topographic visualization of the EEG signal.

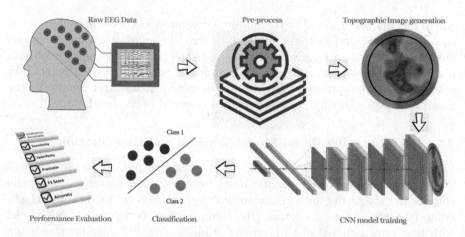

Fig. 1. An overview of the proposed EEG signal data classification framework using topographic image and deep learning-based CNN model.

3. An automatic and efficient CNN model is developed for classification process.
4. Explore the framework's performance with two different EEG datasets.

This is how the rest of the article is organized. Section 2 presents the proposed method. Section 3 presents datasets and performance assessment parameters. Section 4 discusses the experimental results. Section 5 contains closing remarks.

2 Methodology of the Proposed Mining Framework

Here, we have proposed a brain signal data mining framework using topographic image and DL-based CNN model. This framework works in couple of steps as shown in Fig. 1. Details of those steps are discussed below:

2.1 Pre-processing of the Raw Data

In this step, we first resampled the raw data to a 256 Hz sampling frequency, as it is widely used frequency band and computationally less expensive than higher frequency bands [5]. Then, we have divided the data into three-second (3 s) pieces to maximize feature extraction from small signal segments and to increase the dataset [14–16].

2.2 Topographic Image Generation of the Signal Segments

Brain signal topographic image is a neuroimaging technique that is used to plot the activity of the different brain regions using several tones of color [7]. Here, we have used entropy topography where entropy values are extracted using shannon entropy (ShanEn) that quantifies the probability density function of the distribution of values using Eq. 1:

$$ShanEn = -\sum_i p_i log p_i \qquad (1)$$

where i is the likelihood that the amplitude value v_i occurs somewhere in the data time series, and p_i is the probability that the amplitude value v_i occurs anywhere in the data time series. Thus, p_i is the ratio of the number of data points in the data time series with v_i amplitude value to all data points. We have projected the entropy values into topographic plotting after computing the ShanEn for each recording channel of the segmented brain signal.

2.3   Deep Learning Based Model Training and Classification

We have used DL based CNN model for classification purposes as it is a popular model for image based classification problem and has proven exceptionally efficient in categorizing by learning appropriate features on its own and classifying data into various categories [16]. Here, we have developed a CNN model with four convolution (ConV) layer and a fully connected layer for classifying the topographic images. Each ConV layer has 32 filters with karnel size of 5×5 and *relu* activation function, and followed by a batch normalization layer and a max-pooling layer with a pool size of 2×2. Second and fourth max-polling layers are followed by a 25% dropout layer while the fully connected layer followed by a 50% dropout layer. The proposed model is trained using the Adam optimizer and softmax as the classifier, with categorical cross entropy as the loss function.

3   Materials and Parameters for Performance Evaluation

We have used two publicly available EEG datasets of schizophrenia (SZ) disorder for validating the proposed framework. First dataset contains 81 subjects (49 SZ, 32 HC) [6]. EEG data was recorded from 64 electrodes at a sampling rate of 1024 Hz. Second dataset is from the Institute of Psychiatry and Neurology in Warsaw, Poland [4] with 28 subjects (14 SZ, 14 HC). EEG data were recorded 250 Hz sampling frequency from 19 channels of 10–20 international standard EEG system. Details of those datasets can be found in [4, 6]. Performance of the proposed model is evaluated using 10-fold cross-validation technique to reduce over-fitting issue. Finally, the system's performance is evaluated using standard three parameters: sensitivity (Sen), precision (Prec), and accuracy (Acc).

4   Results of the Proposed Framework

Here, we have proposed an EEG data mining system using topographic image and DL based approach. We have tested the model on two different datasets to perform a binary classification (SZ vs HC). Details of the obtained results and their visualization with experimental setups are discussed in below subsections.

4.1   Setup for Experimentation

We have pre-processed the EEG data by resampling it 256 Hz and then segmenting it into 3 s chunks. Then we have generated topographic image for those

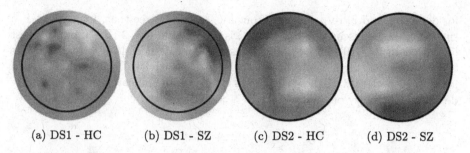

(a) DS1 - HC   (b) DS1 - SZ   (c) DS2 - HC   (d) DS2 - SZ

Fig. 2. Sample topographic images for the tested datasets. a and b are from dataset 1 and c and d are from dataset 2 for HC and SZ subjects, respectively

chunks using ShanEn values. This produces a total of 4728 images for SZ subjects and 3108 images for HC subjects from dataset 1. For dataset 2, those values are 5146 and 4235, respectively. Sample topographic images from the two datasets are given in Fig. 2. For training the CNN model, we have used mini-batch mode (batch size 32, 64, 128 and 256) for training batch size selection.

4.2 Experimental Results of the Proposed Framework

In this study, we have used two different EEG datasets of SZ disorder to validate the proposed framework using 10-fold cross validation technique. We have tested four different training batch sizes to check the impact of the batch size on the proposed CNN model. Table 1 shows the average performance of the framework over 10-fold for the tested datasets with four different batch sizes. Bold marked values in the table are the highest average performance value we have achieved for that evaluation parameter in that dataset over 10-fold cross validation.

From Table 1, we can see that performance of the proposed framework decreases with the increase of training batch size. For dataset 1, highest average sensitivity of 92.94% is achieved using batch size 32, while for dataset 2, it is 97.84% for the same batch size. To check the detail fold wise performance, we have plotted the fold and batch size wise sensitivity value in Fig. 3a and Fig. 3b

Table 1. 10-fold average performance results (mean ± std) for the proposed method on two tested datasets for different batch sizes (BS).

Datasets	Params	BS 256	BS 128	BS 64	BS 32
No. 1	Sen%	91.86 ± 1.17	91.59 ± 0.81	91.71 ± 1.12	**92.94 ± 1.10**
	Prec%	88.50 ± 1.83	89.64 ± 1.25	**90.14 ± 1.46**	89.57 ± 0.84
	Acc%	87.87 ± 1.05	88.54 ± 0.59	88.93 ± 1.24	**89.20 ± 0.81**
No. 2	Sen%	97.80 ± 0.85	97.76 ± 0.47	97.74 ± 0.62	**97.84 ± 0.60**
	Prec%	97.97 ± 0.63	**98.30 ± 0.56**	98.18 ± 0.49	98.22 ± 0.45
	Acc%	97.69 ± 0.42	97.85 ± 0.53	97.77 ± 0.51	**97.85 ± 0.45**

for dataset 1 and 2, respectively. From Fig. 3a we can see that, for dataset 1, a single fold highest sensitivity of 94.43% is obtained in fold 2 (BS 32) and lowest of 89.48% in fold 10 (BS 64). For dataset 2, fold 7 and fold 6 with batch size 256 produces the highest and lowest single fold sensitivity of valued 99.62% and 96.58%, respectively. High sensitivity is desired as it indicates the abnormality detection capability of the model.

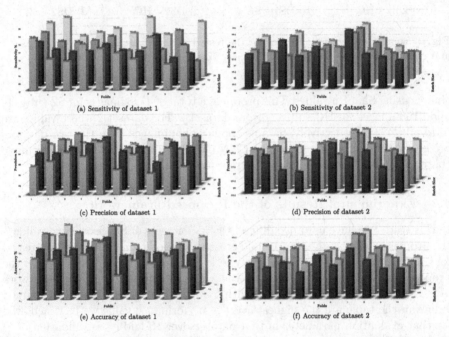

(a) Sensitivity of dataset 1   (b) Sensitivity of dataset 2

(c) Precision of dataset 1   (d) Precision of dataset 2

(e) Accuracy of dataset 1   (f) Accuracy of dataset 2

Fig. 3. Fold wise different evaluation parameters comparison for four training batch sizes over 10-fold for tested two datasets.

Table 2. Performance comparison with existing studies for the same datasets.

Datasets	Comparison for classification accuracy (%)	
Dataset 1	Siuly *et al.* [10] 89.59%	Proposed model 89.20%
Dataset 2	Shoeibi *et al.* [8] 99.25%	Proposed model 97.85%

Next parameter we have analyzed is precision that represents the percentage of relevant instances retrieved. Figure 3c and 3d shows the precision for dataset 1 and 2, respectively. A single fold highest and lowest precision value is achieved in fold 5 (92.77% for BS 64) and fold 8 (85.74% for BS 256), respectively for dataset 1. For dataset 2, those are obtained in fold 7 (99.62% for BS 128) and fold 4 (96.97% for BS 256), respectively. Overall, 10-fold average highest precision for dataset 1 and 2 is 90.14% (BS 64) and 98.30% (BS 128), respectively.

The last parameter we have plotted in detail is accuracy. From Table 1, we can see that for both the tested datasets, BS 32 has produced the best accuracy which are 89.20% and 97.85% for dataset 1 and 2, respectively. Figure 3e and 3f shows the fold and batch size wise accuracy comparison for dataset 1 and 2, respectively. 90.94% is the highest single fold accuracy we have obtained for dataset 1 in fold 5 (BS 64) while 85.84% is the lowest value in fold 6 (BS 256). On the other hand, 99.25% is the highest single fold accuracy obtained in fold 7 (BS 128) and 97.12% is the lowest accuracy value for fold 4 (BS 256).

Finally, performance of the proposed model with the existing works is given in Table 2. Although, our proposed model haven't achieved the best accuracy for the tested datasets but this topographic image based brain signal classification can be used for this kind of signal classification tasks. Moreover, fine tuning the CNN model and also using the transfer learning of the pre-trained popular CNN models can improve the accuracy for the classification process.

5   Conclusion

In this study, a topographic image based brain signal data mining framework is proposed. We have tested the proposed model using EEG brain signal data for classification of schizophrenia disease. EEG data are segmented into small time frames at first and then entropy value for those segments are calculated using shannon entropy. After that, those entropy values are used to produce the topographic plotting for those segments. We have introduced a CNN model to classify those topographic images to two classes of patient verses healthy. Using the proposed framework, we have achieved an accuracy of 89.20% and 97.85% for dataset 1 and 2, respectively. Although, the proposed method could not outperform the existing works on those datasets, but this work can used as a foundation for further research. In future, fine tuning the proposed CNN model and transfer learning technique of existing pre-trained popular models can be used on those topographic images. Other topographic image generation techniques can also be explored to check the classification process.

Acknowledgments. This work is funded by the Australian Research Council Linkage Project (Project ID: LP170100934).

References

1. Al Ghayab, H.R., Li, Y., Siuly, S., Abdulla, S.: Epileptic EEG signal classification using optimum allocation based power spectral density estimation. IET Sig. Process. **12**(6), 738–747 (2018)
2. Dash, M., Liu, H.: Feature selection for classification. Intell. Data Anal. **1**(1–4), 131–156 (1997)
3. Oh, S.L., et al.: A deep learning approach for Parkinson's disease diagnosis from EEG signals. Neural Comput. Appl. **32**(15), 10927–10933 (2020). https://doi.org/10.1007/s00521-018-3689-5

4. Olejarczyk, E., Jernajczyk, W.: Graph-based analysis of brain connectivity in schizophrenia. PLoS One **12**(11), e0188629 (2017)
5. Rivera, M.J., Teruel, M.A., Maté, A., Trujillo, J.: Diagnosis and prognosis of mental disorders by means of EEG and deep learning: a systematic mapping study. Artif. Intell. Rev. **55**, 1209–1251 (2021). https://doi.org/10.1007/s10462-021-09986-y
6. Roach, B.: EEG data from sensory task in schizophrenia (2019). https://www.kaggle.com/datasets/broach/button-tone-sz
7. Sabbatini, R.M.: Mapping the brain (1997). https://cerebromente.org.br/n03/tecnologia/eeg.htm
8. Shoeibi, A., et al.: Automatic diagnosis of schizophrenia in EEG signals using CNN-LSTM models. Front. Neuroinform. **15**, 777977 (2021)
9. Siuly, S., et al.: A new framework for automatic detection of patients with mild cognitive impairment using resting-state EEG signals. IEEE Trans. Neural Syst. Rehabil. Eng. **28**(9), 1966–1976 (2020)
10. Siuly, S., Khare, S.K., Bajaj, V., Wang, H., Zhang, Y.: A computerized method for automatic detection of schizophrenia using EEG signals. IEEE Trans. Neural Syst. Rehabil. Eng. **28**(11), 2390–2400 (2020)
11. Siuly, S., Li, Y.: Discriminating the brain activities for brain-computer interface applications through the optimal allocation-based approach. Neural Comput. Appl. **26**(4), 799–811 (2015). https://doi.org/10.1007/s00521-014-1753-3
12. Siuly, S., Li, Y., Zhang, Y.: EEG signal analysis and classification. IEEE Trans. Neural Syst. Rehabil. Eng. **11**, 141–4 (2016)
13. Skrandies, W.: Electroencephalogram (EEG) topography. In: Encyclopedia of Imaging Science and Technology (2002)
14. Tawhid, M.N.A., Siuly, S., Wang, K., Wang, H.: Data mining based artificial intelligent technique for identifying abnormalities from brain signal data. In: Zhang, W., Zou, L., Maamar, Z., Chen, L. (eds.) WISE 2021. LNCS, vol. 13080, pp. 198–206. Springer, Cham (2021). https://doi.org/10.1007/978-3-030-90888-1_16
15. Tawhid, M.N.A., Siuly, S., Wang, H.: Diagnosis of autism spectrum disorder from EEG using a time-frequency spectrogram image-based approach. Electron. Lett. **56**(25), 1372–1375 (2020)
16. Tawhid, M.N.A., Siuly, S., Wang, H., Whittaker, F., Wang, K., Zhang, Y.: A spectrogram image based intelligent technique for automatic detection of autism spectrum disorder from EEG. PLoS One **16**(6), e0253094 (2021)

Enhancing System Security by Intrusion Detection Using Deep Learning

Lakshit Sama[1(✉)], Hua Wang[1], and Paul Watters[2]

[1] Victoria University, Melbourne, Australia
lakshit.sama@gmail.com, hua.wang@vu.edu.au
[2] Cyberstronomy Pty Ltd., Melbourne, Australia

Abstract. Network intrusion detection has become a hot topic in cyber security research due to better advancements in deep learning. The research is lacking an objective comparison of the various deep learning models in a controlled setting, notably on recent intrusion detection datasets, despite the fact that several outstanding studies address the growing body of research on the subject. In this paper, a network intrusion scheme is developed as a solution of the discussed issue. The four different models are build and are experimented with NSL-KDD dataset. These deep learning models are LightGBM, XGBoost, LSTM, and decision tree. For the validation of the proposed scheme, the proposed scheme is also experimented with UNSW-NB15 dataset and CIC-IDS2017. However, the experiments concluded that the proposed scheme outperforms and the discussion is also illustrated.

1 Introduction

Over the previous ten years, the size, use, and complexity of computer networks have all increased dramatically. Internet of Things have evolved as new sorts of devices and network infrastructures [15,16]. The safety of these networks and systems has grown increasingly important as they grow in size and complexity [7,24]. According to CyberEdge's 2021 Cyberthreat Defense Report, attacks on major enterprise networks have increased over the past five years. Among these attacks, malware, intrusion, spam, and denial of service (DoS) are most common and prominent attacks.

Network intrusion detection is one of the most difficult aspects of network security to deal with [3,22]. Though tremendous progress has been made, the bulk of solutions still use less competent signature-based techniques instead of anomaly detection methods [6,25]. Many factors contribute to this reluctance, including as the high false error rate (and related costs), difficulty in acquiring trustworthy training data, length of training data, and system dynamics [23,29]. There will come a point where the current scenario will lead to inefficient and inaccurate detection as a result of such tactics. For this problem, we must come up with an acceptable anomaly detection method that can keep pace with the ever-changing nature of current networks.

W. Hua et al. (Eds.): ADC 2022, LNCS 13459, pp. 169–176, 2022.
https://doi.org/10.1007/978-3-031-15512-3_14

The implementation of machine learning and deep learning techniques like Naive Bayes, Support Vector Machines, and Decision Trees has been a major focus in Network intrusion research in recent years [4,9]. Improved detection accuracy has been achieved by using these strategies. Expert knowledge is necessary to process data e.g. to find important data and patterns, but these techniques have some drawbacks, such as the relatively high level of human engagement required [27,28]. In addition to the fact that it takes a lot of time and money, this method is also prone to mistakes. Similar to this, in order to operate, a large volume of training data is necessary (together with the corresponding time overheads), which can be difficult in a dynamic context.

Deep learning is a research area that is currently receiving a lot of attention from researchers in a variety of fields because of the above limitations [5,8,19]. An advanced branch of machine learning, this can help overcome the problems with shallow learning. Deep learning's remarkable layer-wise feature learning has so far been shown to outperform shallow learning techniques, if not match them. Using this tool, it is possible to conduct a deeper analysis of network data and identify any anomalies more quickly.

It is possible to analyse network traffic flows through the use of misuse detection, anomaly detection, and signature based analysis techniques. The attacks are detected through the use of predefined signatures and filters, which are known as misuse detection. It dependent on human inputs to keep the signature database up to date on a continuous basis. This method is accurate when it comes to identifying known attacks, but it is completely ineffective when it comes to identifying unknown attacks. Anomaly detection is a technique that employs heuristic mechanisms to identify previously unidentified malicious activities.

The contributions of the paper are:

1. Deep learning models are designed with the objective of intrusion detection.
2. The network intrusion system is built with the deep learning models and validated with the dataset.
3. The validation of the proposed scheme is done by experimenting the proposed scheme with benchmark datasets UNSW-NB15 Dataset and CIC-IDS2017.

The first section of this article laid the emphasis of need of network detection. The second section discusses about the challenges of network issues. Some of the existing work for intrusion detection is also discussed in this section. The proposed scheme is discussed in Sect. 3. The discussion regarding the results of the proposed scheme is discussed in Sect. 4. Finally, Sect. 5 concludes this research work.

2   Related Work

The majority of the work done for the intrusion detection computational modeling section is done using datasets that are similar in both training and testing. It is difficult to generalise real-time events from these datasets because of the nature of the data. As a result, when the bulk of these predictive are exposed to real-world network traffic, their performance measures deteriorate. Different methods for classifying connections with abnormalities in order to detect network intrusions have been proposed, including the use of heuristics.

- According to Shyu et al. [21], an unique scheme based on Principal Component Analysis was presented, with anomalies being treated as outliers. With the KDD'99 dataset, the anomaly detection system performed significantly better. The detection rate increased to ninety nine percent, but the percentage of false alarms plummeted to as low as 1%, according to the results.
- According to Revathi et al. [17], a detailed analysis of the NSL-KDD dataset was carried out using only relevant features, both with and without feature reduction of the dataset, on different classification algorithms, among others. Across both cases, Random Forest was found to have the highest accuracy in test accuracy. Deep learning techniques make it possible to create NIDS that are both versatile and resilient.
- Khaled et al. [1] proposed an integrated approach for intrusion detection that included one hidden layer of Deep Boltzmann Device for unsupervised dimension reduction and Adaboost with multi-class gentle for classification, as well as one hidden units of Restricted Boltzmann Equipment for unsupervised dimension reduction. Using the entire 10% KDD-Cup'99 test dataset, the model achieved a detection rate of 97.9%, surpassing the industry standard. The KDDCup'99 dataset does not represent a challenge that is comparable to that of real-world network traffic in any way.
- Yin et al. [26] suggested a deep learning strategy for intrusion detection based on Recurrent Neural Networks, which they believe will be successful (RNN). The experimental results revealed that the model's performance in both binary and multiclass classification was promising, and that the model was capable of classifying with high accuracy.
- The difficulty in developing a robust NIDS is the lack of real-time network data patterns that include both intrusions and normal network usage, the presence of constantly evolving and changing known attacks, the need for lengthy training periods, and a lack of knowledge about the modifications that should be made to existing datasets. Even though a model may attain great accuracy when compared to test datasets, the model's accuracy always appears to decline when compared to real-world network traffic [18].

The above discussed existing works are summarised in Table 1.

3   Proposed Scheme

The proposed scheme comprises of building a network intrusion detection system (NIDS). The system is designed with four deep learning models, LightGBM, XGBoost, LSTM, and decision tree. Each model is trained with the patches of data and is able to detect the attacks. We have developed the scheme by its validation on NSL-KDD dataset. However, the scheme has been validated with other datasets as well as discussed in next section. Below is the discussion of four models deployed at the proposed scheme. The steps followed are discussed in Fig. 1.

Table 1. Summary of existing techniques

Author	Technique	Model	Dataset	Results
Shyu et al. 2011 [21]	Outlier Detection	Principal Component Analysis	KDD'99	99% Accuracy
Revathi et al. 2013 [17]	Network Intrusion Detection System	Random Forest	NSL-KDD dataset	Improved accuracy
Khaled et al. 2016 [1]	Unsupervised dimension reduction	Adaboost	NSL-KDD dataset	97.9%
Yin et al. [26]	Intrusion detection	Recurrent Neural Networks	NSL-KDD dataset	Improved accuracy
Shone et al. [20]	Intrusion detection system	Deep Auto Encoder	KDD Cup'99 and NSL-KDD	High precision
Sama et al. [18]	Network Intrusion Detection	Deep learning	KDD dataset	Improved accuracy

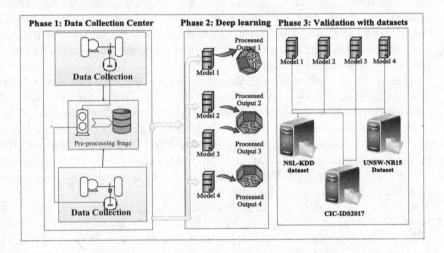

Fig. 1. Steps followed in the proposed work

– LightGBM: Light Gradient Boosting Machine (LightGBM) is a gradient boosting platform which uses algorithms based on tree learning. The segment where LightGBM shines is in the case of big datasets, such as the one used in our implementation. Light is the product of running at a very high speed and using much less memory in LightGBM. LightGBM works to allow complete, effective use of the gradient boosting system by first processing the dataset and making it lighter.

$$x_p = d \sum_{q \in pa[p]} \frac{x_q}{h_q} + (1 - d) \tag{1}$$

$$\hat{V_j}(d) = \frac{1}{n} \left(\frac{\sum x_i A_l \sum x_i B_l}{n_i} \right) \tag{2}$$

Every loss to the network is computed by the above equation. Here, x is the number of features of the proposed scheme.

– XGBoost: EXtreme Gradient Boosting (XGBoost), originated from GBDT. Owing to its accuracy and relatively fast speed compared to traditional machine learning algorithms, it was introduced earlier than LightGBM and is commonly used in machine learning. For performance, XGBoost chooses an algorithm based on histograms. The histogram-based algorithm uses bins that are separated by data point characteristics into discrete types [10].

$$t = \sum n, i = 1 l(y_i, \hat{y}_i(t - 1) + f_t(x_i)) + \omega(f_t) \tag{3}$$

- LSTM: Long-Short Term Memory (LSTM) is commonly used as a deep neural network for Time series data processing, which is an enhanced Recurrent Neural Networks (RNNs) based model. RNN uses an internal state to represent previous input values, allowing temporal background to be captured. For long input sequence, it is not easy to train LSTM. However, compared to RNN, LSTM can capture the background of longer time series [13].

$$e_T = tanh(w_c[h_{T-1}, x_T] + b_c) \tag{4}$$
$$e_T = f_T * e_{T-1} + i_T * \hat{e}_T \tag{5}$$
$$h_T = o_T * tanh(e) \tag{6}$$

- Decision tree: An example of a non-parametric machine learning model, Decision Trees are useful both for classification and regression. If we build them appropriately (which we should), decision trees can generate either a categorical or a numerical forecast depending on the number of characteristics we include in them. Two types of elements, nodes and branches, are used to build them. Data features are examined at each node in the training process or while creating predictions in order to separate observations or to follow a specific path for an individual data point in training [11].

$$E(S) = \sum (c, i = 1) - p_i log_2 p_i E(T, X) = \sum P(c)E(c) \tag{7}$$

Entropy and information gain are the two parameters computed by decision tree. Gain is computed using these two parameters, which decides the position for each instance.

4   Results and Discussion

Dataset-1: NSL-KDD Dataset: Kaggle has a detailed description of the NSL-KDD dataset. When it was first developed in 1999, it was widely used in 2009 for detecting intrusions. The authors [12, 18] now use this dataset as the benchmark dataset. These datasets are named KDDTrainC and KDDTestC, respectively, and are used for training and testing. 41 features are listed for each traffic record and 1 class label.

Dataset-2: UNSW-NB15 Dataset: It is possible to categorise the attacks in the UNSW-NB15 dataset into one normal class and nine attack classes, namely the Analyze class and the Backdoor class and the DoS class and the Exploits class and the Generic class and the Reconnaissance class and the Worms class.

The UNSWNB15 dataset has 257,673 data instances, including 175,341 training data instances and 82,332 testing data instances [14].

Dataset-3: CIC-IDS2017: There are 2,830,743 records in the CIC-IDS2017 database, and each record has 78 features associated with it. The CIC-IDS2017 database contains the latest attacks and the outcomes of network traffic analysis to termed flows depending on the source and destination access technologies and time stamps in the database. An updated intrusion detection database, CIC-IDS2017, covers important criteria such as Botnet, SQL injection, port scan and DDoS [2].

Table 2. Settings of hyper parameters for each deep learning model

Model 1		Model 2		Model 3		Model 4	
LightGBM	Settings	XGBoost	Settings	LSTM	Settings	Decision Tree	Settings
Epoch	50	Epoch	100	Epoch	150	Epoch	250
Error rate	0.001	Error rate	0.001	Objective function	Binary	Level depth	8 nodes, 10 leafs
Batch rate	28	Batch rate	56	Folds	3	Number of splits	5
Data dimension	41	Data dimension	41	Early stopping rounds	50	Nodes shuffling	True

Impact of Deep Learning on the Proposed Scheme

The deep learning models are deployed in the proposed scheme. The experimentation of the models is being done using different datasets. The hyper parameters settings for each model in illustrated in Table 2. The models are experimented with the NSL-KDD dataset.

5   Conclusion

In this paper, we have discussed the difficulties that currently available NIDS techniques face. In response to this, we have proposed our novel NIDS method to the scientific community. We have developed a TensorFlow implementation of our proposed model and conducted extensive evaluations of the model's capabilities. We used the benchmark NSL-KDD dataset for our evaluations, and we were able to achieve very promising results. The four deep learning models are deployed and further experimented with on other benchmark datasets in addition to the one used for this experiment.

References

1. Alrawashdeh, K., Purdy, C.: Toward an online anomaly intrusion detection system based on deep learning. In: 2016 15th IEEE International Conference on Machine Learning and Applications (ICMLA), pp. 195–200. IEEE (2016)

2. Azizan, A.H., et al.: A machine learning approach for improving the performance of network intrusion detection systems. Ann. Emerg. Technol. Comput. **5**(5), 201–208 (2021)

3. Cheng, K., et al.: Secure k-NN query on encrypted cloud data with multiple keys. IEEE Trans. Big Data **7**(4), 689–702 (2017)

4. Ge, Y.F., Cao, J., Wang, H., Chen, Z., Zhang, Y.: Set-based adaptive distributed differential evolution for anonymity-driven database fragmentation. Data Sci. Eng. **6**(4), 380–391 (2021)

5. Ge, Y.F., Orlowska, M., Cao, J., Wang, H., Zhang, Y.: MDDE: multitasking distributed differential evolution for privacy-preserving database fragmentation. VLDB J. 1–19 (2022)

6. Kabir, M., Wang, H., Bertino, E., et al.: A role-involved purpose-based access control model. Inf. Syst. Front. **14**(3), 809–822 (2012)

7. Kabir, M.E., Mahmood, A.N., Wang, H., Mustafa, A.K.: Microaggregation sorting framework for k-anonymity statistical disclosure control in cloud computing. IEEE Trans. Cloud Comput. **8**(2), 408–417 (2015)

8. Li, J.Y., Du, K.J., Zhan, Z.H., Wang, H., Zhang, J.: Distributed differential evolution with adaptive resource allocation. IEEE Trans. Cybern. (Early Access) (2022)

9. Li, J.Y., Zhan, Z.H., Wang, H., Zhang, J.: Data-driven evolutionary algorithm with perturbation-based ensemble surrogates. IEEE Trans. Cybern. **51**(8), 3925–3937 (2020)

10. Makkar, A.: Secureengine: Spammer classification in cyber defence for leveraging green computing in sustainable city. Sustain. Cities Soc. **79**, 103658 (2022)

11. Makkar, A., Kim, T.W., Singh, A.K., Kang, J., Park, J.H.: SecurelloT environment: federated learning empowered approach for securing IoT from data breach. IEEE Trans. Ind. Inform. **16**, 6406–6414 (2022)

12. Makkar, A., Kumar, N., Obaidat, M.S., Hsiao, K.F.: Qair: Quality assessment scheme for information retrieval in IoT infrastructures. In: 2018 IEEE Global Communications Conference (GLOBECOM), pp. 1–6. IEEE (2018)

13. Makkar, A., Park, J.H.: SecureCPS: cognitive inspired framework for detection of cyber attacks in cyber-physical systems. Inf. Process. Manage. **59**(3) (2022)

14. Moustafa, N., Slay, J.: UNSW-NB15: a comprehensive data set for network intrusion detection systems (UNSW-NB 15 network data set). In: 2015 Military Communications and Information Systems Conference (MilCIS), pp. 1–6 (2015). https://doi.org/10.1109/MilCIS.2015.7348942

15. Najam, M., Ahmad, H.F., Wang, H., Anwar, Z., et al.: A novel JSON based regular expression language for pattern matching in the internet of things. J. Amb. Intell. Hum. Comput. **10**(4), 1463–1481 (2019)

16. Qin, Y., Sheng, Q.Z., Falkner, N.J., Dustdar, S., Wang, H., Vasilakos, A.V.: When things matter: a survey on data-centric internet of things. J. Netw. Comput. Appl. **64**, 137–153 (2016)

17. Revathi, S., Malathi, A.: A detailed analysis on NSL-KDD dataset using various machine learning techniques for intrusion detection. Int. J. Eng. Res. Technol. **2**(12), 1848–1853 (2013)

18. Sama, L., Makkar, A., Mishra, S.K., Samdani, Y.: Diadl: An energy efficient framework for detecting intrusion attack using deep learning. In: Proceedings of the 12th International Conference on Computer Modeling and Simulation, pp. 138–142 (2020)

19. Sarki, R., Ahmed, K., Wang, H., Zhang, Y., Wang, K.: Convolutional neural network for multi-class classification of diabetic eye disease. In EAI Endorsed Transactions on Scalable Information Systems, pp. e15–e15 (2022)

20. Shone, N., Ngoc, T.N., Phai, V.D., Shi, Q.: A deep learning approach to network intrusion detection. IEEE Trans. Emerg. Topics Comput. Intell. **2**(1), 41–50 (2018)
21. Shyu, M.L., Chen, C., Chen, S.C.: Multi-class classification via subspace modeling. International Journal of Semantic Computing **5**(01), 55–78 (2011)
22. Sun, X., Wang, H., Li, J., Pei, J.: Publishing anonymous survey rating data. Data Mining Knowl. Discov. **23**(3), 379–406 (2011)
23. Vimalachandran, P., Liu, H., Lin, Y., Ji, K., Wang, H., Zhang, Y.: Improving accessibility of the Australian my health records while preserving privacy and security of the system. Health Inf. Sci. Syst. **8**(1), 1–9 (2020)
24. Wang, H., Wang, Y., Taleb, T., Jiang, X.: Special issue on security and privacy in network computing. World Wide Web **23**(2), 951–957 (2020)
25. Wang, H., Zhang, Y., Cao, J., Varadharajan, V.: Achieving secure and flexible m-services through tickets. IEEE Trans. Syst. Man Cybern. Part A Syst. Hum. **33**(6), 697–708 (2003)
26. Yin, C., Zhu, Y., Fei, J., He, X.: A deep learning approach for intrusion detection using recurrent neural networks. IEEE Access **5**, 21954–21961 (2017)
27. Yin, J., Tang, M., Cao, J., Wang, H., You, M., Lin, Y.: Vulnerability exploitation time prediction: an integrated framework for dynamic imbalanced learning. World Wide Web **25**(1), 401–423 (2022)
28. You, M., Yin, J., Wang, H., Cao, J., Wang, K., Miao, Y., Bertino, E.: A knowledge graph empowered online learning framework for access control decision-making. World Wide Web pp. 1–22 (2022)
29. Zhang, F., Wang, Y., Liu, S., Wang, H.: Decision-based evasion attacks on tree ensemble classifiers. World Wide Web **23**(5), 2957–2977 (2020). https://doi.org/10.1007/s11280-020-00813-y

Challenges in Electroencephalography Data Processing Using Machine Learning Approaches

Ashik Mostafa Alvi$^{(\boxtimes)}$, Siuly Siuly , and Hua Wang

Victoria University, Melbourne, VIC 3011, Australia
Ashik.Alvi@live.vu.edu.au, {Siuly.Siuly,Hua.Wang}@vu.edu.au

Abstract. The future of neuro-science lies in Electroencephalography (EEG). EEG is the latest gold standard for diagnosing most neurological disorders like dementia, mild cognitive impairment (MCI), Alzheimer's diseases, and so on. It is a cheap, portable and non-invasive option to discover neuro-disorders compared to the remaining expensive and time consuming options like computed tomography (CT) scan, positron emission tomography (PET), mini-mental state examination, and magnetic resonance imaging (MRI). Though EEG sounds promising option, but there are some challenges involved in EEG signal processing starting from EEG signal recording till disease classification. This study has reported all the challenges related to the detection of neuro-diseases from EEG data. This study will guide future EEG and neuro-disease investigators to be more attentive to the reported challenges and obstacles, which will ensure smooth and accurate neuro-disease detection models.

Keywords: EEG · Dementia · Mild cognitive impairment · Alzheimer's diseases · Parkinson diseases · Schizophrenia

1 Introduction

Human life expectancy has grown as a result of constant advancements in medical research and technology, and it is becoming increasingly impossible to live without being touched by technology [2,10,11]. To confirm people's life expectancy, more changes in the health-care industry are necessary. However, greater life expectancy increases the risk of developing age-related neurodegenerative illnesses, which have a significant impact on our daily lives.

Brain is the most complex part of the human body and the majority of brain illnesses go unnoticed until they become serious. The primary cause of neuro illnesses and disorders is the dysfunction and death of brain cells. There are more than 600 neuro-diseases which includes Alzheimer's diseases (AD) [13], mild cognitive impairment (MCI) [4,5,8,24], dementias, epilepsy [1,23], stroke, schizophrenia (SZ) [20,21], Parkinson disease (PD) [12], migraine, autism, brain tumors etc. These neurological diseases have an impact on the brain, nerve roots, spinal cord, peripheral nerves, neuromuscular junction, cranial nerves, autonomic nervous system, and muscles [6].

According to World Health Organization's (WHO), nearly one billion individuals worldwide were afflicted with brain illnesses such as Alzheimer's disease, epilepsy, stroke, and headache [6]. This indicates nearly 1 in 6 of world's population suffer from neurological disorders. Regardless of country, gender, age, wealth, or education, these neuro-diseases affect individuals. WHO claims, every year, 6.8 million people die as a result of neurological illnesses, which impact hundreds of millions of people throughout the world: about 47 million people have dementia, and more than 50 million people have epilepsy [15]. These are highly frequent neuro-diseases in the senior population, especially those aged 65 and more, and the severity rate rises exponentially with age [9].

The existing biomarkers to detect these neuro-disorders are: computed tomography (CT) scan, magnetoencephalography (MEG), positron emission tomography (PET), magnetic resonance imaging (MRI), and mini-mental state examination (one-to-one interview procedure). These diagnostic tools are either expensive or time consuming or manual methods. Electroencephalography (EEG) has emerged as a non-invasive, portable, easy, inexpensive, and robust biomarker for investigating neuro-disorders. The electroencephalogram captures the electrical activity in the cerebral cortex throughout time. To capture the electric potentials, electrodes are implanted on the skull. The most common EEG configuration, with about 21 electrodes, is the International 10–20 system [22]. It is worthy to mention that we are dealing with more than 600 neuro-diseases in the current world. In our study, we have focused on the five common and deadliest neuro-disorders detection challenges, which are: dementias, MCI, AD, PD, and SZ.

Rigorous amount of machine learning (ML) techniques [14,16–19] have been used in a number of studies to identify these diseases early on. And it is an ongoing area of research to discover neuro-disorders at the quickest possible time with EEG data. But this is a cross-field area of research that evolves both signal processing and machine learning together. That creates some extra challenges for the researchers. Raw EEG signals have to be taken care of using time or frequency domain methods to get effective and important features out of them. Finally, a promising classifier with adequate parameters to differentiate those disorders from health controls (HCs) is essential.

Previous efforts to detect those indicated five neuro-diseases have suffered from good performance, stability and cost effectiveness in terms of time. It is because of not working with the raw EEG signals properly and not tuning the classifier effectively. In this effort, we have reported those challenges and tuning points which need to be taken care of attentively to ensure an accurate and efficient neuro-disorder detection method. The following is a summary of the key contribution of this effort:

- All the narrow spikes entangle in EEG signal processing have been explored.
- We have investigated the obstacles related to classification and reported here.
- Finally, observing the common challenges both in signal processing and machine learning, we have suggested some solutions.

The following is how the rest of the article is organised: all the relevant challenges and obstacles in detecting the mentioned neuro-diseases are reported in Sect. 2. A detailed discussion where effective solutions, suggestions and limitation of this study are outlined in Sect. 3. This study ends with talking about the conclusion in Sect. 4.

2 Challenges in Identifying Brain Disorders

EEG signals are not periodic and stationary like other regular signals. There are certain features and attributes in EEG signals. It has five frequency bands: delta (δ) from 0.1 Hz to 4 Hz, theta (θ) from 4 Hz to 8 Hz, alpha (α) from 8 Hz to 12 Hz, beta (β) from 12 Hz to 30 Hz, and gamma (γ) > 30 Hz [6]. Possible challenges starting from EEG recording to EEG classification are reported below:

2.1 Challenges in EEG Data Recording

Managing medical data for conducting research is quite hard. So, initial challenge is to find good number of case subjects and normal subjects. Here, case subjects indicate patients with any neuro-diseases which we want to automatically differentiate from normal subjects. And normal subjects mean humans of any gender without brain diseases. Researchers need to find a sufficient number of subjects to conduct the EEG recording sessions. While selecting the subjects, there are some exclusion criterion need to be followed:

- Head trauma
- A yesteryear of major psychiatric disorders
- Substance misuse
- Any medication that affects cognition
- Other special requirements based on the case
- Other significant medical condition

The Petersen criteria means a neuropsychiatric interview named the Mini-mental State Examination (MMSE) has to be performed for each of the subjects. Usually, the MMSE score of the normal subjects stays higher than 26, and less than 26 is the score of the case subjects. After all these criterion have met, ethical approval has to be taken from each of the subjects and the hospital or managing authority. After doing so, an EEG cap can be placed on the scalp of the subject. Just before that, it has to be fixed how many electrodes will be used to record the electrical activity of the brain. There are a couple of options like the international 10-20, 10-10, 10-5, etc. systems are available. They have 21, 64, and 128 electrodes set up respectively. To find out the perfect set up according to the work is a big challenge in EEG recording. Figure 1 illustrates the positioning of the 21 electrodes (Fp1, Fp2, F7, F3, Fz, F4, F8, A1, T3, C3, Cz, C4, T4, A2, T5, P3, Pz, P4, T6, O1, O2) used according to the international 10-20 system, and it is the most widely accepted and used set up to conduct EEG recordings.

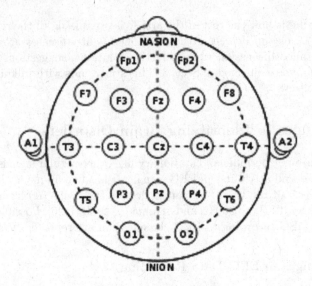

Fig. 1. Electrodes position according to international 10-20 system.

Next thing to work on before recording is to set the electrodes skin impedance. It is preferable to set fewer than 5 kΩ, otherwise there might be some white noise included in the signal. Then, choosing the right sampling frequency is another decision to make. The standard sampling frequency for the aforementioned five neuro-diseases studies is 128–256 Hz. Finally, and lastly, the most challenging part of EEG recording is to keep the subject conscious as it may last for 10–30 min.

2.2   Challenges in EEG Signal Pre-processing

This stage is to process the raw data before feeding it into the classifier for classification. Raw EEG recordings are frequently contaminated by artifacts or "unwanted signals". Some of the most typical reasons for contaminating an EEG recording are outlier readings, baseline drift, electrode-pops, power supply fluxes and interference (50 Hz), breathing, eye blinking, or muscle electrical activity, among others. If we want to create an accurate detecting system, we must first remove the noise from the recording. Now the initial struggle begins with the noise reduction algorithm. There are several ways for removing artifacts that have been proven to work. Buttherworth filtering, Wavelet Transform (WT), Fourier Transform (FT), Independent Component Analysis (ICA), Wavelet Enhanced Independent Component Analysis (wICA) etc. are some of the common options for noise and dimensionality reduction. Figure 2 is a showcase of an MCI subjects (a) raw EEG signal and (b) de-noised signal.

Based on the classifier and computational resources, the next steps vary. If a traditional machine learning classifier is picked, then it requires features from the data to be manually extracted using time, frequency, or time-frequency domain

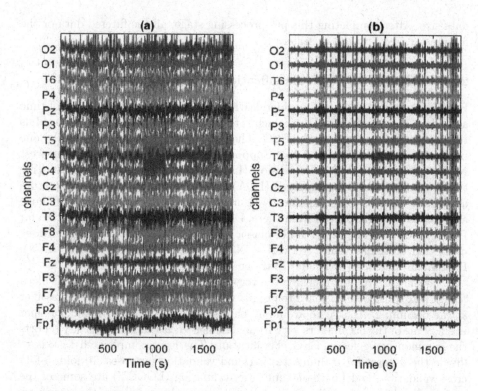

Fig. 2. EEG recording of an MCI subject (a) raw EEG signal (b) de-noised EEG signal of the same MCI subject [5].

methods. Some of the time-domain options for feature extraction include: Phase Locking Value (PLV), P300, Event Related Potential (ERP), Auto regressive (AR) coefficients, etc. are some of the time-domain options for feature extraction. Candidate Feature Vector (CFV), Relative Power (RP), Hilbert Transform (HT), Fast Fourier Transformation (FFT) etc. are widely used frequency domain methods. WT, MUSIC-Empirical Wavelet Transformation (EWT), Continuous Wavelet Transform (CWT), Discrete Wavelet Trans-form (DWT) etc. are some time-frequency domain analysis methods.

Now, considering the computational power, some extra pre-processing is required, like segmentation, compression or down-sampling. The motivation for these steps is to break down the massive EEG dataset while not losing important features. There is no well-established method for segmentation. Segmentation is mostly done based on epoch size. E.g. rom 30 min of EEG recording of a subject, we will consider each epoch of 5 s in duration, which will be a temporal segment. For compression Piecewise Aggregate Approximation (PAA) is a widely used method for EEG data. Well-known average [3] or median filtering [7] can be used for down-sampling. But it is not recommended to down-sample the data as it compromises important features if the computational power can handle the data size. After completing this pre-processing stage, all the filtered data or the features are fed into the classifier.

2.3   Challenges in EEG Classification

Establishing and improving machine learning algorithms has taken a lot of time and effort. Deep Learning (DL), which is the latest branch of ML, has enabled us to work with huge datasets like EEG. Though there has been a lot of work done using classical ML classifiers like Support Vector Machine (SVM), K-nearest Neighbor (KNN), Logistic Regression (LR), Naïve Bayes (NB), Decision Tree (DT), Linear discriminant analysis (LDA) etc. Due to their shallow architecture and linear pattern, these classical ML algorithms struggle to deal with huge amounts of EEG data. And from there, DL comes to enhance its support. So far DL methods have not explored like classical ML methods. Few studies have done using Convolutional Neural Network (CNN), Recurrent Neural Network (RNN), Boltzmann Machine (BM), and Extreme Learning Machine (ELM).

Choosing the right classifier is the very first challenge here. Though it is like a "Black Box" problem. It is hard to predict the performance of the chosen classifier at the beginning. And there are many parameters associated with the classifier itself. Some of the parameters vary from classifier to classifier. This study reports the common struggles in EEG classification. The least complicated task is to divide the dataset for training, testing, and validation purposes. 10-fold, 5-fold cross validation, and Leave-one-out cross-validation (LOOCV) are some of the preferred and accepted validation methods to prove the stability of the classifiers. Fine tuning the parameters of the classifier can increase the performance. But it requires a lot of time. To reduce the training time, normalization can be done with the dataset. It will reduce the size of the data and provide redundancy over the main memory. Fine tuning involves changing the kernel, order, batch size, number of epochs, activation function, window size etc. Another challenge lies in the coding. MATLAB and Python-based editors like Pytorch, Spider, Pycharm, and Jupyter Notebook are some of the commonly used tools for EEG classification. As Python has better support for DL, recent studies are mostly done in a Python environment.

3   Discussion

EEG analysis has drawn the attention of many researchers for neuro-disease detection. Multiple EEG classification framework have been demonstrated in [4,5,8]. All the steps discussed in this study have taken part inside [4,5,8]. But there are certain things which need to be taken care of carefully to ensure a qualityful detection mechanism. It all starts with the EEG data recording. Arranging a sufficient number of subjects for the study is one of the big challenges here. Certain exclusion criterions are there to eliminate illegible subjects from the study. As the EEG recording goes on for a long time, keeping the selected subjects stable and quite for a long time is another challenge.

After EEG signal recording, the artefacts have to be removed from the signal for further processing. Removing these noises with a proper noise filter is a hard task. Further processing involves feature extraction, segmentation, compression, etc. If a DL-based classifier is chosen, then just right after de-nosing, the data is ready to be fed into the classifier. Otherwise, features have to be manually extracted using some time or frequency domain algorithms. Selecting the right feature extraction algorithm is challenging, and the quality of the extracted features mostly depends on the quality of the data after de-noising. Segmentation and compression are done to reduce the computational overhead.

The classification stage does not have the huge challenges of the previous stages if the EEG data is processed properly. The classifier may struggle to perform well. But proper fine tuning can increase the performance, which is the challenging part. There are lots of parameters when we talk about fine tuning a classifier. Parameters include: kernel, order, batch size, number of epochs, activation function, window size etc. These have an impact on the learning rate of the classifier as well as the training time.

4   Conclusion

EEG has opened a new door towards brain disease research. There has been an extensive amount of work going on to detect different brain diseases at an early stage. Some neuro patients only live after 5–8 years after being medically confirmed. And EEG is a very easy biomarker to investigate. This study is a pathway for upcoming EEG research. Challenges and common struggling points are discussed, along with possible solutions. New studies will find it interesting and easy to work with EEG data.

References

1. Akut, R.: Wavelet based deep learning approach for epilepsy detection. Health Inf. Sc. Syst. **7**(1), 1–9 (2019). https://doi.org/10.1007/s13755-019-0069-1
2. Alvi, A., Tasneem, N., Hasan, A., Akther, S.: Impacts of blockades and strikes in Dhaka: a survey. Int J Innov Bus Strat **6**(1), 369–377 (2020)
3. Alvi, A.M., Basher, S.F., Himel, A.H., Sikder, T., Islam, M., Rahman, R.M.: An adaptive grayscale image de-noising technique by fuzzy inference system. In: 2017 13th International Conference on Natural Computation, Fuzzy Systems and Knowledge Discovery (ICNC-FSKD), pp. 1301–1308. IEEE (2017)
4. Alvi, A.M., Siuly, S., Wang, H.: Developing a deep learning based approach for anomalies detection from EEG data. In: Zhang, W., Zou, L., Maamar, Z., Chen, L. (eds.) WISE 2021. LNCS, vol. 13080, pp. 591–602. Springer, Cham (2021). https://doi.org/10.1007/978-3-030-90888-1_45
5. Alvi, A.M., Siuly, S., Wang, H.: A long short-term memory based framework for early detection of mild cognitive impairment from EEG signals. IEEE Trans. Emerg. Top. Comput. Intell. , Early Access 2022
6. Alvi, A.M., Siuly, S., Wang, H.: Neurological abnormality detection from electroencephalography data: a review. Artif. Intell. Rev.**55**, 2275–2312 (2022)

7. Alvi, A.M., Siuly, S., Wang, H., Sun, L., Cao, J.: An adaptive image smoothing technique based on localization. In: Developments of Artificial Intelligence Technologies in Computation and Robotics: Proceedings of the 14th International FLINS Conference (FLINS 2020), pp. 866–873. World Scientific (2020)
8. Alvi, A.M., Siuly, S., Wang, H., Wang, K., Whittaker, F.: A deep learning based framework for diagnosis of mild cognitive impairment. Knowl. Based Syst. **248** (2022)
9. Duthey, B.: Background paper 6.11: Alzheimer disease and other dementias. A public health approach to innovation, vol. 6, pp. 1–74 (2013)
10. Hasan, M.A., Tasneem, N., Akther, S.B., Alvi, A.M.: A study to find the impacts of strikes on students and local shopkeepers in Bangladesh. In: Proceedings of the ICITST-WorldCIS-WCST-WCICSS-2019, pp. 81–86. Infonomics Society (2019)
11. Hasan, M.A., Tasneem, N., Akther, S.B., Das, K., Alvi, A.M.: An analysis on recent mobile application trend in Bangladesh. In: Barolli, L., Takizawa, M., Xhafa, F., Enokido, T. (eds.) WAINA 2019. AISC, vol. 927, pp. 195–204. Springer, Cham (2019). https://doi.org/10.1007/978-3-030-15035-8_18
12. Heyn, S., Davis, C.: Parkinson's Disease Symptoms, Signs, Causes, Stages, and Treatment, NIH (2020)
13. International, A.D.: The global voice on dementia: Dementia statistics (2020)
14. Lee, J., Park, J.S., Wang, K.N., Feng, B., Tennant, M., Kruger, E.: The use of telehealth during the coronavirus (Covid-19) pandemic in oral and maxillofacial surgery-a qualitative analysis. In: EAI Endorsed Transactions on Scalable Information Systems, pp. e10–e10 (2022)
15. Organization, W.H.: Neurological Disorders: Public Health Challenges. World Health Organization, Geneve (2006)
16. Pandey, D., Wang, H., Yin, X., Wang, K., Zhang, Y., Shen, J.: Automatic breast lesion segmentation in phase preserved DCE-MRIs. Health Inf. Sci. Syst. **10**(1), 1–19 (2022)
17. Paul, S., Alvi, A.M., Nirjhor, M.A., Rahman, S., Orcho, A.K., Rahman, R.M.: Analyzing accident prone regions by clustering. In: Król, D., Nguyen, N.T., Shirai, K. (eds.) ACIIDS 2017. SCI, vol. 710, pp. 3–13. Springer, Cham (2017). https://doi.org/10.1007/978-3-319-56660-3_1
18. Paul, S., Alvi, A.M., Rahman, R.M.: An analysis of the most accident prone regions within the Dhaka metropolitan region using clustering. Int. J. Adv. Intell. Paradig. **18**(3), 294–315 (2021)
19. Sarki, R., Ahmed, K., Wang, H., Zhang, Y., Wang, K.: Convolutional neural network for multi-class classification of diabetic eye disease. In: EAI Endorsed Transactions on Scalable Information Systems, p. e15 (2022)
20. Siuly, S., Khare, S.K., Bajaj, V., Wang, H., Zhang, Y.: A computerized method for automatic detection of schizophrenia using EEG signals. IEEE Trans. Neural Syst. Rehabil. Eng. **28**(11), 2390–2400 (2020)
21. Spitzer, R.L., Md, K.K., Williams, J.B.: Diagnostic and Statistical Manual of Mental Disorders. American Psychiatric Association. Citeseer (1980)
22. Supriya, S., Siuly, S., Wang, H., Cao, J., Zhang, Y.: Weighted visibility graph with complex network features in the detection of epilepsy. IEEE Access **4**, 6554–6566 (2016)
23. Supriya, S., Siuly, S., Wang, H., Zhang, Y.: Epilepsy detection from EEG using complex network techniques: a review. IEEE Rev. Biomed. Eng. (2021)
24. Yin, J., Cao, J., Siuly, S., Wang, H.: An integrated mci detection framework based on spectral-temporal analysis. Int. J. Autom. Comput. **16**(6), 786–799 (2019)

Database States Exhibiting Tree Projection Necessity

Oded Shmueli[✉] [iD]

Technion - Israel Institute of Technology, Technion City, 32000 Haifa, Israel
oshmu@cs.technion.ac.il
https://www.cs.technion.ac.il/~oshmu

Abstract. Consider determining whether the join of n relations with relation schemas $\mathbf{R}_1, \ldots, \mathbf{R}_n$ is non-empty. Abstracting the essence of many query processors, we may form new m intermediate relations, with relation schema $\mathbf{S}_1, \ldots, \mathbf{S}_m$, then repeatedly use in-place semijoins to obtain an overall pair-wise compatible database state, and finally test that this state is non-empty. Recently, it was proved that if the relation schemas $\mathbf{S}_1, \ldots, \mathbf{S}_m$ guarantee a correct solution, i.e., for any initial database state, then there must exist an acyclic database schema (tree schema), say over relation schemas $\mathbf{R}_1, \ldots, \mathbf{R}_n, \mathbf{U}_1, \ldots, \mathbf{U}_q$ such that each relation schema $\mathbf{U}_i$ is a subset of some relation schema $\mathbf{S}_j$, $1 \leq i \leq q$, $1 \leq j \leq m$. Such an acyclic database schema is called a *tree projection* of $\mathbf{R}_1, \ldots, \mathbf{R}_n, \mathbf{S}_1, \ldots, \mathbf{S}_m$ with respect to (w.r.t.) $\mathbf{R}_1, \ldots, \mathbf{R}_n$. Suppose such a tree projection does not exist. The proof provides no mechanism, except for exhaustive search, to exhibit an initial database state over which the non-emptiness problem is solved incorrectly. Constructing such a database state is interesting combinatorially and it may also prove useful in testing query processors. We construct such a database state for two classes of cyclic database schemas: Arings and Cliques. Constructing such database states for arbitrary cyclic database schemas remains an open problem.

Keywords: Cyclic scheme · Acyclic scheme · Hypergraph · Tree projection · k-partite graph · Join · Semijoin

1 Introduction

Consider a simple SQL query $J_\mathbf{X}$ which computes the natural join of its From Clause relations projected on attributes $\mathbf{X}$ of its Select Clause. The Where Clause contains only conjunctions (only the AND operator). The first abstraction is considering all the relations mentioned in the query as a database, over database schema $\mathbf{D}$, and the query itself as a projection on attributes $\mathbf{X}$ out of the natural join of all database relations.

The next abstraction we consider is solving $J_\mathbf{X}$ by a finite straight-line program P, i.e., a finite sequence of statements such that in each statement a new

© The Author(s), under exclusive license to Springer Nature Switzerland AG 2022
W. Hua et al. (Eds.): ADC 2022, LNCS 13459, pp. 185–192, 2022.
https://doi.org/10.1007/978-3-031-15512-3_16

relation (with a new name) is created from existing ones by applying either project or natural join operations. Such programs provide a useful abstraction of the execution methods used by many query processing algorithms as we are interested in schema structural requirements and not the specific details of processing algorithms. Program P creates relations, possibly over additional relation schemas. The relation computed in the last step of P is the desired result. In [4], it is shown that if P solves $J_{\mathbf{X}}$ then P must create an *extended database state E* whose *extended database schema* **E** satisfies the following property. There exists an acyclic (i.e., tree) database schema **TP**, consisting of the relation schemas of the relations mentioned in $J_{\mathbf{X}}$, the relation schema of the result relation **X**, and potentially additional relation schemas, such that the attributes of each such additional relation schema are a subset of some relation schema in the extended database schema **E**. This tree database schema is called a *tree projection* [4] of the extended database schema w.r.t. $J_{\mathbf{X}}$. This highlighted the central role of tree projections in relational query processing.

Suppose that, prior to its final projection statement, P uses a *semijoin loop* by executing all possible semijoin statements *in place* (i.e., modifying existing relations) until there are no further changes. The work of [4] treats finite database states and finite straight-line programs *without* a semijoin loop. If database states may be *unrestricted* (i.e., finite or infinite), then forming a tree projection w.r.t. **D** is necessary in order for P augmented with the semijoin loop to solve $J_{\mathbf{X}}$ [6]. For strictly *finite* database states, the necessity of creating a tree projection, for general original and extended database schemas, remained an open problem for about 35 years. This problem was finally settled (in addition to other open problems) in 2017 [5]- there must be a tree projection **TP** of **E** w.r.t. **D** $\cup$ **X**.

Whereas the fundamental question is settled, there are additional problems worth exploring. The basic proof of [5] establishes that if a tree projection does not exist then there is a finite database state D such that P does not solve $J_{\mathbf{X}}$ on D. However, no effective construction of such a state was provided (except for perhaps exhaustive enumeration). An effective state construction is useful for (i) examining the combinatorial properties of such states and their potential use in proofs, (ii) gaining intuition which may yield new query processing strategies, and (iii) "planting" such states D within test suites for query processors as a test mechanism. Interestingly, effective constructions are known for cyclic schemas wherein a finite database state may be constructed that is semijoin-reduced (locally consistent) yet the join of all relations is empty [1,2] .

We focus on the structure of **D** and **E** and assume that **X** is empty. In this setting we can unambiguously say that P augmented with the semijoin loop, or the extended database schema **E** it produces, solves **D** rather than that P solves $J_{\mathbf{X}}$. We can also use the *solves* terminology w.r.t. specific database states D. We consider cyclic database schemas whose adjacency graph (see Sect. 2) is either a simple cycle graph, called *Arings* (attribute rings), or a clique, called *Cliques*. Consider a program P over a database D with schema **D** forming a database state with database schema **E**. We construct a "small" database state D for an Aring or Clique schema **D** such that (i) $\bowtie_{R \in D} R = \emptyset$, and (ii) if P does not form a tree projection of **E** w.r.t. **D**, *no original tuple* of D is eliminated in the extended database state E by executing the semijoin loop augmented program P, rendering P incorrect. This corroborates the result of [5]. We note that in [6], the tree projection necessity result for *Acliques* (a subset of Cliques) database schemas was erroneously attributed to Aviel Klausner (unpublished)[1].

Prescribing effective state constructions to arbitrary initial cyclic database schemas remains an open problem. Such constructions may rely on the general construction technique we present, of deriving a construction of a database state for a cyclic database schema **D** from a construction of a state for a *binary* database schema corresponding to the adjacency graph of **D**.

2   Terminology

2.1   Relational Databases and Operators

A *relation schema* **R** is a finite subset of attributes (taken from a *universe* **U**), and a *database schema* **D** is a set of named relation schemas. We denote a database schema **D** as $(\mathbf{R}_1, \ldots, \mathbf{R}_n)$, where each $\mathbf{R}_i$ is the distinct name of a relation schema within the database schema **D**. We blur the distinction between the set of attributes of a named relation schema and the name of a named relation schema and use the $\mathbf{R}_i$'s also as the underlying sets of attributes. A database schema **D'** is a *sub-schema* of database schema **D** if **D'** is obtained from **D** by removing some named relation schemas. **U(D)** denotes the set of all the attributes in schema **D**. A database schema **D** may also be viewed as a hypergraph over **U(D)**.

For database schema $\mathbf{D} = (\mathbf{R}_1, \ldots, \mathbf{R}_n)$, a database state is denoted as $D = (R_1, \ldots, R_n)$ where each R_i is a relation for $\mathbf{R}_i$. Tuple r over relation schema **R** *matches* tuple s over relation schema **S** if they have identical constants for all attributes in **R**∩**S**. The (natural) *semijoin* of relations R and S, denoted $R \ltimes S$ is defined as the relation containing all tuples of R which match some tuple in S. Observe that $(R \ltimes S) \subseteq R$. Therefore, the semijoin is called a *reduction operator*. A database state D is *join reduced (JR)* if for each relation R with relation schema **R** in D, $R = \Pi_\mathbf{R} \bowtie_{S \in D} S$. A pair of relations R and S are *compatible* if each tuple in R matches a tuple in S, and vice versa. A database state D is *semijoin reduced (SJR)* if each pair of relations R and S in D are compatible.

2.2   Tree and Cyclic Schemas

By 'undirected graph' we mean one without self edges. A *subgraph* $G' = (V', E')$ of an undirected graph $G = (V, E)$ is an undirected graph such that $V' \subseteq V$ and $E' \subseteq E$; we say that G' is *contained* in G. Let $G = (V, E)$ be an undirected

---

[1] Apparently Klausner showed an example (unfortunately it cannot be located) of a query (i.e., database schema) with multiple Arings in which a tree projection was constructed for each Aring, individually, yet the query as a whole was not solved.

graph whose nodes are in one-to-one correspondence with the relation schemas of a database schema $\mathbf{D}$. For an attribute $A \in \mathbf{U}(\mathbf{D})$, we say that G is A-connected if the subgraph of G induced by relation schemas (nodes) containing attribute A is connected (i.e., for any two nodes in the induced subgraph, there is a path connecting them in the induced subgraph). For a set $\mathbf{X}$ of attributes, G is $\mathbf{X}$-connected if for all $A \in \mathbf{X}$, the graph G is A-connected. G is a *qual graph* for $\mathbf{D}$ if it is $\mathbf{U}(\mathbf{D})$-connected [2]. If a qual graph G is a tree then we call G a *qual tree*. $\mathbf{D}$ is a *tree schema* (equivalently, *acyclic hypergraph*, *acyclic scheme*) if some qual graph for $\mathbf{D}$ is a tree; otherwise, $\mathbf{D}$ is a *cyclic schema* (equivalently, *cyclic hypergraph*, cyclic scheme).

The *adjacency graph* of a database schema $\mathbf{D}$, $AG(\mathbf{D})$, has the attributes of $\mathbf{D}$ as nodes and two nodes are connected via an edge if the corresponding attributes appear together in a relation schema of $\mathbf{D}$. A cyclic database schema $\mathbf{D}$ is a *Clique* of *size* n, if $AG(\mathbf{D})$ is a clique over n nodes. A database schema $\mathbf{D}$ is an *Aring* (attribute ring), of *size* n, if it is isomorphic to the schema $\mathbf{A} = (\{A_1, A_2\}, \{A_2, A_3\}, \ldots, \{A_{n-1}, A_n\}, \{A_n, A_1\})$ where by isomorphic we mean there is a 1-1 mapping ϕ from the attributes of $\mathbf{U}(\mathbf{D})$ to $\{A_1, \ldots, A_n\}$ such that when ϕ is naturally extended to relation and database schemas, $\phi(\mathbf{D})$ is identical to $\mathbf{A}$. All Aring database schemas are cyclic schemas. We succinctly write an Aring $\mathbf{A}$ as a sequence of attributes, that is Aring $\mathbf{A}$ is simply written as $\mathbf{A} = (A_1 A_2 \ldots A_{n-1} A_n)$.

A database schema $\mathbf{D}$ is a *projection of* database schema $\mathbf{E}$, denoted $\mathbf{D} \leq \mathbf{E}$, if for all relation schemas $\mathbf{R} \in \mathbf{D}$ there exists a relation schema $\mathbf{S} \in \mathbf{E}$ such that $\mathbf{R} \subseteq \mathbf{S}$. Note that $\leq$ is a transitive relationship.

Database schema $\mathbf{TP}$ is a *tree projection* (*TP*) of database schema $\mathbf{E}$ (extended) w.r.t. $\mathbf{D}$ (original) if $\mathbf{U}(\mathbf{TP}) = \mathbf{U}(\mathbf{D})$, $\mathbf{TP}$ is a tree schema and $\mathbf{D} \leq \mathbf{TP} \leq \mathbf{E}$ [4]. Intuitively, a tree projection is a tree schema which is "sandwiched" between the original and extended database schemas.

Example 1. *Consider the following database schemas:*

$$\mathbf{D} = (\{A, B\}, \{B, C\}, \{C, D\}, \{D, E\}, \{E, F\}, \{F, A\})$$

$$\mathbf{TP} = \mathbf{D} \cup (\{C, D, E, F\}, \{F, A, B, C\})$$

$$\mathbf{E} = (\{A, D\}, \{F, A, B, C\}, \{C, D, E, F\})$$

Database schema $\mathbf{D}$ is an Aring of size 6 and hence cyclic, $\mathbf{E}$ is cyclic due to the embedded Aring over attributes $\{A, C, D\}$ and $\mathbf{TP}$ is a tree schema. $\mathbf{D} \leq \mathbf{TP} \leq \mathbf{E}$, and therefore $\mathbf{TP}$ is a TP of $\mathbf{E}$ w.r.t. $\mathbf{D}$.

If $\mathbf{TP}$ is a tree projection of $\mathbf{E}$ w.r.t. $\mathbf{D}$, then, from now on, we assume that $\mathbf{D} \subseteq \mathbf{TP}$, i.e., all the original relation schemas of $\mathbf{D}$ are also in $\mathbf{TP}$. Therefore, from here onward, $\mathbf{TP}$ is denoted as $(\mathbf{R}_1, \ldots, \mathbf{R}_n, \mathbf{S}_1, \ldots, \mathbf{S}_m)$, i.e., the first n relation schemas, the *base* relation schemas, are those of $\mathbf{D}$ and the rest are *non-base* relation schemas (i.e., extended relation schemas, or subsets thereof).

An undirected graph is *chordal* if each simple cycle in the graph of length greater than 3 has a *chord*, i.e., an edge connecting two nodes that are not adjacent in the cycle. A database schema $\mathbf{D}$ is *conformal* if each clique in $AG(\mathbf{D})$ is a subset of some relation schema in $\mathbf{D}$. Database schema $\mathbf{D}$ is a tree schema if and only if $AG(\mathbf{D})$ is chordal and $\mathbf{D}$ is conformal [3].

Lemma 1. *If there is a tree projection* $\mathbf{TP}$ *of a database schema* $\mathbf{E}$ *w.r.t. an Aring schema* $\mathbf{D}$ *of size* $n \geq 3$ *then there is a tree projection* $\mathbf{TP3}$ *of* $\mathbf{E}$ *w.r.t.* $\mathbf{D}$ *with up to three attributes per relation schema.*

3   Constructing (k-1)-Complete k-Partite Graphs

The database state construction we introduce encodes a specific type of graph, a $(k-1)$-complete k-partite graph, that we shortly define. An *undirected k-partite graph* is an undirected graph $G = (V, E)$ such that $V = V_1 \cup \ldots \cup V_k$ where the sets V_i, $i = 1, \ldots, k$ are disjoint and are called the *partitions* of the graph, and there is no edge that connects nodes in the same partition.

A k-partite graph $G = (V, E)$ is *(k-1)-complete* if (1) no clique of size k is a subgraph of G, and (2) each edge e in E is part of exactly $(k-2)!$ cliques of size $(k-1)$ where each clique is over vertices drawn out of a set of $(k-1)$ partitions, that is, drawing from the 2 partitions of the edge e plus $(k-3)$ additional partitions. For example, for $k = 5$, there are 5 partitions and each edge is required to be part of $(5-2)! = 6$ cliques of size 4.

We now show that such graphs exist for all $k \geq 2$. We provide an algorithm for constructing a $(k-1)$-complete k-partite undirected graph G^k given k as input. The algorithm, *Construct(k)*, has the following steps:

1. For $i = 1, \ldots, k$, let $V_i = \{(i, 1), \ldots, (i, (k-1))\}$. That is, each partition i has exactly $(k-1)$ distinct vertices, each of the form (i, b).
2. For each pair of distinct partitions, V_i and V_j, $i < j$, for $u = 1, \ldots, (k-1)$, for $v = 1, \ldots, (u-1), (u+1), \ldots, (k-1)$, form an undirected edge $\{(i, u), (j, v)\}$. That is, connect every pair of vertices from different partitions via an edge unless they are of the form (i, b) and (j, b) (the same constant b).

Let $G^k = (V^k, E^k)$ be the k-partite undirected graph resulting from executing *Construct(k)*.

We now prove that the algorithm correctly constructs a $(k-1)$-complete k-partite graph.

Lemma 2. *Consider the graph* $G^k = (V^k, E^k)$ *formed by Construct(k). The graph contains no edge of the form* $\{(a, b), (c, b)\}$ *for any* a, b, c.

Proof. The two *for loops* of the algorithm specifically prohibit constructing such an edge. □

Lemma 3. *Algorithm Construct(k) constructs a* $(k-1)$-complete graph $G^k = (V^k, E^k)$.

G^k *encodes* a database state over 2-attributes (i.e., 2 columns) relation states. The tuples in this database state are the edges of G^k. An edge connecting a vertex (m, a) in partition V_m to vertex (n, b) in partition V_n, both partitions are subsets of V^k, gives rise to a tuple $t = ((m, a), (n, b))$ in a relation state R_{mn} whose relation schema is $\mathbf{R}_{mn}$ and whose schema's attributes, namely columns, are A_m and A_n. Let D^k be the database state composed of all these relation states and $\mathbf{D}^k$ be its database schema. As $AG(\mathbf{D}^k)$ is a clique, $\mathbf{D}^k$ is a Clique.

Suppose one would like to compute (*) the natural join of all the relation states in D^k projected on a set of attributes, say $\mathbf{X} \neq \mathbf{U}(\mathbf{D}^k)$. One can employ a program P with join and project statements, construct an extended database state, apply a semijoin loop to achieve a SJR state and then project the desired result from a relation state whose schema contains $\mathbf{X}$. Clearly, if the extended database schema $\mathbf{E}$ includes a relation schema $\mathbf{U}(\mathbf{D}^k)$, the computation is correct as the extended state includes all the original relation states of D^k. So, suppose that this is not the case. However, suppose P performed "maximum effort", i.e., the extended schema $\mathbf{E}$ includes relation schemas over all cardinality $(k - 1)$ relation schemas. This is "maximum effort" because *any* other such possible extended schema $\mathbf{E}'$ satisfies $\mathbf{E}' \leq \mathbf{E}^2$.

Because of Lemma 3, each $(k - 1)$ clique $C = (V_c, E_c)$ of G^k provides the constants for a tuple t for the relation state S whose schema $\mathbf{S}$ is the partition of the $(k-1)$ vertices in V_c and where t's constants for the attributes are the $(k-1)$ vertices in V_c themselves. In other words, all initial database tuples (i.e., edges in E^k) whose attributes are contained in a relation schema $\mathbf{S}$ will "survive" the join operations in constructing the corresponding relation S and the semijoin loop, and give rise to a final state tuple in S.

However, the construction of $\mathbf{E}$ has not solved our initial problem (*). The reason is that all the relation states with which we end up are not empty and from this final state we deduce result tuples for $\mathbf{X}$. In contrast, we claim that the join of all initial relations is actually *empty*. For the sake of deriving a contradiction, suppose the join of all initial relations is not empty. Consider a tuple $s = (a_1, \ldots, a_k)$ in the join result, over attributes $A_1, \ldots, A_k$. Each pair (a_i, a_j) must be an edge in G^k for otherwise it would have been eliminated in the overall join. However, this implies the existence of a size k clique in G^k. This contradicts Lemma 3 which ensures that no such cliques exist. The conclusion is that the only way to compute (*) using a straight line program P with join and project operations, followed by a semijoin loop until convergence, is constructing a relation with all k attributes. We summarize the above discussion in the following theorem.

Theorem 1. *Let the k-partite graph G^k be formed by Construct(k). Let D^k be the database state, over database schema $\mathbf{D}^k$, in which every pair of attributes (partitions) forms a relation schema and the tuples are the edges in G^k connecting the nodes in the corresponding partitions. If database schema $\mathbf{E}$ solves D^k then $\mathbf{E}$ must include a relation schema $\mathbf{U}(\mathbf{D}^k)$.*

---

[2] And hence the reductive effect of $\mathbf{E}'$ is subsumed by that of $\mathbf{E}$.

4   The General Construction Theorem

A database schema $\mathbf{D}$ is *binary* if all relation schemas in $\mathbf{D}$ consist of two attributes. Let $\mathbf{D}$ be a database schema and $(\mathbf{U}(\mathbf{D}), \mathbf{G_D}) = AG(\mathbf{D})$ its adjacency graph. We can think of $\mathbf{G_D}$ as a *derived binary database schema* with each of its relation schemas consisting of the vertices (attributes) of an edge in $AG(\mathbf{D})$. We can now state the following *general construction Theorem* which shows that a state construction for $\mathbf{D}$, exhibiting tree projection necessity, is obtainable from a state construction for a binary database schema derived from $\mathbf{D}$.

Theorem 2. *Let $\mathbf{D}$ be a cyclic database schema. Let $\mathbf{G_D}$ be the binary database schema derived from $AG(\mathbf{D})$. Let D_G be a database state for $\mathbf{G_D}$ such that in order to solve $\mathbf{G_D}$ on database state D_G a tree projection w.r.t. $\mathbf{G_D}$ must be formed. Then, a database state D, such that in order to solve $\mathbf{D}$ on state D a tree projection w.r.t. $\mathbf{D}$ must be formed, can be constructed as follows: for each relation schema $\mathbf{R}$ in $\mathbf{D}$, construct a state R for $\mathbf{R}$ by joining all the relation states in D_G such that both of their attributes are contained in $\mathbf{R}$.*

5   Aring Database Schemas

Consider relation R over relation schema $\{A\}$. We add a new type of statement that intuitively duplicates a column: (duplicate) $RNEW \leftarrow R.AA'$ where $RNEW$ is a new relation name, A' is a new attribute, $\mathbf{RNEW} = \{A, A'\}$ is the relation schema of $RNEW$, and there is no previous duplicate statement involving attribute A. The semantics is as follows: each tuple t of R gives rise to exactly one tuple t' of $RNEW$, the constant assigned to A' in t' is identical to the one assigned to A in t. A' is called a *synonym* of A. Consider a database schema $\mathbf{D}$. Define directed graph $G(\mathbf{D})$ whose nodes are $\mathbf{U}(\mathbf{D})$ and whose edges are of the form (A, B) such that B is a synonym of A. Attribute B is a *transitive synonym* of attribute A if $A = B$ or there is a path from A to B in $G(\mathbf{D})$. If a program P is allowed to use duplicate statements we say that P *is duplicate-enabled*.

Example 2. *Consider relation state $R = \{(1), (4), (5)\}$ over relation schema $\{A\}$. Consider the duplicate statement $RNEW \leftarrow R.AA'$. The result is $RNEW$ which equals $\{(1, 1), (4, 4), (5, 5)\}$ over relation schema $\{A, A'\}$.*

Consider a database state A for $\mathbf{A} = (A_1, \ldots, A_n)$ such that the relation state for relation schema $\mathbf{S_1} = \{A_1, A_2\}$, called the *switching relation*, is $\{(0, 1), (1, 0)\}$, and for all other relation schemas it is $\{(1, 1), (0, 0)\}$. This database state was conceived in [1]. This SJR state is called the *standard state* for $\mathbf{A}$ and the join of all relations in it is empty.

Claim. Let $\mathbf{A} = (A_1 \ldots A_n)$ be an Aring database schema of size n and A the standard state for $\mathbf{A}$. Let P be a duplicate-enabled program creating a database schema $\mathbf{D}$ such that $\mathbf{D}$ solves A. Program P must form a relation state R whose schema $\mathbf{R}$ contains three transitive synonyms of consecutive attributes A_i, A_{i+1} and A_{i+1+1}[3] of $\mathbf{A}$ where $1 \leq i \leq n$.

---

[3] $n + 1 = 1$.

Theorem 3. *Let* **A** *be an Aring schema of size n and A the standard state for* **A***. Let P be a duplicate-enabled program creating a database schema* **D** *such that* **D** *solves A. Then, there exists a tree schema* **TP** *such that* $U(TP) = U(A)$*,* **A** *is contained in* **TP** *and for every relation schema* **R** *in* **TP** *there is a relation schema* **S** *in* **D** *such that each attribute of* **R** *has a transitive synonym attribute in* **S** *(i.e.,* **TP** *is a TP of* **D** *w.r.t.* **A***).*

Proof. W.l.o.g., we may assume that a semijoin loop until stabilization is applied after *each* statement of P as this will not affect the final result. The proof is by induction on n, $\mathbf{A} = (A_1 \ldots A_n)$. □

It follows that if duplicate statements are not used at all in program P then solving the standard state A for an Aring **A** necessitates constructing a tree projection w.r.t. **A**.

6   Conclusions

We consider database schemas **D** whose adjacency graph (with attributes as nodes and edges corresponding to co-occurring attributes) is a clique or a simple cycle. We construct a database state for such a schema such that the join of all relations in the database state is empty. Yet, a straight line program, with project and join statements, followed by a semijoin loop until convergence, that extends the state (and schema) without forming a tree projection in the process, will fail to completely reduce the state (to empty relation states). This provides explicit state constructions, for such schemas, which exhibit the necessity to form a tree projection. Such constructions are of a theoretical interest and may also have practical applications in testing query processors. Towards such constructions, we prove that a state construction for a cyclic database schema is obtainable from a state construction for a binary database schema derived from that database schema.

References

1. Bernstein, P.A., Chiu, D.W.: Using semi-joins to solve relational queries. J. ACM **28**(1), 25–40 (1981)
2. Bernstein, P.A., Goodman, N.: Power of natural semijoins. SIAM J. Comput. **10**(4), 751–771 (1981). https://doi.org/10.1137/0210059, https://doi.org/10.1137/0210059
3. Goodman, N., Shmueli, O.: Syntactic characterization of tree database schemas. J. ACM **30**(4), 767–786 (1983). https://doi.org/10.1145/2157.322405, http://doi.acm.org/10.1145/2157.322405
4. Goodman, N., Shmueli, O.: The tree projection theorem and relational query processing. J. Comput. Syst. Sci. **28**(1), 60–79 (1984). https://doi.org/10.1016/0022-0000(84)90076-X, https://doi.org/10.1016/0022-0000(84)90076-X
5. Greco, G., Scarcello, F.: The power of local consistency in conjunctive queries and constraint satisfaction problems. SIAM J. Comput. **46**(3), 1111–1145 (2017). https://doi.org/10.1137/16M1090272, https://doi.org/10.1137/16M1090272
6. Sagiv, Y., Shmueli, O.: Solving queries by tree projections. ACM Trans. Database Syst. **18**(3), 487–511 (1993). https://doi.org/10.1145/155271.155277, http://doi.acm.org/10.1145/155271.155277

Comparative Study of Transformer Models

Ashwin Sankar$^{(\boxtimes)}$ (iD) and R. Dhanalakshmi (iD)

KCG College of Technology, Karapakkam, Chennai, Tamil Nadu, India
ashwins1211@gmail.com

Abstract. Machine Reading Comprehension (MRC) is the process where computers or, machines are taught to understand a paragraph or more technically called a context. Like humans, machines also need to be evaluated for their understanding on question answering. MRC is one of the formidable sub-domains in the Natural Language Processing (NLP) domain, which has seen considerable progress over the years. In recent years, many novel datasets have tried to challenge the Machine Reading Comprehension (MRC) models with inference based question answering. With the advancement in NLP, many models have surpassed human-level performance on these datasets, albeit ignoring the obvious disparity between genuine human-level performance and state-of-the-art performance. This highlights the need for attention on the collective improvement of existing datasets, metrics, and models towards "real" prehension. Addressing the lack of sanity in the domain, this paper performs a comparative study on various transformer based models and tries to highlight the success factors of each model. Subsequently, we discuss an MRC model that performs comparatively better, if not the best, on question answering and give directions for future research.

Keywords: Transformer · Natural language processing · Reading comprehension · Question answering · Deep learning

1 Introduction

There is a humongous amount of data over the internet which cannot be retrieved spontaneously. Machine Reading Comprehension (MRC) could be leveraged to tackle this problem by feeding the model the abundant data. We do a thorough analysis on Extractive Question Answering (EQA) based techniques and models. EQA based models have seen considerable progress; so far as to be included in search engines to produce better results. This can be attributed to the development of Transformer based architectures and the self-attention mechanism that has the ability to capture the context. Novel datasets such as SQuAD, DuoRC and NewsQA have challenged Machine Reading Comprehension (MRC) models with inference based question-answer pairs and unanswerable questions. With the introduction of common sense, inference and reasoning based datasets, it becomes challenging to generalize previous well-performing MRC models over newer datasets.

© The Author(s), under exclusive license to Springer Nature Switzerland AG 2022
W. Hua et al. (Eds.): ADC 2022, LNCS 13459, pp. 193–200, 2022.
https://doi.org/10.1007/978-3-031-15512-3_17

Before Transformer, approaches like Bag-of-Words, and sequence-to-sequence models prevailed. After Transformer took over, models such as BERT [2], which were based on Transformer architecture, have proven to have the ability to generalize to various NLP tasks such as Named Entity Recognition, multiple choice question answering, Extractive Question Answering, classification, summarization, translation and much more. With the increase in accessibility to the computational power, newer NLP models based on BERT and Transformer have been proposed.

In this paper, we will analyze various approaches to solving this problem and identify a model based on existing work and provide reasons as to why it works better than its competitors.

2   Models

2.1   BERT

Bidirectional Encoder Representations from Transformer (BERT) is a language representation approach that uses unlabeled text to train deep bidirectional representations. With just one more layer, BERT can be fine-tuned to produce models for downstream tasks. BERT bypasses the limitation of uni-directionality by using Masked Language Model (MLM). MLM "randomly masks some of the tokens from input, and the goal is to accurately predict the vocabulary id of the word solely based on its context" [2].

BERT is structured as a multi-layer bidirectional Transformer encoder with primarily two model sizes, i.e., $BERT_{base}$ and $BERT_{large}$ which vary on the number of Transformer blocks, hidden units, and self-attention heads. BERT uses self-attention to effectively achieve what bidirectional cross attention does by concatenating the text pair. For pre-training, BERT model trains on two prediction tasks, i.e., masked token prediction and Next Sentence Prediction (NSP).

2.2   XLNet

XLNet [8] was designed to address the problems of BERT, which neglects the inter-dependency of positions of masked tokens and suffers a setback from pretrain-finetune discrepancy. XLNet is a generalized autoregressive pre-training method that enables the model to learn bidirectional contexts. It transcends BERT by addressing the limitations using the autoregressive formulation. It is found to outperform BERT on twenty tasks by a large margin under similar experimental conditions. To address the ineffective approach of an autoregressive language model, XLNet introduces permutation language modelling that allows models to capture bidirectional context while retaining the advantages of autoregressive models.

XLNet uses relative positional encoding scheme and segment recurrence mechanism on top of Transformer-XL, which overcomes the sequence length limitation of Transformer. XLNet combines the benefits of Auto Regressive and Auto Encoding approaches by using permutation language modelling.

2.3   RoBERTa

Replication study on BERT exposed that the model was significantly under-trained. Robustly optimised BERT approach (RoBERTa) [6] presents a better strategy for training BERT that can match or even outperform the then existing post-BERT methods. RoBERTa proposes some changes over vanilla BERT by "training the model longer with a bigger batch size, removing the NSP objective, training on longer sequences and dynamically changing the masking pattern applied to the training data" [6]. RoBERTa establishes a new SOTA performance on four of the nine GLUE tasks. RoBERTA uses a novel dataset, CC-News, to control the effects of the size of training set.

RoBERTa uses full-sentences based training approach without NSP, in which each input consists full sentences sampled continuously from at least one document to make the total length at most 512 tokens. RoBERTa's findings include performance improvement by training for a longer period of time, with bigger batches of data while removing the NSP, and dynamic change of the masking pattern.

2.4   ALBERT

A Lite BERT (ALBERT) [4] is a smaller condensed version of BERT, which has similar or even superior performance than BERT, designed to address compute limitations. To achieve this, ALBERT introduces two parameter reducing techniques which lowers memory consumption and speeds up the training of BERT: the first one being factorized embedding parameterization and the other being cross-layer parameter sharing [4]. Sentence Order Prediction (SOP) focuses on sentence-coherence and was created in response to the NSP's failure.

ALBERT architecture inherits a lot from its parent architecture, BERT. ALBERT factorizes the embedding parameters, breaking them into two smaller matrices. This parameter reduction is significant when the number of hidden units, H is significantly larger than WordPiece embedding size. ALBERT uses cross-layer parameter sharing as a parameter reducing technique with growing depth of the network. As the NSP objective was replaced, the loss function was also replaced with inter-sentence coherence loss.

2.5   DistilBERT

DistilBERT [7] is a strategy for fine-tuning a smaller general-purpose language representation model with high performance on downstream tasks by pre-training it. DistilBERT uses knowledge distillation methods during the pretrain phase, reducing the size of BERT by 40% and making it faster by 60% while retaining 97% of its parent's performance. DistilBERT proves that it is possible to have a high performance system that is also fast, cheap and light, on many downstream tasks with a relatively smaller model size with Knowledge Distillation (KD).

DistilBERT takes some crucial design choices that make it smaller than BERT by a factor of 2, being removal of token-type embeddings and pooler. Major operations used in the Transformer architecture are optimized using modern linear algebra frameworks.

2.6 BART

Bidirectional Auto Regressive Transformer (BART) [5] is a deionizing auto-encoder for pretraining sequence-to-sequence models. It is trained by corrupting the text with an arbitrary noise function and learning to reconstruct the original text. BART is found to be comparable to RoBERTa in terms of performance with similar training resources on GLUE and SQuAD and performs well on abstractive dialogue, question answering, and summarization.

The $BART_{base}$ uses 6 layers in the encoder and decoder while $BART_{large}$ uses 12. In BART, each layer of decoder performs an additional cross-attention over the final hidden layer of the encoder. It also drops the feed-forward neural network that BERT uses before word prediction.

2.7 ConvBERT

Detailed studies performed on BERT found that all its attention heads query on the whole input sequence which incurs computational cost. To explicitly model local dependencies, ConvBERT [3] substitutes some of the attention heads with an unique Span-based dynamic Convolution (SDC). These new convolution heads, in conjunction with self-attention heads, forms a mixed attention block that proved to be more effective in capturing both global and local context.

The model was designed with a bottleneck structure to reduce the number of attention heads. This removes the redundancy and improves the efficiency. Additionally, for the feed forward module, a grouped linear operator is used, which minimizes parameters while being competent in representation power.

2.8 ELECTRA

Efficiently Learning an Encoder that Classifies Token Replacements Accurately (ELECTRA) [1] replaces the masked token detection objective with Replaced Token Detection (RTD). In this approach, instead of corrupting the input tokens by masking the input sequence, ELECTRA corrupts the input sequence by swapping out tokens with suitable replacements chosen from a generator network, and then learning to discriminate between the genuine tokens and the alternatives.

ELECTRA architecture primarily consists of two blocks, i.e., a Generator and a Discriminator. The Generator is trained to perform MLM and predict the original identities of the masked-out input while the Discriminator is trained to discriminate the replaced tokens from the generator samples. Further studies showed that the efficiency of ELECTRA can be improved by introducing weight sharing between the Generator and Discriminator networks.

2.9 Retrospective Reader

In the recent years, MRC models primarily focus on the encoder end and not on the task specific modules like answer verification and, question-passage interaction. But, studies show that better task specific module architectures have a significant impact on MRC performance, no matter how strong the encoder is.

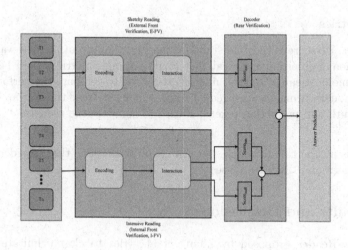

Fig. 1. Architecture of Retro-Reader

Retro-Reader [9] introduces the Sketchy Reader, which briefly interacts with the question and context, and the Intensive Reader, which substantiates the answer, involves verification steps which helps in distinguishing unanswerable questions as well as predict accurate answers for answerable questions (Fig. 1). These blocks have verification modules called Internal Front Verification and External Front Verification. It is found that having either of these verification module boosts the scores on the baseline models, but having both of these verification modules works the best.

3 Methodology

3.1 Retro-Reader Based Question Answering System

We identify an architecture based on Retrospective-Reader in conjunction with ELECTRA that has achieved a SOTA performance on SQuAD 2.0. This end-to-end architecture is trained on SQuAD and NewsQA that relies more on reasoning and comprehension. Initially, the context, question and answer are obtained and is fed into the model where it goes through the Sketchy Reader and Intensive Reader. The Sketchy Reader and Intensive Reader computes the External Front Verification and Internal Front Verification values. These two verification steps in combination, called Rear Verification, will be used for the final prediction of the answer (Fig. 1).

Once the data is fed to the model the starting and ending positions of the answer are predicted and the span is extracted. Since a computationally competent and a lighter model than most transformer based models is used, we reduce on the computational requirements while not sacrificing performance.

3.2 Metrics

F1-Score. F1-score is the gold standard metric for information retrieval. It is a combination of precision and recall metrics into a single metric is the F1-score. It is the harmonic mean of the two metrics. It is used to compare the performances of MRC models. A macro-averaged F1 score, which measures the overlap between ground truth and prediction tokens, is used to compare the models.

EM. This metric calculates the percentage of predictions that are identical to any of the ground truth responses.

4   Results and Discussions

The Retro-Reader proposed by Zhang et al., tries to closely imitate human behaviour with a verification modules. The Retro-Reader introduces the Sketchy Reader and the Intensive Reader. The Sketchy Reader module performs External Front Verification and the Intensive Reader module performs Internal Front Verification. Combined, these form Rear Verification which is responsible for the boost in performance of the model with respect to others as indicated by Table 1 and Fig. 2.

Table 1. Performance comparison of various BERT based models on SQuAD 2.0 Dev set

Model	EM	F1
Human	86.8	89.5
BERT	78.98	81.77
XLNET	87.9	90.6
RoBERTa	86.5	89.4
ALBERT	83.1	86.1
BART	86.1	89.2
ConvBERT	80.6	83.1
ELECTRA	80.5	83.3
Retrospective Reader		
on ALBERT	87.8	90.9
on ELECTRA	**88.8**	**91.3**

The SOTA performance of Retro-Reader on Electra are due to the verification modules which it has, compared to its contemporaries which doesn't, which is apparent in the comparison in Fig. 2.

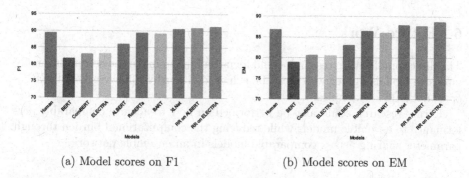

(a) Model scores on F1   (b) Model scores on EM

Fig. 2. Figure 2a shows the comparison of various models on F1 score and Fig. 2b shows the comparison of various models on EM score

5   Conclusion

Vaswani et al. pioneered a way to build models around attention called Transformer. Using this, Devlin et al. proposed a way to represent bi-directional context efficiently, using stacked Transformer encoders, called BERT. BERT used MLM as one of its pre-training objectives while the other was NSP which was later found to be a flawed combination.

Yang et al. proposed XLNet, combining the advantages of auto-regressive and auto-encoding approaches using permutation language modelling. Liu et al. found that BERT was significantly undertrained and with the proper tuning it could outperform most of the post-BERT models and proposed RoBERTa.

To address the issues in BERT, Lan et al. proposed ALBERT, which replaced NSP with SOP and used inter-sentence coherence loss to improve the performance. Lewis et al. proposed a deionizing auto-encoder approach called BART which uses a combination of text infilling and sentence permutation to record SOTA results.

Although there were advancements towards improving the performance of the models, it also gave rise to increasing compute demands. Sanh et al. proposed DistilBERT which leveraged knowledge distillation to develop smaller, faster and cheaper models for inference. Jiang et al. also tried to replace the costly attention heads with dynamic span-based mixed attention blocks with ELECTRA's RTD as the pre-training objective which gave some promising results.

Clark et al. identified the weakness of MLM and replaced MLM with RTD and proposed ELECTRA. Also, ELECTRA does not use NSP owing to its flaws discussed in XLNet and RoBERTa.

While comparing 11 different models one model showed strong results on the F1 and EM metrics. It is observed from Table 1 that Retro-Reader on ELECTRA sets a precedent on F1 and EM scores. This can be attributed to Retro-Reader's Rear Verification module which aids in making appropriate decisions.

6   Future Work

The direction of future research could focus on how to make the computationally intensive models lighter which can be achieved either by following DisitlBERT's or ConvBERT's examples.

Future research could also be performed on how to achieve comparable performance to ensemble models while reducing the computational burden through parameter sharing across comparable models in an ensemble network.

References

1. Clark, K., Luong, M.T., Le, Q.V., Manning, C.D.: ELECTRA: Pre-training Text Encoders as Discriminators Rather Than Generators, pp. 1–18 (2020). http://arxiv.org/abs/2003.10555
2. Devlin, J., Chang, M.W., Lee, K., Toutanova, K.: BERT: pre-training of deep bidirectional transformers for language understanding. In: NAACL HLT 2019 – 2019 Conference of the North American Chapter of the Association for Computational Linguistics: Human Language Technologies - Proceedings of the Conference, vol. 1, issue number Mlm, pp. 4171–4186 (2019)
3. Jiang, Z., Yu, W., Zhou, D., Chen, Y., Feng, J., Yan, S.: ConvBERT: improving BERT with span-based dynamic convolution. In: Advances in Neural Information Processing Systems 2020-Decem (NeurIPS), pp. 1–17 (2020)
4. Lan, Z., Chen, M., Goodman, S., Gimpel, K., Sharma, P., Soricut, R.: ALBERT: A Lite BERT for Self-supervised Learning of Language Representations, pp. 1–17 (2019). http://arxiv.org/abs/1909.11942
5. Lewis, M., et al.: BART: Denoising Sequence-to-Sequence Pre-training for Natural Language Generation, Translation, and Comprehension, pp. 7871–7880 (2020). https://doi.org/10.18653/v1/2020.acl-main.703
6. Liu, Y., et al.: RoBERTa: A Robustly Optimized BERT Pretraining Approach, p. 1 (2019). http://arxiv.org/abs/1907.11692
7. Sanh, V., Debut, L., Chaumond, J., Wolf, T.: DistilBERT, a distilled version of BERT: smaller, faster, cheaper and lighter, pp. 2–6 (2019). http://arxiv.org/abs/1910.01108
8. Yang, Z., Dai, Z., Yang, Y., Carbonell, J., Salakhutdinov, R., Le, Q.V.: XLNet: generalized autoregressive pretraining for language understanding. In: Advances in Neural Information Processing Systems (NeurIPS), vol. 32, pp. 1–18 (2019)
9. Zhang, Z., Yang, J., Zhao, H.: Retrospective Reader for Machine Reading Comprehension (Lm) (2020). http://arxiv.org/abs/2001.09694

Removing Performance Bottleneck of Timestamp Allocation in Two-Phase Locking Based Protocol

Tatsuhiro Nakamori[1], Jun Nemoto[2], Takashi Hoshino[3],
and Hideyuki Kawashima[1(✉)]

[1] Keio University Faculty of Environment and Information Studies, Tokyo, Japan
{t19601tn,river}@sfc.keio.ac.jp
[2] Scalar, Inc., Tokyo, Japan
jun.nemoto@scalar-labs.com
[3] Cybozu Labs, Inc., Tokyo, Japan
hoshino@labs.cybozu.co.jp

Abstract. Concurrency control ensures the correctness of databases when transactions are processed in parallel. Bamboo is a state-of-the-art concurrency control protocol. One problem of Bamboo is that it requires transactions to fetch timestamps from a single centralized atomic counter. To replace the concentrated access to it, each transaction should generate timestamps independently. This paper proposes two methods of decentralization to address the problem. The first is the thread-ID method (TID): transactions use thread IDs as their timestamps. In high-contention settings, the performance of TID plummets, but proposed optimization FairTID sustains the performance. The second method (RandID) allocates timestamps using random-number generators. Experiments indicated that there were up to 60% and 34% improvement in throughput from Bamboo with FairTID and RandID, respectively. In high-contention settings, TID recorded 24% degradation, but FairTID and RandID showed 19% to 31% and 12% to 22% improvement from Bamboo, respectively.

Keywords: Database system · Transaction processing · Concurrency control · Two-phase locking · Single centralized atomic counter

1 Introduction

1.1 Motivation

Transaction processing has been used in many situations such as in banks, for credit card payments, and in distributed file systems for big science [6]. The rise of many-core architecture has led to a growing interest in faster concurrent-transaction processing. It is necessary to ensure the correctness of the resulting database after the execution of the transactions. Concurrency control takes this role, ensuring the isolation of transactions.

© The Author(s), under exclusive license to Springer Nature Switzerland AG 2022
W. Hua et al. (Eds.): ADC 2022, LNCS 13459, pp. 201–208, 2022.
https://doi.org/10.1007/978-3-031-15512-3_18

Concurrency control is mainly divided into two categories: pessimistic and optimistic. One of the most scalable protocols is the two-phase locking protocol (2PL), which is pessimistic and suited for contended workloads [5].

Bamboo [1], an extension of 2PL, is designed for highly contended workloads. Its main idea is to release the acquired locks at an early stage to reduce the blocking time and aggressively operate dirty reads to increase concurrency. Bamboo can be faster than other state-of-the-art concurrency-control protocols under conditions in which hotspot accesses limit transaction throughput.

1.2 Problem

Bamboo implements the wound-wait method for deadlock prevention among transactions [1,8]. Wound-wait resolves deadlocks by making transactions of higher priority abort other transactions. The priority is determined by the timestamp that each transaction receives at the start of its execution.

One problem with the wound-wait implementation of Bamboo on modern many-core architecture is that it requires transactions to fetch timestamps from a *single centralized atomic counter*. The atomic counter is a data structure that allows only one thread to access at one time in CPU instruction level. In certain settings where transactions contend to fetch timestamps, only one transaction accesses the counter while the other transactions must wait for that one transaction to receive the timestamp. Consequently, the Access to the centralized counter can become a bottleneck, as described in a previous study [5].

1.3 Contribution

To avoid the concentrated access to the centralized counter, each transaction should have a structure that generates timestamps independently.

This paper proposes two methods of decentralization to improve the performance of Bamboo. We first propose *thread-ID method* (**TID**) to decide the orders: threads are assigned IDs at the start of concurrency control, and transactions use the thread IDs as order-deciding timestamps. In high-contention settings, the performance of TID plummets. Proposed optimization **FairTID** sustains the performance even in high-contention settings. The second proposed method *random-ID method* (**RandID**) enables transactions to fetch timestamps from random-number generators.

The experiments with CCBench [5] measured that the throughput increased from that of Bamboo by up to 57%, 60%, and 34% with TID, FairTID, and RandID, respectively. Our code is available online for reproduction [3]. This paper is an extension of our poster [4].

2 Proposal

Bamboo [1] is an extension of the wound-wait variant of 2PL. Wound-wait is one type of deadlock [8] prevention that makes transactions of higher priority

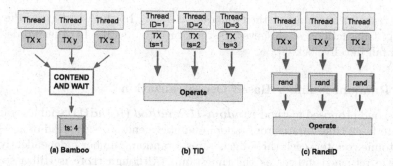

Fig. 1. Bamboo, TID, and RandID (a) Bamboo. Needs a centralized atomic counter that incurs contentions. (b) Proposed method TID. Decentralized timestamp fetching by using thread ID. (c) Proposed method RandID. Decentralized timestamp fetching by using random number.

abort other transactions. The priority is determined by the timestamp that each transaction receives at the start of its execution. One problem with Bamboo is that it requires transactions to fetch timestamps from a single centralized atomic counter. Using the centralized atomic counter is convenient to determine the orders between the transactions, but it is problematic because transactions contend to fetch timestamps. When many transactions need to access the centralized atomic counter simultaneously, all the other transactions must wait for the one transaction to complete the access to the counter, leading to performance bottleneck (Fig. 1).

To avoid the concentrated access to the centralized counter, each transaction should have a structure that generates timestamps independently. Such decentralized data structures will enable the transactions to fetch timestamps without waiting for one another. In the following sections, the two proposed methods of decentralization to improve the performance of Bamboo are discussed. Our proposal is based on the fact that the timestamp in Bamboo is only used to decide orders between transactions and is not representative of actual time.

2.1 Thread-ID-Based Decentralization

We first propose *thread-ID method* (**TID**) to decide the orders: threads are assigned IDs at the start of concurrency control, and transactions use the thread IDs as order-deciding timestamps. Since each thread continuously executes incoming transactions, the assignment of IDs as timestamps is not only decentralized but also done only once as the threads and IDs are kept for the duration of the concurrency control and not dependent on the lifetime of transactions. Therefore, the overhead due to fetching the timestamp and waiting for the access to the atomic counter does not occur altogether with this method.

One weakness of this method is that the priority of the transactions assigned to threads with high IDs is always low. Under highly contended workloads, these low-priority transactions would have to yield to other transactions even if the other transactions started their operations later. In the worst case, the low-priority transactions would never get their turn to operate. In other words, they would fall into livelock [8].

2.2   Random-Number-Based Decentralization

The second proposed method *random-ID method* (**RandID**) enables transactions to fetch timestamps from random-number generators. Instead of accessing one atomic counter, each thread generates a random number independently and uses the returned integer as the timestamp. Although there is still a step to fetch a timestamp in every transaction, transactions no longer contend with each other to receive the timestamp to begin actual operations. Unlike TID, RandID reduces the chance of livelock by making transactions fetch new random numbers as timestamps every time transactions terminate (i.e. commit or abort). Consequently, even when a transaction fetches a maximum random number that can be generated by a random-number generator and has the lowest priority possible, it fetches a new timestamp after it terminates. Transactions constantly change their timestamps so their priority would never be the same, reducing the chance of livelock.

The determining factor regarding the performance improvement with this method is how long the random-number generator takes to return an integer. Performance will not improve even though the fetching process is decentralized if random-number generator takes long time to return integers. The quality of the generated random numbers also affects the overall performance improvement. If the random numbers that transactions fetch follow the same pattern, their timestamps may coincide too often to the extent that the transactions constantly abort each other and do not progress. To minimize such problems, the experiments for this study involved Xoroshiro128+, a high-speed random-number generator that outputs quality random numbers suitable for parallel computing.

2.3   Optimization: Increment ID in Commit Phase

Livelock hinders the performance of TID. It happens because the threads that have high IDs would never be prioritized over other transactions. Ideally, threads that have low priority should eventually be prioritized so that all threads would have a fair chance to execute transactions. One solution to ensure such fairness among threads is to increment the ID of a thread by the number of active threads when it commits a transaction (**FairTID**). For example, suppose there are 5 threads with ID 1, 2, 3, 4, and 5. At the beginning of concurrency control, thread (ID = 1) has the highest priority so it has the greatest chance to commit a transaction. When thread 1 commits a transaction, if its ID is unchanged, its priority would remain the highest, leading to other threads not being able to commit transactions. However, if thread (ID = 1) increments its ID by the number of active threads (i.e. 5) to become thread (ID = 6), it would be least prioritized among all the threads, allowing other threads to have higher probability to commit transactions. Similarly, all the other threads increment

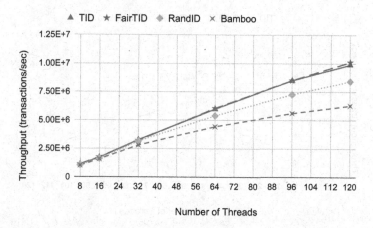

Fig. 2. Number of threads vs. throughput in low contention –16 operations, read ratio = 0.5, 1 million tuples, tuple size = 4 bytes, skew = 0, writes in the first 20% of accesses retired, hash table indices.

their IDs by the number of threads upon the commit phase of their transactions so that other threads would be more likely to commit a transaction. As the example suggests, the threads take their turn to have higher priority, so all threads commit transactions fairly. Therefore, the livelock would not occur in FairTID, leading to better performance even in high-contention settings.

3   Evaluation

Experiments were conducted on a machine with 4 CPU Xeon® Platinum 8276 CPUs (2.20 GHz, 28 cores) and 512 GB of DRAM. Each core can run 2 threads with hyperthreading and total number of logical cores is 224.

The experiments in this study used Yahoo! Cloud Serving Benchmark A (YCSB-A) workload to measure the performance of the original Bamboo and the proposed method. YCSB-A controls Zipfian distribution with parameter skew. A higher skew indicates that transactions access some tuples more frequently. That is, the workload is more contended. The first experiment involved measuring the results in which transactions are in low contention (skew = 0) and the second and third involved this in high contention (skew = 0.99). Detailed settings are written in the captions of the corresponding figures of the experiments.

3.1   Low-Contention Setting

Figure 2 shows the results in a low-contention setting. Compared with Bamboo, the proposed methods showed better scalability. The throughput increased by 57%, 60%, and 34% at 120 threads with TID, FairTID, and RandID, respectively.

The proposed methods showed improvement in throughput because the level of contention was low. Lower contention means that there are less opportunities

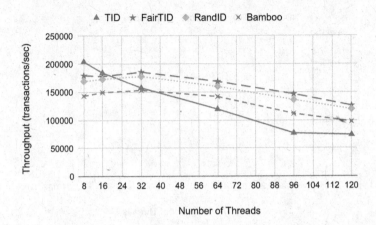

Fig. 3. Number of threads vs. throughput in high contention - Skew = 0.99, writes in the first 85% of accesses retired, backoff enabled, other settings being equal.

for transactions to compare their timestamps and wound each other. Therefore, cutting the overhead of fetching timestamps was directly reflected in the results of this experiment. There is a difference in performance between TID and RandID because while TID can completely ignore the process of fetching timestamps, RandID is affected by it as generating random numbers still requires CPU resources.

3.2   High-Contention Setting

Figure 3 illustrates the results of the experiment in a high-contention setting. 42% improvement in throughput from Bamboo was obtained with TID at 8 threads. However, as the number of threads increased, the performance improvement with TID decreased. TID was worse than Bamboo starting at 64 threads, and at 120 threads, it recorded 24% degradation from Bamboo. Contrastingly, FairTID and RandID showed improvement between 19% to 31% and 12% to 22% in the experiment in Fig. 3, respectively.

Figure 4 shows the number of transactions that each thread committed in the high-contention setting. As discussed in Sect. 3.1, when too many threads contend, less-prioritized threads fall into livelock, hindering the ability of them to commit transactions. Consequently, the threads would have an unfair amount of work done, as TID in Fig. 4 shows. In detail, the first 13 threads with IDs 0–12 committed 51% of the transactions whereas the last 13 threads with IDs 107-119 only did 2%. In low-contention settings, TID does not cause livelock of transactions because transactions do not contend and wound each other frequently, so the threads can utilize the CPU resources efficiently. In high-contention settings, however, the chance of transactions to fall in livelock is high, leading to the imbalance of work done between each thread: the majority of the threads would waste the CPU resources while only few threads work. As a result, the throughput of TID became extremely low as the number of threads increased in Fig. 3.

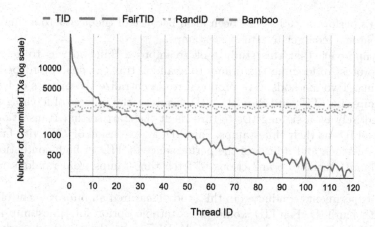

Fig. 4. Number of committed transactions of 120 threads (log scale) - The data is obtained from the same experiment as in Fig. 3.

The threads in Bamboo, FairTID, and RandID share the amount of work more fairly. Most notably, FairTID displays a straight line in Fig. 4, suggesting that the threads commit almost equal amounts of transactions. The near perfect fairness may have contributed to the improved performance of FairTID in comparison to others when the number of threads were greater than 16.

4   Related Work

The problem of the centralized counter on many-core architecture has been addressed in previous papers [5,7]. Though the decentralization of the process of fetching timestamp was proposed in Cicada [2], it did not address the fairness for worker threads. Fairness among threads can affect performance as shown in Fig. 3 and 4 in which TID performed worse than Bamboo and FairTID because the threads in TID had an unfair amount of work done. Furthermore, while FairTID completely abandons the cost of fetching timestamp, the decentralized timestamp allocation in Cicada still has some overhead. FairTID not only accounts for the fairness among threads to commit transactions but also dismisses the process of timestamp allocation altogether.

The proposed methods are effective on protocols that implement timestamp to decide orders between transactions. However, the effectiveness is unknown for protocols that need timestamp to represent actual time (e.g. multiversion timestamp ordering). In such protocols, the installation of the proposed methods may not lead to better efficiency, although it may not affect the correctness, because transactions cannot infer time from timestamps in proposed methods.

5   Conclusion

The purpose of this study was to improve the performance of Bamboo which is a wound-wait variant of 2PL that enables transactions to release locks early.

Bamboo's performance has not been ideal because of the access to a single centralized atomic counter to fetch timestamps.

The approach that this study took to improve Bamboo was to decentralize the process of fetching timestamp to abandon transactions' interdependence on waiting. Two methods were proposed to decentralize the process of fetching timestamps, i.e., TID and RandID. TID dismisses the process of fetching timestamps entirely by assigning IDs to threads at the start so that transactions use the thread IDs as their timestamps. FairTID, an extension of TID with fairness, prevents livelock and improves the performance of TID in high-contention settings. RandID enables transactions to fetch timestamps from random-number generators.

The experiments conducted in this study measured an improvement of up to 60% with FairTID. FairTID would be a suitable option for timestamp allocation in two-phase locking based protocols. We expect the proposed methods to accelerate transaction processing worldwide. Our code is available online [3].

Acknowledgement. This work is partially supported by JSPS KAKENHI Grant Number 22H03596 and a project, JPNP16007, commissioned by the New Energy and Industrial Technology Development Organization (NEDO).

References

1. Guo, Z., Wu, K., Yan, C., Yu, X.: Releasing locks as early as you can: Reducing contention of hotspots by violating two-phase locking. In: SIGMOD Conference, pp. 658–670 (2021)
2. Lim, H., Kaminsky, M., Andersen, D.G.: Cicada: dependably fast multi-core in-memory transactions. In: SIGMOD Conference, pp. 21–35 (2017)
3. Nakamori, T.: Tatzhiro/ccbench: concurrency control benchmark (2022). https://github.com/Tatzhiro/ccbench
4. Nakamori, T., Nemoto, J., Hoshino, T., Kawashima, H.: Decentralization of two phase locking based protocols. In: HPDC (poster) (2022)
5. Tanabe, T., Hoshino, T., Kawashima, H., Tatebe, O.: An analysis of concurrency control protocols for in-memory databases with CCBench. Proc. VLDB Endow. **13**(13), 3531–3544 (2020)
6. Tanaka, M., Tatebe, O., Kawashima, H.: Applying Pwrake workflow system and Gfarm file system to telescope data processing. In: CLUSTER, pp. 124–133 (2018)
7. Tu, S., Zheng, W., Kohler, E., Liskov, B., Madden, S.: Speedy transactions in multicore in-memory databases. In: SOSP, pp. 18–32. ACM (2013)
8. Weikum, G., Vossen, G.: Transactional Information Systems: Theory, Algorithms, and the Practice of Concurrency Control and Recovery. Morgan Kaufmann Publishers Inc., San Francisco (2001)

Performance Prediction of Songs
on Online Music Platforms

Dolly Sharma[✉], Sonia Khetarpaul, S Mohit Kumar,
Ambreesh Parthasarathy, and Sparsh Agarwalla

Department of Computer Science and Engineering, Shiv Nadar University,
Delhi-NCR, India
dolly.sharma@snu.edu.in

Abstract. The Billboard magazine is a world renowned music
publication since 1984 and it releases a weekly ranking of the top 100
songs in various categories such as rock, pop, hip-hop, etc. Several studies
have determined that it is possible to predict the approximate bucket
of ranks that a song is likely to chart in using social and subjective
indicators. The definitions of these indicators however can change over
time, thus rendering the previous classifications erroneous. Here, we
report successful results from our experiments in predicting the ranks
and the number of weeks the songs are likely to stay on the charts, using
objective and well-defined features, obtained from Spotify's Web API.
It extends existing research about classifying songs into rank buckets of
Top-10 and Top-40 using these objective features, demonstrating that
it is possible to predict exact ranks of the songs within a root-mean-
squared-error of 28 ranks and the number of weeks of charting within
a root-mean-squared-error of 7 weeks, demonstrating definitive trends
between individual features and the ranks of the songs, demonstrating
that objective metadata about the songs serve as good indicators about
the trends in the Billboard charts, and can be used to predict a song's
performance on the charts within acceptable error rates.

Keywords: Song rank prediction · Hit song science · Music data
analysis · Machine learning · Ensemble learning

1 Introduction

Billboard magazine has published various charts since 1913 such as best sellers,
playtime, etc. Since 1958, the Billboard Hot 100 Charts[1] have proven to be a
definitive weekly ranking for the commercial success of America's most popular
songs and is accepted by people associated with the music community, such
as music artists, record labels and the audience. This ranking helps track
the commercial success and popularity of songs as well as albums. Given the
enormous amounts of money invested in this industry, understanding what

---

[1] Billboard's Hot 100: billboard.com/charts/hot-100.

© The Author(s), under exclusive license to Springer Nature Switzerland AG 2022
W. Hua et al. (Eds.): ADC 2022, LNCS 13459, pp. 209–216, 2022.
https://doi.org/10.1007/978-3-031-15512-3_19

actually makes a song a hit would provide tremendous commercial benefits for the music industry.

This work aims to analyze Billboard's Hot 100 Charts from 1970 to 2018 and the song feature set from Spotify's Web API[2] as inputs with the following objectives: (i) to identify trends and correlations between song parameters and their chart ranks, and (ii) to model these features to predict the song's performance on the charts. This paper extends existing research on hit song science by applying machine learning methods to classify songs into the Top-10 and Top-40 buckets of rank. Finally, it demonstrates the efficacy of objective song metadata from Spotify's API to predict the overall performance of a song on the Billboard charts. Further, regression techniques were applied to compute three parameters to quantitatively predict the performance of the song being analyzed - the peak rank achieved by the song, its rank on its last week in the chart, and the number of weeks it charted. Additionally, this paper also investigates if objective metrics can reveal anti-musicological influences in a song's success.

Problem Statement: The objective of this work is to predict the rank of a song in the Billboard Hot 100 charts by using historical chart data with music metadata from Spotify's web API. Here we attempt to select the peak position attained by the song on the charts, the rank at which it exits the charts, and the number of weeks it features on the charts as the specific elements to define the song's performance.

The key contributions of this paper are as follows:

- A new approach to hit song science is proposed using primarily song metadata alongside cultural indicators of success as opposed to the traditional methods using social and subjective indicators.
- Creation of ensemble models that can accurately predict chart positions of songs after being trained on song metadata.
- Analysis of data trends to see how the various objective features of trending songs have changed over the years, and also how they vary across ranks.

2   Related Work

Hit Song Science (HSS) aims to predict whether a given song will become a chart-topping hit. François Pachet [1] studied how music and its commercial success can be linked via patterns. Shin and Park [2] presented a framework to identify factors that determine the on-chart success dynamics. The framework drew insights into the success and decline of songs with the specific focus on external factors that affect the trajectories of songs. Ni et al. [3] in their work on Hit Song Science, tried to separate the extremely popular songs on the UK Top 40 charts (1–5) from less popular songs (30–40). Jakubowski et al. [8] and their analysis on INMI trakcs, show that their positions are dependent on intra as well as extra-musical factors and attempt to track popularity as an important parameter.

---

[2] Spotify Web API: developer.spotify.com/documentation/web-api.

Aranjo et al. [9] attempted to predict whether a song would crack the Spotify Top 50 global ranking after a certain point in time, creating a base expectation on our classification by using simple methods. Dhanaraj and Logan [5] and Herremans et al. [7] both try to predict the formulaic parameters of a hit, with acoustic and rhythmic parameters. Fan et al. [6] and Prey et al. [13] explain the cultural aspects. The former comparing the Chinese and US charts, and the latter talking about the role of streaming services in how songs are perceived. Karydis et al. [10] created a comprehensive track popularity dataset that compiled data from various streaming services. Yang et al. [11] approached the topic using a deep learning model on auditory features. Zangerle et al. [12] performed a differentiation and analyses of High-Level and Low Level audtitory features.

3   Proposed Approach

To predict chart positions, we use a customized method to account for both objective and subjective factors. In our approach, we take objective song metadata from Spotify's API for the charting songs. The data is then processed to ensure standardization across the features. We then engineer the data to help us predict Spotify's popularity metric from the given auditory features. This predicted popularity is then used in tandem with the other features to predict the song's performance.

3.1   Data

For this study, the Billboard top 100 hot-hits of every week from December 12, 1970, to June 21, 2018 were used. This data was retrieved from a dataset on data.world. Each song is then passed as a query into the Spotify API to retrieve the musicological features of the songs. After removing the songs with missing features, 19581 tracks were left. Figure 1 shows the various preprocessing stages.

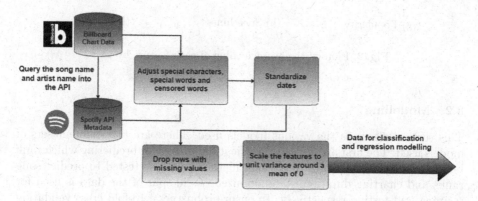

Fig. 1. Preprocessing stages

To understand the trends in the features, line-plots of the mean values of all the features were computed, grouped first by year (as seen in Fig. 2) and then by peak rank. Through this we see an increase in the track's danceability, proportion of lyrical content, loudness and overall energy over the course of time. We also see a decrease in acousticness and instrumentalness can be seen. A decrease in valence suggests that songs are increasingly conveying negative emotions like sadness and anger. Finally, the inverse relation between instrumentalness and speechiness may also indicate the increasing popularity of single artists over bands.

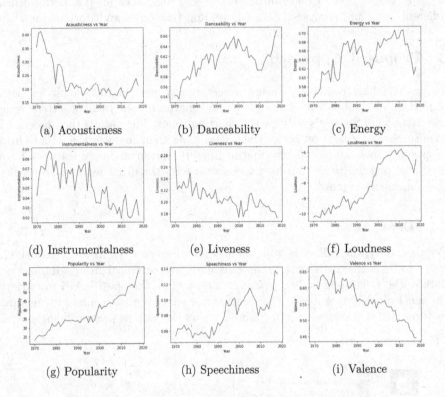

    (a) Acousticness   (b) Danceability   (c) Energy

  (d) Instrumentalness   (e) Liveness   (f) Loudness

    (g) Popularity   (h) Speechiness   (i) Valence

Fig. 2. Plots of the average value of each feature by year

3.2   Modelling

This section discusses the various models used. There are two different sets of models used. The first are a set of classification models for predicting which rank bucket a song will fall into. Regression methods are also tested to predict song ranks and charting duration. A randomized 80–20 split of the data is used for training and testing respectively. To ensure robustness, 10-fold cross validation was also done.

3.3   Predicting the Spotify Popularity Metric

Spotify generates a popularity score based on the number of recent streams. The features from the Spotify API, the year of charting were encoded into unique labels, and out of Ridge Regression, Random Forest Regression and a Deep Neural Network, the Random Forest model gave the best result, with a mean absolute error of 5.70 and a root mean square error of 7.07. This resulting prediction was then used as a feature in all the subsequent tests. To predict the various rank buckets that songs can fall in, single-class and multi-class classifiers were used:

- The top 10 ranked songs, 10–40th ranked songs, and 40+ ranked songs. This was done because top 10 and top 40 are the most coveted spots on the Billboard charts, and are therefore of the most utility.
- The songs that would rank in the top 10.
- The songs that would rank in the top 40.

Due to the high dimensionality and variability within the data, we primarily tested the following models: Random Forest Classifier (RFC), XGBoost ClassifierGaussian SVM. All the class weights were balanced to account for the imbalance in the class distributions in the dataset. To predict the complete snapshots of a song's chart duration, peak and exit rank, the following models were tested:

- Ridge Regression with alpha values in the range of 10^{-3} to 10^3.
- Deep Neural Network with 4 dense hidden layers, the first containing 128 nodes and the other 3 containing 256 nodes were used. Each hidden layer node used the ReLU activation while the output layer, containing 1 node used the linear activation function to predict the rank. For training the model, the batch size was set to 32 and the model trained for 400 epochs.
- Random Forest Regression with 100 estimators and a minimum split condition of 2 samples. Mean squared error was used as the criterion
- XGBoost Regression, with XGBRegressors that were programmed to use to use 100 estimators and the gbtree booster to predict our target variables.

4   Results

This section summarizes the results of all the models applied for the classification and regression tasks, and presents the insights inferred from all the experiments. The best result for Top 10/11–40/40+ Classification was obtained from the Random Forest Classifier, with an accuracy of 56.2%. The best result for Top 10/10+ Classification was obtained from the XGBoost Classifier, with a whopping 82.0% accuracy. The best result for Top 40/40+ Classification was obtained from the Random Forest Classifier, with a decent 63.8% accuracy. The comparison can be seen in Table 1. The results obtained from the regression models have been detailed in Table 2. There were significant deviations in the results, but the Random Forest models performed best across all 3 target variables.

Thus, for a given song, the peak position can be successfully predicted within a range of ± 24 ranks, the exit rank within a range of ± 14 ranks and the number of weeks it shall stay on the chart within a range of ± 6 weeks. The proposed approach along with a combination of musicological features, tracking metadata and predicted popularity, we created various predictive models that attempt to predict chart positions. When comparing across the same dataset, our Top-10 classifier predicts results with an accuracy of 82.0% using the Random Forest Classifier, which is significantly higher than Herremans et al.'s 65% accuracy with the Naive Bayes classifier [7] in a Top-10 classification using the Echo Nest data. The proposed Random Forest model shows an accuracy of 56.2% and a precision of 54%. Fan and Casey perform the same experiment with a Support Vector Machine, and achieve an accuracy of 56% on a similar dataset [6]. Additionally, Datla and Vishnu perform a similar multi-class experiment on lyrical data where they achieve predictions with a 79% precision [4]. Predicting exact song ranks using musicological features is an under-researched area.

Currently, Zangerle et al. use high and low level audio features like mood, emotion, instruments involved etc. as inputs into a neural network model. They achieve a root mean squared error (RMSE) of 55.45 ranks [12]. Our experiments surpass this result, with an RMSE of 27.96 for predicting the peak rank, and 18.07 for the exit rank. While both datasets contain musicological features, the actual features used are starkly different.

As shown in the visual analysis there seem to be trends that are linked to external cultural factors. These cultural factors, along with the combination of musicological features, drive production of songs in a certain direction, and give us a "recipe" for a hit song. The fact that the Top 10 was much easier to predict than the Top 40 leads us to believe in two things. Firstly, the existence of a varied set of niches (possibly derived from the most popular niche) that may not be the most popular but still command airtime. Secondly, the existence of a super popular niche that has almost a formulaic distribution of the features shows that these hit songs have roughly the same blueprint musical features wise, even though the implementation of these can be achieved in different ways.

Table 1. Classification results

Model	Top 10,10–00,40+ Classification		Top 10 Classification		Top 40 Classification	
	Accuracy (Weighted average)	Precision (Weighted average)	Accuracy (Weighted average)	Precision (Weighted average)	Accuracy (Weighted average)	Precision (Weighted average)
RFC	0.562	0.54	0.819	0.81	0.638	0.64
XGB	0.545	0.5	0.82	0.81	0.626	0.63
SVC	0.524	0.5	0.807	0.78	0.625	0.64

Table 2. Regression results

Target attribute	Models	MAE	RMSE
Peak Position	RR	25.4305	29.2049
	DNN	24.0867	28.4211
	RF	**23.7752**	**27.9609**
	XGB	24.8387	28.6761
Exit Rank	RR	16.9713	20.4216
	DNN	68.4997	71.8630
	RF	**13.9865**	**18.0686**
	XGB	14.2701	18.3426
No. of Weeks	RR	6.5520	8.2823
	DNN	6.0173	8.0113
	RF	**5.9468**	**7.7197**
	XGB	6.2771	7.9394

5 Conclusion

By using ensemble modelling methods, we get excellent results with respect to Accuracy and Precision in our classification as well as in regression problems. Significant progress has been achieved with the regression models, which attempt to predict the exact rank of songs. It can also be shown that simply relying on musicological features is insufficient, as there are cultural factors that influence a songs popularity, which can be seen by the incorporation of the popularity metric. This could give valuable insights and can lead to better decision making during the production and promotion of songs.

By achieving an 82.0% accuracy score in our Top 10 classification test, we have managed to perform better than the previous approach that used just musicological features. For predicting a song's performance on the chart, it can be seen that the random forest models tend to give the best scores. The model can predict the peak positions of songs with a mean absolute error of 23.7, the exit rank with an error of 13.9 and the number of weeks the songs will stay on the chart with an error of 5.94, enabling us to accurately predicting numerical ranks for a song based on objective song data. These results imply that there exist certain trends and patterns in music that influence a song's commercial success.

References

1. Li, T., Ogihara, M., Tzanetakis, G. (eds.): Music Data Mining, vol. 20. CRC Press, Boca Raton (2012)
2. Shin, S., Park, J.: On-chart success dynamics of popular songs. Adv. Complex Syst. **21** (03n04), 1850008 (2018)

3. Ni, Y., Rodriguez, R., Mcvicar, M., De Bie, T.: Hit song science once again a science. In: 4th International Workshop on Machine Learning and Music (2011)
4. Datla, V., Vishnu, A.: Predicting the top and bottom ranks of billboard songs using Machine Learning. arXiv preprint arXiv:1512.01283 (2015). arxiv.org/abs/1512.01283. Accessed 12 Mar 2020
5. Dhanaraj, R., Logan, B.: Automatic prediction of hit songs. In: Proceedings of the 6th International Conference on Music Information Retrieval, vol. 11, No. 15, pp. 488–491 (2005)
6. Fan, J., Casey, M.: Study of Chinese and UK hit songs prediction. In: Proceedings of the International Symposium on Computer Music Multidisciplinary Research, pp. 640–652 (2013)
7. Herremans, D., Martens, D., Sörensen, K.: Dance hit song prediction. J. New Music Res. **43**(3), 291–302 (2014)
8. Jakubowski, K., Finkel, S., Stewart, L., Müllensiefen, D.: Dissecting an earworm: Melodic features and song popularity predict involuntary musical imagery. Psychol. Aesthe. Creat. Arts **11**(2), 122 (2017)
9. Araujo, C.V.S., Pinheiro de Cristo, M.A., Giusti, R.A.: Predicting music popularity using music charts. In: 2019 18th IEEE International Conference on Machine Learning and Applications (ICMLA), pp. 859–864. IEEE (2019)
10. Karydis, I., Gkiokas, A., Katsouros, V.: Musical Track Popularity Mining Dataset. In: Iliadis, L., Maglogiannis, I. (eds.) AIAI 2016. IAICT, vol. 475, pp. 562–572. Springer, Cham (2016). https://doi.org/10.1007/978-3-319-44944-9_50
11. Yang, L.-C., S.-Y., Chou, J.-Y., Liu, Y.-H.Y., Chen, Y.-A.: Revisiting the problem of audio-based hit song prediction using convolutional neural networks. In: 2017 IEEE International Conference on Acoustics, Speech and Signal Processing (ICASSP), pp. 621–625. IEEE (2017)
12. Zangerle, E., Vötter, M., Huber, R., Yang, Y.-H.: Hit song prediction: leveraging low-and high-level audio features. In: ISMIR, pp. 319–326 (2019)
13. Prey, R., Valle, M.E.D., Zwerwer, L.: Platform pop: disentangling Spotify's intermediary role in the music industry. Inf. Commun. Soc. **25**(1), 74–92 (2022)

Author Index

Printed in the United States
by Baker & Taylor Publisher Services